Edward Everett Hale

June to May

The Sermons of a Year Preached at the South Congregational Church in Boston in

1880 and 1881

Edward Everett Hale

June to May
The Sermons of a Year Preached at the South Congregational Church in Boston in 1880 and 1881

ISBN/EAN: 9783337085872

Printed in Europe, USA, Canada, Australia, Japan

Cover: Foto ©Lupo / pixelio.de

More available books at **www.hansebooks.com**

JUNE TO MAY.

THE SERMONS OF A YEAR.

PREACHED AT THE SOUTH CONGREGATIONAL CHURCH
IN BOSTON, IN 1880 AND 1881,

BY

EDWARD E. HALE.

BOSTON:
ROBERTS BROTHERS.
1881.

PREFACE.

THIS volume is the fourth in a series of sermons preached in the South Congregational Church in Boston, and printed week by week at the wish of some of those who heard them.

Every parish minister will understand that there is a certain convenience in having in print a few copies of a sermon, which he may wish to send to some who did not hear it. This convenience has been enough to justify the continuation of this series.

For the additional convenience of preservation, a few copies are now bound and published together,— not because they are on one subject, but rather because they are not; not because they have any literary claim for preservation, but rather because they have not. They simply represent the affectionate counsels which a minister who has spoken to one congregation for a quarter of a century has a right to offer on every theme to the people who come to hear him,— people most of whom have heard him long, but who are, in general, younger than he is.

The sermons preached on Communion Sundays have generally been reserved for another collection.

EDWARD E. HALE,
Minister of South Congregational Church.

JULY 3, 1881.

CONTENTS.

The Sunday Laws,	delivered	June 27, 1880,	. . .	3
Subsoiling,	"	Oct. 31, "	. . .	13
Law and Gospel,	"	Nov. 28, "	. . .	20
Men of Gadara,	"	Dec. 5, "	. . .	29
These Three Abide,	"	Dec. 12, "	. . .	36
Christ the Giver,	"	Dec. 25, "	. . .	44
Christ the Friend,	"	Dec. 26, "	. . .	52
All Things New,	"	Jan. 2, 1881,	. . .	61
The Abolition of Pauperism,	"	Jan. 9, "	. . .	70
Things Above,	"	Jan. 16, "	. . .	78
Not Less, but More,	"	Jan. 30, "	. .	86
Christian Realism,	"	Feb. 6, "	. . .	76
Thomas Carlyle,	"	Feb. 13, "	. . .	104
God is a Spirit,	"	Feb. 20, "	. . .	113
Send me,	"	Feb. 27, "	. . .	122
The Religion of America,	"	Mar. 6, "	. . .	127
Parable and Bible,	"	Mar. 13, "	. . .	137
Indifference,	"	Mar. 20, "	. . .	146
The Possible Boston,	"	Mar. 27, "	. . .	154
Increase of Life,	"	Easter Sunday,	. . .	162
The King's Work,	"	Palm Sunday,	. . .	168
I must see Rome,	"	Apr. 24, 1881,	. . .	185
Honor and Idolatry,	"	May 1, "	. . .	192
The Unitarian Principles,	"	May 8, "	. . .	199
The Œdipus Tyrannus,	"	May 15, "	. . .	208

THE SUNDAY LAWS.

"The Son of Man is lord of the Sabbath."—LUKE vi., 5.
"The Sabbath was made for man, and not man for the Sabbath."—MARK ii., 27.

WITH the change of social habits, some curious difficulties have appeared in the construction and use of our Sunday laws, which will of necessity challenge the attention of all conscientious people. That has happened which often happens,—that the part of a law which was once of little importance seems important, and that it is invoked in an interest quite apart from that which passed it. The sections now of special interest are the first six. The present revision dates from 1860.

SECTION 1. Whoever keeps open his shop, warehouse, or workhouse, or does any manner of labor, business, or work, except works of necessity and charity, or is present at any dancing or public diversion, show, or entertainment, or takes part in any sport, game, or play on the Lord's day, shall be punished by a fine not exceeding ten dollars for every offence.

SECTION 2. Whoever travels on the Lord's day, except from necessity or charity, shall be punished by fine not exceeding ten dollars for every offence.

SECTION 3. Whoever, keeping a house, shop, cellar, or place of public entertainment or refreshment, entertains therein on the Lord's day any persons not being travellers, strangers, or lodgers, or suffers such persons on said day to abide or remain therein, or in the yards, orchards, or fields appertaining to the same, drinking or spending their time idly or at play, or in doing any secular business, shall be punished by fine not exceeding five dollars for each person so entertained or suffered so to abide and remain; and, upon any conviction after the same, by fine not exceeding ten dollars; and, if convicted three times, he shall thereafter be incapable of holding a license; and every person so abiding or drinking shall be punished by fine not exceeding five dollars.

SECTION 4. Whoever is present at a game, sport, or play, or public diversion, except a concert of sacred music, upon the evening of the Lord's day, or upon the evening next preceding the Lord's day, unless such game, sport, play, or public diversion is licensed by the persons or board authorized by law to grant licenses in such cases, shall be punished by fine not exceeding five dollars for each offence.

SECTION 5. No person licensed to keep a place of public entertainment shall entertain or suffer to remain or be in his house, yard, or other places appurtenant any persons not being travellers, strangers, or lodgers in such house, drinking and spending their time there, on the Lord's day or the evening preceding the same; and every such innholder or other person so offending shall be punished by fine not exceeding five dollars for each offence.

SECTION 6. No person shall serve or execute any civil process on the Lord's day; but such service shall be void, and the person serving or executing such process shall be liable in damages to the party aggrieved, in like manner as if he had no such process.

SECTION 7. Whoever on the Lord's day, within the walls of any house of public worship, behaves rudely or indecently, shall be punished by fine not exceeding ten dollars.

These statutes are in substance those of the year 1791. I believe their history will be found to be that in the increased liberty and liberality of the new-born State it was resolved to give to the citizen every privilege on Sunday, except that of annoying other people, or forcing them to work for him. You will observe that here is none of the old Puritan law, so called, enforcing church attendance. In fact, that was English law, as well as Puritan. It appears as distinctly in Charles I.'s proclamation, as it does in any New England statute. I should like also to say, in passing, that the attendance on worship of the old times is, as I believe, generally greatly exaggerated. The first meeting-house in Salem — the only one for a generation — was twenty feet by twenty-five. There is not a village of that size to-day which would not have two or three churches four times as large. And, though these would not be half full on Sunday, we can hardly believe that the fathers wholly failed to provide for such attendance as they had on days of public worship.

It is no longer with the desire to compel people to go to meeting or to church that our present statutes are devised. All that effort has been weeded out from them. It is rather with the intention to leave everybody free to go to public worship, and free to rest if he wants to rest. It is an effort to relax all chains on that day. I am old enough to remember when poor debtors, who had to reside in the jail limits on week-days, availed themselves of this statute on Sunday, and went where they chose on visits to their friends. That liberation is a type of the whole plan. The apprentice could not be compelled to work, nor the journeyman. Stage-drivers, ferry-men, hostlers, and grooms even, were at large. People who lived in and near taverns were not to be annoyed by the racket of revellers. Churches were not to be annoyed by the passage of vehicles. I am fond of telling my children the story of the arrest by one of their ancestors of the Russian ambassador and his party who had landed in some seaboard town here, and were crossing the country. Ignorant or indifferent to our laws, they pressed their way to the seat of government on the Lord's day. But they found that a Connecticut tithing-man stopped them. He held that the journey was not one of charity or of necessity. Of which the latent desire was not that the ambassador should go to meeting, but simply that those that did should not be annoyed by the rattle of his wheels; that the people of the inns should have only the minimum of care, and, in general, that everybody should be as free to rest himself as he chose, on Sunday, as was possible, under every condition short of a return to barbarous life. I hope you observed, when I read the Old Testament lesson from Deuteronomy, that the observance of the Jewish Sabbath is there put on the ground of a memorial of the emancipation of the Hebrews from slavery. "You shall let your slave be free from work one day in seven. Remember that you were slaves yourselves." Our Massachusetts statute is, in like wise, a statute for emancipation from common cares. It is an effort to secure one day, with as few mutual claims as possible. You may not ask me to pay my money debts on the Lord's day. And you may not ask me to fulfil any other of my ordinary obligations. So far as possible, the law makes me a free man on that day. If I am a blacksmith, on other days I must set your horse's shoes: on the Lord's day, you may not compel me to. If I am an innkeeper, on other days I must prepare your meals, when you travel: on the Lord's day, you cannot compel me to. If I am a common carrier, on other days I must carry your trunk or your merchandise: on the Lord's day, you cannot compel me to. And so through all the ranges of human duty. Our present Sunday law was made to secure human freedom, as far as human freedom can be secured and the outward machinery of society maintained.

Nor was this so difficult in a little State, separated almost by nature from other communities. It was when that separation ended, that the first difficulties came in. There is preserved among the memorials of this church the sign-board on which the drivers of the Providence mail-coach were requested to walk their horses as they passed our meeting-house on the afternoon of Sunday, coming by with the New

York mails from Providence; for it was very soon held that the carrying of the mail was a work of necessity. And as the Jews, under Judas Maccabæus, found that, in spite of themselves, they must fight on the Sabbath, so the community found that it had no right to stop any man's work in Maine or in New York on Monday or Tuesday, under the pretext that we were giving a Massachusetts man a rest upon Sunday from carrying the mail. A kindred instance is that of the daily newspaper, and it illustrates the whole difficulty. You do not wish to have your newspapers sold on Sunday, and therefore the custom came in of having no newspaper on that day. But the consequence is that, in the quiet of the printing-office, the compositors and the editors are at work on the newspaper which you read on Monday morning. Such exceptions as come in under the justification of necessity and charity are so frequent that it is unnecessary that I should repeat them. The last real battle that was made in this community was in the discussion regarding the opening of the public library. Here the city solicitor said that the work of the attendants on the library was neither a work of necessity or charity, and that the library could therefore not be opened under the statute. But, other legal advisers in other cities having held that the work was both necessary and charitable, these libraries were opened; and we have followed their example. A curious instance was that of the necessary labor at the public baths. Here it has been conceded at the beginning that the cleanliness and health insured at the free bathing establishments were enough to justify the employment of the people who serve them. Yet it is clear enough that these are all exceptional instances. They all run contrary to the theory of the statute, which is that on the Lord's day we shall return, as far as we can, to the condition which we suppose to be the condition of Arcadian freedom and simplicity. Let me repeat it, there is no effort now on the part of people who believe in religious worship to secure by force attendance on what they consider religious instruction. It is rather the determination of a newly emancipated people that no habit or custom shall come in on this day of rest, shall break in upon the rights even of the lowest and poorest of their number. And granting that there must be certain persons, like lamplighters, policemen, apothecaries, and preachers, whose duties must be fulfilled on the Lord's day, still the intention of the statute is that for the world at large it shall be a day of rest, or a day when each individual may choose his own method of filling the time. It follows, however, that he must choose that method in such a way as shall not compel the attendance or assistance of another. Strictly speaking, for instance, the rule is followed out, when the father says to his son on Sunday: "Yes, you may go to ride; but you must saddle and bridle your own horse, and you must groom him when you come home. For I will not, on the Lord's day, compel the attendance of a servant, in order that you may be entertained."

It is now nearly twenty years since the practical question presented itself in this community, whether among these exceptional cases, in which we certainly escape the old construction of the Sunday laws, we were to include the use of the street cars on Sunday. There were many people who, in the cause of religion, wanted to say that the street cars should not run on Sunday, as, if you will remember, the street omnibuses had never done. All that I have been saying as to the rights of inn-keepers, hostlers, and common carriers applied in this case. The man who did the necessary work on the street railroad had unquestionably the right to the same protection which under the law a blacksmith has, or a wheelwright. If the street railways were to run, it was by an exception to the old interpretation. As a matter of history, I think I may say that the permission to the street railways to run was a permission in this community caused by the intervention of people who saw their advantages for facilitating religious worship. We, who were then clergymen in Boston, were approached both by the president of the Metropolitan Railway and by an eager Orthodox clergyman, who wanted to suppress the practice, for our opinion upon the subject. Of course, we formed that opinion with care. I think the experience of twenty years has justified it. We said that we thought church attendance was a good thing, that we thought church attendance would be increased by the Sunday use of the cars. We said that certainly, if the rich man had a right to ride to church in his carriage, the poor man had a right to go in the street cars; and we deprecated any attempt even to obtain the decision of the courts on the question whether the running of the street cars was a work of necessity or charity. But such a decision was subsequently obtained in a case where a woman received injury from an accident on Sunday; and the courts held that, if she had not been going to attend worship, or for any purpose of charity which could be proved, or other necessity, she could not have recovered damage from a company which was violating the law, if it carried her on Sunday for any other purpose. Under the statute, therefore, now the running of the street cars is justified, simply on the plea that it is a work of necessity or charity. I am quite sure that, as our civilization goes, the running of these cars is not to be called travelling, in the ordinary sense of that word; but that it has become one of the necessities of our social system,— a necessity as distinct as that by which in a country town a farmer should drive his wife from one part of the town to another, on a visit to her mother or her sister.

What has followed from this has been that the public eye is so familiar with the idea of public carriages on Sunday that the public is gradually forgetting the steady effort of the statute to protect people in their freedom on the Lord's day. But we ought to remember that all these exceptions have been taken under the plea of necessity. Necessity is at best but the tyrant's plea. Nothing can be more certain than that the laboring man, for whom Sunday is the only free day, may, under the statute, use his Sunday with his family to go where he pleases, whether to visit a sister or a brother, or to spend the day in the open air. If he finds the street car running, nothing is more certain than that he will use it, and ought to use it. But he, of all men, is the man who should be most careful how he removes from over his head that very protection without which he would have no holiday at all. Let not any workman try his separate power at negotiating with his master, if no such law were behind him. Let no man try to engage himself in a mill or workshop, with the condition that he is to have every Wednesday free to himself. Yet that is the danger which impends, if some such statute does not regulate the order of daily occupation.

In one case, the next step now attempted is the most natural in the world. Why not take one of the large steamships, released from daily service, precisely because the statute will not let them go to sea for travellers on Sunday, and because men's habits will not let them travel? Why not fill her with passengers for a Sunday excursion in the bay, land somewhere at mid-day, and come home at night? If you have stretched the law so far as you have, will you not stretch it thus much further? The first result of this effort which the general public saw was that a body of North End roughs, enlisted in such an enterprise, stormed the town of Marblehead one Sunday last summer. The Marblehead people proved too much for them, and drove them back, like so many pirates, to their ship. The incident was natural enough and characteristic enough to show that the Sunday law had an intelligible and defensible basis. These Marblehead people have certain rights. One of them is to a quiet Sunday. The law asserted itself at once to protect them; and, if anybody had supposed that it was a dead letter of Puritan folly, he saw his mistake. I think the decision of the good sense of the people and of the authorities, will be to resist any change of law which will lead to making the Sunday excursion more easy. I think so, and I hope so. I think that is the true decision. The principle of the statute is as good for 1880 as it was for 1790. We will hold this one day in seven a day for as large freedom as we can have, — we and everybody else. I will not buy my enjoyment by compelling twenty other people to work for me. They shall be free as well as I. And, by precisely the same sacrifice with which my father ate a cold dinner rather than have his cook work on Sunday, will I abstain from the voyage to Marblehead and back, rather than have twenty firemen and twenty deck hands work on Sunday. The principle shall still be the principle of freedom, not to one, but to all. We admit that there must be exceptions; but we will hold to it that these are necessary exceptions.

In the present vagueness of opinion on these points, I think I must go much further. I think that every conscientious man, or, as I said before, every leader of society, must make up his mind whether he thinks public worship one day in seven a good thing or a bad thing, and whether he considers this Sunday rest, as protected by statute, a good thing or a bad thing. As matter of feeling or theory, most men agree here. Most young lawyers would say they are glad there is one day when they need not go to their offices; most young clerks, that they are glad that on that day they need not go to their stores, and so on. As matter of feeling and theory, yes. Nay, as matter of feeling and theory, almost all these persons would be sorry to have public worship abandoned,— most,— not all. Some people would not care. Addressing those who do care, I should say: " You must make this a matter of action also. You have no right to take the comfort of Sunday, and then to leave to the ministers, to your father and mother, and to the women of the community, the maintaining of Sunday. When a club of high-minded, moral, and intelligent young men mount their bicycles on Sunday morning, by public appointment, and ride to Newport on Sunday, they say far more distinctly than any words or votes could say that, so far as they are concerned, they mean that the next generation shall have no Sunday. Courts are not to be closed, stores shut up, sheriffs kept back from executing writs, in order that young gentlemen may ride all day on bicycles. The institution of Sunday, if it is to be maintained at all, will be maintained for the nobler purposes of the higher life. And, while it is quite legitimate to urge that the Art Museum, the Public Library, the concert on the Common may tend to this higher life, nobody will accept the plea which says that a feat of laborious athletics is a bit of the higher life. Every such effort to get over the line helps the way to the secularization of all days, when there will be no time at all.

Some of you heard at the Music Hall the careful appeal of Mr. Howard Brown to this point. I wish all those people could have heard it who are not here to-day, nor in any other place of public worship. A man says he does not go to church, because church-going does him no good. Who said it did? What has that to do with it? Is my question to be always that miserable question of my good? The doctor asks me to hold an artery, while this man's life-blood is ebbing away. Shall I say, "No, I thank you: it does me no good"? The law sends for me as a witness, that justice may be done to two strangers. Shall I say, "It does me no good"? You spent Friday in teaching a child her letters. What good did that do you? That man spent it in laying rails for the railway. What good did that do him? Have we come to that sink-hole of hoggishness that we will do nothing that we are not paid for on the nail? What we say is that public worship is a necessity to the noblest life of the community. If you say so, and I think you do, you must act so also. You must visibly, and with personal sacrifice, enlist yourself on that side. What good did it do you, when you went to a ratification meeting and cheered for Garfield? or you, when you went to another and cheered for Hancock? Thank God, you went without any such mean usurer's question. You went to show your colors, to throw yourself into the common cause. You knew that your country wanted more than your ballot. That, of itself, is a trifle. She wanted more than your touch on a trigger in the very improbable contingency of her sending you to battle. She wanted you. And, when you cheered for your candidate, she found you. All the more she wants you to show that you believe in the eternal laws on which all paper laws are founded, on the eternal institutions without which her constitutions are sand-heaps. She wants you to commit yourself personally, heartily, regularly, to maintain those institutions,— not for the good it does you, poor creature, but for the good it does mankind. Central among these institutions is the institution of public worship. She wants you visibly and practically to maintain that institution.

And just at this moment, when people scatter to summer homes, let me say a word in regard to our summer Sundays. They are to be for rest, yes. To the men who work here all the week, and run down to their families by a Saturday train peculiarly for rest, yes. But days of religious obligation all the same. In that little country village, where your holiday is spent, there are a congregation and a minister who are trying to level up the community around them. The church bell on Sunday rings not for Orthodoxy or Methodism or Unitarianism so much as it rings for public spirit, for mutual regard, for human freedom. Into that town, you come for Sunday. If you choose to go sailing all day, or to go off to "worship God on the mountains" all day,— as I observe is the cant phrase,— or to spend the Sunday in fishing or hunting, you do practically all you can to break down that institution. If, on the other hand, you and yours note the Sunday also, just as you say you want these villagers to do; if in the hotel parlor you sit at the piano yourself to lead the hymn; or if the wagon which on Saturday went to Paradise or Purgatory goes on Sunday to the village church with those who are spending their holiday,— you are doing your share to keep that village what you found it, and to maintain the social order which has made New England what it is.

I have refrained from any argument of the divine appointment of Sunday. I have been discussing the worth not of the Hebrew Sabbath, but of the Massachusetts Sunday, which is a very different thing. I do not urge that you should rest from labor one day in seven, because God rested after six acts of creation. But I ought to say that, so far as history avouches law as divine, all the history of Sunday pleads for the sort of rest which I am urging. More suggestive than any thunder of Sinai, and more convincing than any argument of Moses, is the steadiness with which the seventh day of rest worked itself into the civilization of Europe. Men despised the Jews: they ridiculed and caricatured them, they spurned them in the street, they degraded them in society, but they took from them this institution. Before Christianity got its hold on Rome, the one day in seven captured Rome. A nation which gave masters power to crucify their slaves was not strong enough to keep slaves from the enjoyment of this rest one day in the week. No movement of our times for a ten-hour system, for an early-closing system, for the relief of children in factories, ever approached this great determination of a working world, that it would rest from its labors when a seventh day came round. Observe, no statesman directed that movement. No philosopher suggested it. Only a few dirty and despised Jews, on the wrong side of the Tiber, if they were in Rome, rested on the seventh day. The good sense of the thing, the good effect of the thing, captured even the scoffers and the tyrants; and they accepted the boon, which proved to be the new life of their social order. I only ask you to look round you to-day, and see if that lesson is not re-enforced on every side. By their fruits shall ye know institutions as well as man. Is not the town or village where workman and prince, boy and man, rest heartily on Sunday, and make Sunday a day for the refreshing of man's best nature,— is it not a place palpably and certainly in advance of the other community, wherever you find it, which struggles against this stream of a world's experience, and tries to reduce Sunday to the common level?

"To labor is to pray," the monkish proverb says. Sometimes it is, sometimes it is not. The motive makes it prayer — or devil service. Of course, I may say the same of rest from labor. It may be the nastiness of Circe's style. But every one of us knows it may bring the closest vision, it may bring the noblest resolution, it may bring the highest life. To leave the clatter of my own anvil; nay, to turn from the echoes of my own thoughts, to go away from friends or disciples, it may be, as the Prince of Men retired in his need,— this is to seek God. And they who seek him, surely, they shall find him, if thus they seek for him with all their hearts.

SUBSOILING.

Do men gather grapes of thorns, or figs of thistles? — MATT. vii, 16.

No, they do not; but they try to. They are always trying to obtain their grapes and figs by some such short-hand process. But the only successful way is to dig deep the trench, to manure it richly, to plant well-selected roots, to train carefully the vine, and to prune the leaves and the branches. People are always hoping to find some other way. And they will even sell you wine made out of all sorts of substitutes, and hope to persuade you that it is from the true grape of a true vine.

Thus, when this nation was born, men thought that farmers from the plough, so they had only guns in their hands, could meet and conquer soldiers. But they could not. It was not till a Continental army of trained soldiers was made by all the care of Knox and Greene and Washington that the work of an army was done. When the Rebellion was to be crushed, and the first enthusiasm of loyalty seemed chilled, men thought by large bounties you could bribe mercenaries to fill the vacant places of brave men who had been killed. Figs from thistles, indeed! The brave soldier is not to be had at that price; and so many a failure proved. Experiences in history these, which only confirm every man's experience in manufacture, agriculture, or trade. If you want fruit, you must have root and stem. If you want a good table or chair, you must have seasoned wood. If you want oats or wheat, you must subsoil your land, drain it, pulverize the soil, clean out the stones, and weed. You must begin at the beginning.

In the relief of local poverty, which is the duty we are to consider to-day, this same preparation is necessary, unless we mean always to do the same thing to-morrow as to-day, and the next year as this year. Child's play to relieve poverty, unless we mean to prevent pauperism. It is to break off the thistle-head or the blossom of white-weed, and to suppose that the root will not trouble you next month or next year. Alms-giving in itself, therefore, is not charity. Your charity only begins with alms-giving; and unless you go forward to eradicate your thorns, to cut the tap-roots of your thistles, and to plant grape-vines in soil which you have underploughed, it is not a charity which deserves the name. To these sub-soiling processes, therefore, the church directs its effort with the most zeal. It is in such work as this that Channing and the other liberal leaders of this community led the way fifty and sixty years ago, and the results have been encouraging. While every effort to reduce pauperism and crime by any mere economical process fails, every effort to reduce them by levelling up men and women, by raising the quality of the material, has steadily succeeded. The way seems open for larger successes in the same directions.

Statistics are not attractive. But you must let me give you the figures which show how far, both in England and in New England, the steady work of men and women, who have applied pure ideal methods of relief to the diseases which we call crime and pauperism, have succeeded. Of England I will take the last twenty years. In that period, the annual number of boys and girls committed to prison for crime has been reduced from 8,801 to 6,810. The population of England, in the mean time, has increased almost as rapidly as the juvenile crime has decreased, so that the gain is forty per cent. in twenty years. I must not go into detail. But it is known to all the students of the subject that this gain is due to the work of such people as Miss Carpenter and the rest, who have been establishing and improving the reform schools and similar establishments. They undertook simply and squarely to abate the amount of crime among the young, and they have so far succeeded. They have had also the great help of the enlargement of the public system of common school education. The diminution of crime punished by imprisonment is so great that they have been able to sell some of their prisons in England, and use them for other purposes. We are apt to say that this is because they send the criminals over here; and this is one reason. But the other reason, and the greater reason, is that they have cut off the root so largely as they have, and have reclaimed so many of their juvenile offenders.

When we ask how much has been done here, the answer

is embarrassed by two difficulties. There is no question but that everything is improving. But we cannot, tell, *first*, how much the improvement is due to the return of the nation to the habits of peace from the habits of war; and, *second*, we cannot tell how far the emigration to America of criminals from Europe affects our condition unfavorably. Both these causes have a large effect; but, as you see, they operate against each other. That I may not claim results due only to the present prosperity in business, let me go back before the financial depression,— to the prosperous year 1872 and the beginning of 1873. We had then in Massachusetts thirty-six hundred prisoners in all. After four years of famine which then followed, and three years of prosperity which followed them,— with a large emigration out of Massachusetts, and another large emigration in,— we have now only thirty-five hundred prisoners in all. The number of prisoners has diminished one hundred, while the population has increased about twenty per cent. In the last year alone, the number of paupers in our pauper establishments has fallen from thirty-one thousand to eighteen thousand. But this decline must be ascribed mostly to the return of business prosperity. The diminution of crime does not follow the same law. On the other hand, petty crime — such as stealing from shops, stealing from the person, and the like — materially diminished in Boston during the year of the most severe business depression. The Chief of Police assured me that this was because people were so poor that they were more careful. He said there was less to steal, more care taken of it, and therefore less stolen. He said, also, that men had less spending-money; that they therefore drank less, and there was less crime produced by intoxicants.

I hope I have not tired you with these figures. I want to show that we who are idealists, we who are called dreamers, fanatics, and unpractical, have all along known what we were about, and that we have done what we tried to do. We are at work all along on the subsoiling process. We want real figs and real grapes, and are not satisfied with thistle figs or thorn grapes. We do not permit ourselves to be discouraged when an avalanche or land-slide stops almost every factory in Boston, and for a year, perhaps, throws out of employment laboring men. But in such years we cannot speak of results. For me, I do not want to claim all the gain of commercial prosperity as being due to the intelligent supervision of public and private charities. But I do want to encourage those who have liberally forwarded such charities, by showing that they have not labored in vain.

Now, I am going to ask you to contribute for our charity work of the winter; and, though we shall make other appeals to you, this is our principal appeal. By the contribution of to-day, we are to gauge our scale of work for the winter. You know sufficiently well by what enginery this work will be done. I have, thank God, no such statement to make to you as I had in the winter with which 1875 began and ended,—when the great workshops were all stopped; when every honest merchant and manufacturer was reducing the numbers of his hands; when this church had more families on its poor-list for relief than it had since it was a church. All that has changed. What is more, the sister-churches, and the different private and public charities of the town, are now knit together in an organized system, which grew out of the necessity of a period of famine; and in the Associated Charities there is a working power for the relief of poverty, simply, that the city has never had organized before. Precisely this improvement of system leaves us free to some details of the work of a church which I have never dared undertake before, but which I believe are now within our power.

They run in this line of subsoiling of which I spoke. It is our duty, and I believe it is in our power, to reduce the causes of pauperism and crime in this district which is intrusted to us. This work falls first of all on the Church of Christ; and, in our case, it falls particularly on this church.

It falls on us, because we are the Established Church for this region. These Catholics, Episcopalians, Methodists,—excellent good people, all of them.—came in after us. They are not to the manor born. The Congregational Church made Boston and the institutions of Boston. The South Congregational Church — this church — is the first church established this side Castle Street. Glad as we are to see new-comers entering on our field, all the same we acknowledge that they are new-comers; and for one I do not scruple to say that we understand the field and the methods of working it better than they do. By this, I mean to say that Boston is still an American city. Its institutions, through and through, are democratic. To train men to its life and to raise that life as it is lived by the mass of its people is to continue the work laid out by the men who made Boston. According to this doctrine, the subjects of an Italian prince, though he be an ecclesiastical prince, will not succeed in developing that life. Nor will men succeed who are studying English patterns. Nobody will succeed who turns his back on the future and worships any setting sun. We of this church ought to have peculiar facilities in dealing with the duty which in this town the church has in hand.

So far as one of those duties is the mere relief of hunger and cold, I have said already that I think it is well done. The city system of relief is admirable, the system of the Associated Charities is admirable. Less and less of such work devolves on a separate congregation. Where we spent a thousand dollars for such a purpose, in the war or in the panic, we do not need to spend a hundred dollars now. We are able to leave that unsatisfactory work of picking thistle-heads, as I called it, and to address ourselves more to the subsoiling processes. By this, I mean that we can study the district assigned to us by our conference, and see how we can prevent pauperism and crime.*

I shall be glad this winter, if we can so clearly follow the proceedings of the criminal courts as to know the circumstances of each arrest and conviction for crime in our district. I think we ought to be able, on the day when a man is imprisoned, to go to his family and see after them. Then is the time for that sort of care which shall see that his children do not follow the father's example. When he returns from his imprisonment, we ought to be able to meet him, to watch over him, and to be sure that he does not fall into bad company again. The second imprisonment is the disgrace of a Christian civilization. I think we can do a good deal — by sympathy and care, acting in regular system — to make such relapse of crime unnecessary.

Again, I want to have that kind watchfulness through the district that we may set on foot a system of home nursing, when sickness invades the poor man's dwelling. The dispensary gives medicine and medical advice. The diet kitchen gives food. But care, the proper care of the child in diphtheria or the mother in typhus, is just what our present charities do not give. The Sisters of Charity in the

---

*The "District" is bounded on the north by the Albany Railroad, on the south by Northampton Street, on the east side Washington, and by Pelham Street on the west side. In the other direction, the "District" extends to Tremont Street on the west, and to the harbor on the east.

older countries supply this work to a certain extent. I believe it is possible so to organize it here as to relieve sickness, when it comes to the poor, of its worst horrors.

I speak of these two lines of work in detail, because they involve certain novelties for our charity work here, in which we shall need the sympathy and help of every one who is here. I need not speak in detail of the familiar methods of work for those who are in need, which have all along occupied the South Friendly Society and your Board of Charities. The principle is fixed. As Dr. Ellis states it: "You do a man no good, unless you make him better." If you think it worth while to cut out garments and give out sewing, it is not in the foolish wish to compete with dealers: it is simply that you may teach the woman to sew well who, when she comes to you, cannot sew at all. You try to do her good by making her better,—a better seamstress; and, in short, our effort is by calling on as large a number of kindly people to help as is possible; to infuse, wherever we can get a chance, the light and life which the spirit of God carries, wherever a kind heart goes. The loneliness of life in cities makes the curse of cities. To break up that loneliness, to bring about sympathy, friendliness, mutual support between the old resident and the stranger, between the sick and the well, between the ignorant and those who know something, this is the application of Christian principle. When I was asked to speak on this subject at Philadelphia, I said: "There is the whole story. If, by such agencies as I have hinted at, those to whom much has been given have, without condescension, but in the real spirit of Christian brotherhood, opened the doors for an easy intercourse with those to whom less has been given; if the rule of give and take, teach and learn, lend and borrow, help and be helped, fairly works itself into the society of large cities, as it already exists in the simpler social order of the country,—there will be no socialism but Christian socialism, and no communism but the communism in which a man bears his brother's burdens." And I asked, What is the spell on life in cities which does not exist on life in the country, which compels us to deal only with people whose clothes are bought at the same shops with ours, while in the country we are permitted to deal with all the sons and daughters of our Father, God?

And no one answered me.

I do not believe that that spell is omnipotent. Love is

omnipotent. The man who has once engaged in setting on his feet the puzzled exile from another land finds that his work is well worth pursuing, and that life itself has enlarged, from the moment when he left the daily rut of horse-car, office, exchange, and club, for the wider duty in which he lent a hand to this exile, because he was his brother, entered into his life and bore his burden. The woman who left her novel that she might be sure that the beef-tea was rightly made for a girl in fever, was quite sure as she came home at night-fall that the romance she had played a part in was the better worth of the two. It was more artistic, and it had more of the divine life. Both of them won the Christian victory. Each of them learned that the quality of mercy blesses him that gives as him that takes. Or, as the same truth stands in an older text,

"Blessed are the merciful, for they shall obtain mercy."

With every exercise, the power grows.

LAW AND GOSPEL.

All things work together for good to them that love God.— ROMANS viii., 29.

It is only one of the outbursts of delight of which this letter and, indeed, all Paul's letters are full. To us, such enthusiastic joy is indeed remarkable. It contrasts sharply enough with the grave decorum of our religious exercises. As you came to church to-day, you did not see people hurrying, thronging, singing, and cheering,— eager to be first at the place of service, and in whatever way to attest their joy that they have found an infinite Father and a Saviour of perfect love. Yet that is the tone of feeling recorded here. And it has been recorded again and again through history. The memory of the campaign of Francis Davidis, in Transylvania, has lately been recalled. He was one of the first of the Unitarian preachers. He was a foreigner, who could not have spoken the Magyar tongue very well. He was not a priest, and he spoke in a Catholic country. But so well he spoke, with such transport did he show to men what it is to have a Father in heaven, and no one between us and him,— what joy and blessedness it is to know that the Saviour of mankind is indeed one of ourselves, that God himself asks nothing better than man who is man indeed, when he has a revelation to make,— with such joy and enthusiasm did Davidis speak, that the people thronged about him, wherever he went. He should not speak in the open air at street corners. They stormed the churches. They turned the priests out-doors. This was purer religion, and better, than their religion. He and his with their simple creed — God is our father and Jesus is our brother — were bidden to enter into those churches and to preach there, in place of the Roman priesthood. And so it has been there to this day.

There is, in truth, nothing in the nature of the Christian

religion to make people shy in the proclamation of it, sad in their profession of it, doubtful about its future, gloomy in their general view of life, or in any sort low-toned or depressed. True, the decorums of establishments — nay, the fear of making sacred things seem trivial — all unite to give seriousness and often dulness to our religious statement and profession. But there is every reason now, which existed in the beginning, why the common people should hear Jesus Christ gladly, why the gospel should be regarded as glad tidings, why men should exult, with whatever expression of their enthusiasm, in the liberty with which Christ makes them free. Indeed, the Church has probably given itself no blow so dangerous as by the effort — which it has made so often, as fast as it achieved secular power — to restrict general or popular amusement. Nor does it ever make a greater mistake than when it insists that its own exercises — as its meetings, its music, its books, its exhortations — shall be sorry rather than glad, or hopeless rather than cheerful.

> "Religion never was designed
> To make our pleasures less."

The distinction between sombre religion and joyous religion is likely to underlie all the distinctions drawn by the theologians. There is every reason why it should. For, whether the theologians say so or no, here is the root of the matter. Either God loves all his children, and means that they shall all be saved, or, in the midst of a certain technical love for all of them, he has predetermined that the greater part of them shall be damned. According as the one of these suppositions is true, or the other, we can well imagine that men shall be very sad or very cheerful. Or, again, either all men are my brothers, with whom I may and ought to seek communion, — in which case my life will be social and glad, — or, on the other hand, the greater part of mankind is incapable of good, unable to pray even, — in which case I ought to be reserved, and shy of society. Or, once more, I have in Jesus Christ really a brother of my brotherhood, a friend, a well-wisher, a teacher, an example, an inspirer, who knew really my temptations, and gives me practical guidance and common-sense help, or I have in him a being wholly unlike all other beings, whom my imagination must not depict, whose life I cannot conceive of, at whose very name I must bow my head, and who, in a word, is to be to me the most unreal person in history. It follows, of course, that as I take one of these views or the other will my religion be cheerful or the other. Our own poet, Dr. Holmes, notes an essential distinction, and not a mere superficial badge, when, in discribing a Sunday in Boston, he contrasts

> "The cheerful Christian of the Liberal fold"

against him whom he meets in the street,

> "Severe and smileless, he that runs may read
> The stern disciple of Geneva's creed."*

It is six years since I received a letter from a stranger, which I read, with my answer, in this pulpit, because I thought he probably expressed the feelings of others. He said: "I want light.... What is the truth? I was brought up amid the strictest orthodox surroundings. My parents, my wife, and my intimate friends are strong Calvinists. I cannot doubt but they are sincere and happy in their faith; but it does not satisfy my heart.... I wish I might believe as you do; for you seem to have faith in your faith.... If you will tell me what you believe to be the truth, or refer me to books (not very expensive ones, for I cannot afford to buy them) from which I can learn it, you may help me out of the darkness, and will certainly earn and receive my gratitude." To this letter, I replied at once. I told him he needed no book but the New Testament. Even if he could not read that, it was enough to know that God is our Father, and that we all are brethren. I told him that from this truth all other truth, religious or social, flowed; that, as for faith, he must use such faith as he had, and, using it, he would find more. I heard no more of my correspondent for six years.

It happened a few weeks ago that I lighted on his letter; and as I have often thought of him, and as often prayed God for him, I wrote to him again, now I had found the address, to ask him how he fared. In reply, I have a

---

* "By the white neck-cloth, with its straightened tie,
The sober hat, the Sabbath-speaking eye,
Severe and smileless, he that runs may read
The stern disciple of Geneva's creed.
Decent and slow, behold his solemn march :
Silent, he enters through yon crowded arch.
A livelier bearing of the outward man,
The light-hued gloves, the undevout rattan,
Now smartly raised, or half-profanely twirled,
A bright, fresh twinkle from the outward world,
Tell their plain story. Yes: thine eyes behold
A cheerful Christian from the Liberal fold."

[The arch was the entrance to Marlboro chapel, since destroyed.]

cordial letter. Perhaps I had better not read it to you, even with the omission of his name. It is simply a little autobiography, which gives a short account of the moral experience from boyhood. It is clear enough that he was a good boy, who wanted to obey his father and to please him. And the pathetic thing is that his love for his father wrought the misery of his life. For his father was a sincere member of the Presbyterian Church. When the boy was fourteen years old, a revival swept along, and all his young companions joined the church. He also knew that it would please his father, if he would do the same,—nay, he also wanted to serve God and to please him. Now, it is here that the old oppression of a Law comes in. For the minister told him, his father told him, everybody he loved told him that he must assent to a covenant which carried all the Westminster Confession with it. Of course, he did not understand it. Why, nobody understands it, far less a child of fourteen. What he did understand he did not believe. But all the same he was told that this was not his affair. I suppose he was told that he would come to it. At all events, he was told that great and good men had determined on it, and that a boy like him must not set up his own will. So he assented to it, — that is, he said he believed it; and in that moment his moral fall began. He traces the steps distinctly in his letter. The efforts that he made to silence his conscience there taught him how to silence his conscience in other things. The purity of decision and the strength of will were gone. He traces the moral decline till he actually violated a trust committed to him. Then, in the horror for what he had done, he fled from his family, fled from his friends, he changed his name, if I understand him, and exiled himself from all he loved.

It is in this exile that this man finds out that God is his Father, and that all men are his brethren, and comes at the clear sight that this is really the whole of religion. In this exile, he sees what is the Liberty in which Christ makes him free. He sees that God never meant to have him strain his conscience or force his will by those old creeds and catechisms. Yes; and, in this exile, his father's love follows him. His father covers his crime, so that it shall not be known by the world. His father promises him welcome among the friends he had deserted. He joins his family again, in another city. And for all of them a new life begins.

But why does it begin? Here is the moral of this story. It is because, in this city, the pastor of the Evangelical church which he seeks, in the true spirit of Christ, meets him and welcomes him. The poor repentant tells him, squarely, that he can make nothing of the covenant and does not believe the creed. He believes God is his Father, and man his brother, and in that belief rejoices. And this friend says, as Paul would have said, that this is all he wants, or any man wants, as assurance of religion. From that welcome, forward, the poor fellow has found his life happy and his steps sure. Sorrows? Yes, plenty of sorrows; but, all along, the heavenly strength which bears sorrow. His wretchedness and failure began in this horrid struggle to obey a dogmatic law. His joy and peace begin in the moment when he yields to the loving-kindness of a free gospel.

A man is living in light and cheerfulness, who was in darkness and wretchedness. What was it which made him wretched? Simply, it was his effort to conform to a religious statement which he did not believe. This not only made him wretched, it made him wicked. It broke the moral sense with which he started. How does he regain this moral sense? He regains it by repentance and by squarely giving up the effort to hold on by these old standards, which were, after all, only so much inherited lumber which had come down to him from his fathers. The case is precisely like the case of Paul, and those of so many of Paul's converts. This man has tried to be saved by a law. It is the law of the Westminster Confession. A very stiff law it is. For my own part, having been born, thank God, quite outside both of them, I think I had rather take my chance to obey that old Jewish law — which Paul hated so — than to try to conform to this system of John Calvin's. This man had tried to live by this Westminster law; and he had wholly failed. It had made him a hypocrite. It had made him a bad man. Then he found out that God was his Father and all men were his brothers. When he found this out, he found that this is enough. He found that this is the liberty with which Christ makes men free. And his whole letter has the jubilee ring of Paul's enthusiastic words about the deliverance from that old bondage. And his life, according to his own account of it, is all lighted and fired by the gladness of true religion. I do not say by its peace, merely: I mean more than peace. Here is a man who has found out that, if you live with God, and live for man, it is joy and gladness and victory to live.

Now, I do not tell that story for any good that it may do to the chiefs of the Presbyterian Church. I have no doubt that they hear such stories themselves, and have to consider their morals; and I do not suppose that any of such chiefs are hearing me now. I will not descend to that cheap courage which teaches absent people their duty. I think such a letter as that has a warning and a lesson for us who are here. I have a right to say, in passing, that every such letter shows to every pulpit and every preacher the danger of overstatement, the terrible risk which teachers or counsellors run, when they try to tune the strings too high which are given to their care. If such a string cracks, it is not the maker of the string who is guilty. The *North American Review*, a few months ago, was bitterly assailed, by what is called the religious press of the country, for asking me to warn the preachers of this country of the danger of insincerity, the danger of overstatement. The *Review* was told — and I was told — that we must mind our own business; that, if we were insincere, we must mend our ways, but that we must leave other people to theirs. Now, I think a letter like this shows how far this danger travels, and how the penalty for the overstatement strikes far away from the preacher. This man had done his best to profess a creed which was unintelligible to him. There is no doubt he had been told that he must profess it or be damned. He did profess it, and found he was damned then. And not till he disowned it before God and man did he escape the penalty. At last, observe, he found in the pulpit a man who told him that this creed of the Church was of no sort of consequence. He found a man who was satisfied with his love of God and love of man. He found a man not guilty of the overstatement which had ruined years of this poor fellow's life and made the name of religion hateful to him. Surely, that is a warning to you and to me that, when we attempt to lift others into a religious life, we never substitute what we would be glad to know for what we do know, what we wished men believed for what they must believe, what is supposed for what is proven.

Do not say that there are not five preachers in this house now. There is not a person here who has not some duty in the inculcation of religion; and every parent here, every elder brother and sister, every Sunday-school teacher, and every day-school teacher, quite as much, has a great deal to do in this line. Now, just this experience of Paul's, between the religion of law and the religion of love, is an experience by which you ought to be warned in the every-day religious teaching, where you have chances worth a thousand-fold the chance which the pulpit gives to me. Your child or your pupil may grow up in the love of God and in the love of man, or he may grow up in the dread of God and the fear of man. That is, he may grow up under the law, instead of growing up under the gospel. It is your business to see that his whole notion of religion is gospel. He ought to have no sense of terror in his prayer, in his Sunday, in his reading of the Bible, or in his notion of duty. Duty is not to be something which he does because he will be beaten or burned, if he fail to do it. Duty is his glad part in the joyful work of a joyful world. A Father, who is full of love in the midst of his blessings to the world, is glad to have his children round him all the time, helping in his work, and taking their little share. That is the child's privilege, which we call his duty.

And surely we have a duty to the world. When we know that half Christendom is still groaning under this pressure of a law, of a written creed or code which somebody this side of Jesus Christ has established, surely our duty is clear to do something that they may enjoy the liberty to which we were born. I had a letter from the mountains of Tennessee the other day, admirably written,— as well written as any man could write. But the writer told me that he had had to fight his way through alone, from the hardest shell of strict Baptist theology. He had little enough help from the thirty-nine articles, of course,— he had no help from the Westminster Catechism,— as he came into the real freedom of the real gospel. No difficulty, of course, if he had been left with his simple gospel, to read it. But every authorized expounder of it told him that it did not mean what it seemed to mean. Every authorized expounder told him that he was wrong in taking its apparent simplicity for the truth. He did fight his way through. And, after he had got through, some accident, some scrap in a secular newspaper, told him that some people called Unitarians believed the Bible when it said that man was made in the likeness of God, and believed Jesus Christ when he said we might all trust the Holy Spirit. So he wrote for some of our books, and he wanted to know if we had no preacher who would go there. I confess I was not well satisfied with the attitude of our Church toward a man like that. I wondered he did not say: "Why did you leave me to fight my own battle? Why was there no man of you who was willing for the truth to come and tell us the truth? Why did no church of you take Tennessee for a field, where you might scatter at least the seed of printed truth, that those of us who were under this bondage of a man-made law might rejoice in the same liberty in which Christ had set you free?" The man did not say so. He was too good a Christian for that. But when, a few weeks after, a member of this church, an old Sunday-school teacher of ours, wrote to me that he was going down to East Tennessee to preach the real glad tidings there, I did not feel quite so meanly as before in writing to my unknown friend. It is a good thing to live in a city like this, where a man may enjoy his religion and have faith in his faith. But it is a good thing which we owe to the courage of men who lived long ago. And it seems to me a very mean thing so to live, if we do not forecast the future, if we do not study the world outside of us all the time, and, while we enjoy the love of God, do what we can that others may. While we take the comforts of our freedom, we are bound — in mere honor bound — to lift others into the liberty in which Christ wants to make them free. Shall we sit upon our rocks of safety, and be all indifferent while the shipwrecked vessels there go down?

Nor is it for our own time only that we have this duty. Who wants to leave his children in bondage from which his fathers wrenched themselves free? Mrs. Wells is quite right in the essay which some of you heard at the Second Church. We do want to prejudice our children in favor of good and truth and love. And, among the necessities for these realities, we want to prejudice them in favor of simple religion, of freedom. They will soon enough be tempted the other way. But do we want them to yield to the temptation? You send your girl to a great boarding-school. With the first spring term, the inevitable revival comes round, foreordained by the principal and led up to. And in the throng of those,— first anxious, then inquiring with tears, and then redeemed, your daughter is naturally enough swept along,— swept along to say she believes this and that which she does not understand, this and that of which she can know nothing, and this and that, indeed, of which she never dreamed. At first, of course, she has your tender sympathy, because you see she is earnest and true. But her time of trial is not now. It is by and by. Her time of trial will come five years hence, ten years hence. You have let her put on these pretty bracelets, because the other girls put them on. And then her arms have grown, her wrists have grown; and the golden bands are agony. Nay: if they are not cut off, they are death. Surely, it is your duty, before that child leaves your house, that she shall know that she is the free child of a loving God. She cannot be too young for you to teach her that, with her own prayer, in her own way, she may come to him. And, if you are wise, you will early show to her what an escape was that in which such men as Paul and his friends escaped the bondage of the Jewish law; how such women as you can tell her stories of escaped the bondage of the Roman law; how her own fathers escaped the bondage of a ritual and ceremonial law; and how people all around her have to struggle in agony and tears to escape the bondage of a doctrinal law. Show to her, too, that all these with a great price obtained this freedom, but that she is free-born.

Most of all, perhaps, does the duty press on us for our own lives; that with every enjoyment, every holiday, every new book, every glad success, we so associate our gratitude to God that religion shall come to mean joy, and joy religion. Religion shall not mean the carving of reading-desks or the embroidery of table-cloths or the architecture of steeples. Religion shall not mean the meeting of a synod or the discussion of a catechism. Religion shall mean life,— life full of God, and happy because full. It is the certainty, fixed in one's own experience, that "all things work together for good to those that love God."

THE MEN OF GADARA.

They began to pray him to depart out of their coasts. — MARK v., 17.

WE persuade ourselves that we should have welcomed such a Saviour as Jesus Christ. A child of God, so true to that great name that we should be willing to call him the son of God, — kinder than the kindest, stronger than the strongest, braver than the bravest, wiser than the wisest, more practical than the most practical, and all the time in perfect sympathy with us all, — we know and we say that this is just what we need. If he would come now, how he would bless us, and how we would welcome him! Hidden in the tangle of the wicked prejudice against the Jewish race is anger that they killed this Saviour. If it took form in words it would be to say that they are people so stupid and so bad at once that, when at last the prayer of all ages was answered, — when men saw for once, for a few months, the divine order of man's life, — these brutes could do nothing better than kill him who showed it. For ourselves, so thoroughly has the world learned in eighteen centuries that here is God's way for man's life that we go to Palestine for traces of it. A pebble from the beach at Capernaum is, and ought to be, more sacred than any other pebble. And a picture of the old olive-trees at Gethsemane is, and ought to be, a daily benediction to the man who sees it. What, then, would be the rapture of our greeting, if this Saviour took human form again, — came to us in our Boston, and showed us how to live?

There are different ways of finding answers to that question. Nay, in different moods, we should answer it differently. Little question what answer any of us would make to it, in the hush of a darkened house, where lay the body of a child, a sister, or a father, waiting for its burial. Different answers, in different needs and in different moods, there would be. Will you follow me now, in some thought as to the risks of our repeating history? Suppose we were in the old temptations, should we make the old answer? And are the old temptations done away?

In trying to work out any of these stories, we are apt to be deceived by our own wishes and prepossessions. But, in truth, these people were not all sitting, waiting for a Messiah. They did not know that they lived in a crisis of history, — excepting in this notion which men always have, that to-day is all-important, and its sufferings intolerable. They were about their daily work and daily play, just as we are ; and daily work and daily play filled a very large place in their eyes. These people of Gadara — "on the other side," as they are always called — were perhaps less interested in Jerusalem politics and Hebrew jealousies than the people on the Capernaum side. On either side, the population was from all nations. It was "Galilee of the Gentiles"; and the old staple of Hebrewism had, at Capernaum, about as much and about as little part in the web and woof of society, as the old staple of English Puritanism has in Boston, among Irish emigrants, Germans, Frenchmen, and Italians, people who are attached to European habits and people who are proud to be mistaken for Englishmen. From Capernaum, Jesus crossed over to this Gadara, precisely because he wanted to escape from the enthusiasm of those he knew at home. There he found a population less Jewish and more indifferent. There was more Gentile and less Hebrew. Yet it was not far away. Only a sail of five or six miles.

But there are sickness and distress everywhere, and he is Saviour. That is what he is for. Where there is suffering, he must help. As he lands, here comes a poor wretch, laden with fetters, — who shall say how long ? — living among the tombs because no one will house him elsewhere. The tombs are there to this day, caves in the rock that the poor wretch had found refuge in. As Jesus lands, he comes rushing down to abuse him. But the Saviour, with the inevitable power which he carried with him always, soothes the madman to gentleness, turns his whole life, indeed, till now so bedevilled and dispirited ; and, where there was this wild outcast, there stands a man, gentle and grateful, ready to be clothed again, and all in his right mind.

So far, it is easy to see how we should welcome a visitor,

a Saviour, who came to us with such blessings. Let it be announced to-morrow that a stranger had arrived here to-day who met at once some howling maniac, had not avoided his insults, had not sought to restrain him, but by the pure majesty of his person, and the calm, overruling divinity of all he said and was, had set this madman on his feet, had restored him strong, cheerful, and all right to his friends, all of us would want to know more. Some would not believe a word of it, but even those would be curious. They who had seen, and were sure, would be grateful, would be eager to see more of the stranger, and would seek to give him welcome. All this, so far as we know, the people of the city of Gadara would have felt. That is the way people felt in other towns where Jesus came, and, in his commanding way, overawed evil in whatever form. Gadara might have felt so, also.

But in Gadara the matter was complicated. In some way,— we know not how, for the accounts are as confused as they are fragmentary, — an immense herd of swine, feeding on the table-land above the lake, rushed off into the sea, and were drowned, at the moment when the poor maniac was restored. He thought himself that his cure was connected with their destruction. The bystanders thought so. Forty years after, the evangelists, writing their narrative, thought so ; and, so far as testimony goes, we cannot say they were not right. Two thousand swine were lost.— The man was saved. Yes. But the swine were lost. This loss, as I say, complicates the incident in the minds of the people, and abates the warmth of their welcome. "Two thousand swine lost!" Where will the rest of our swine and sheep and cattle go? They seek Jesus at once, respectfully,— timidly, very likely,— but they beseech him to depart. They will have none of him. The sooner he can go, the better ; and he goes. That is the way in which, in fact, men received then a Saviour, in whose power they believed.

We give the true colors to the incident, I suppose, if we understand that on the western side of the Lake public opinion was so strongly Jewish that men could not keep herds of swine there. Still there would be a market for pork in the Roman garrisons, and among other indifferent foreigners. It is easy to see that that market would somehow be supplied. On the other side is some stock-raiser who defies Jewish law and Jewish prejudice at once, by raising swine for this convenient market. I can remember when we had just such a case here. Our police in Boston was so strong that men dared not keep large numbers of stolen dogs together. But our police had no authority in Cambridge,— indeed, Cambridge was in another county. So unprincipled men found it quite worth while to keep in Cambridge a corral of dogs stolen in Boston, expecting that, when a man found his dog there, he would buy him again. The success of liquor-dealers in keeping up their business in face of prohibitory laws gives a perfect analogy. The early critics of the Gospels were swift to show that the destruction of these animals was probably a part of some vindication of insulted Jewish law.

From that day to this, their name has been used to denote people who will not endure sound doctrine, unless it is pleasant. The people who are indifferent about the saving of men, if the saving be mixed up with the loss of swine, are called, in many of the serious writers, Gadarenes. Instances will occur to you at once. The Chinese government implores England not to send opium to China. The Christian men of England take up the appeal and bring it to Parliament. The government and press acknowledge that the appeal is rightful and humane. "But," they say, "we have £6,000,000 of East Indian revenue involved. Do not talk sentiment. Tell us how to find this revenue elsewhere." And so the opium-trade goes on. You cannot save the men, and keep the swine. Up till our civil war, our status regarding slavery was like that. The enthusiasts said,—

"That on the day
You make a man a slave, you take his life away."

But the South said: "Yes, but you must have cotton. And, if you free these slaves, you risk your cotton." Again, the lives of men were measured against the value of swine. The whole liquor-discussion is complicated in the same way. Loss of revenue to government, ruin of vested interests, destruction of trade,— all these dangers press men's action, though perhaps they do not dare express them in words, when we who believe in men insist that the saving of men is the one reality for which government exists, or laws. Nay, you see it in the concerns of individuals. How often you see a worn-out old farm which has thus been the curse of the man who inherited it! His brothers were so fortunate as to have no inheritance. They went off to live as their training or their tastes directed, or the providence of God. But this man had this millstone of a farm around his neck, and has carried it, round-shouldered, till he died. He has never been able, alas! to do anything but carry the farm. The man was lost that the farm might be saved. Here are instances, in the humblest affairs, or in the largest works of nations, of the rejection of the Idea, of that which saves and makes alive, that one may hold on to the thing, to what has been, to the institution. Men send away a Saviour, that they may keep their swine.

One's fancy hovers over Gadara a moment to ask what it might have been, if only any ten men there had seen the blessing that came to them, if they had welcomed this master of men, at once so strong and so tender. What if he had made his home with them, and to their children's lives given a new spring! And, when the wider duty to a world called him to other cities, or the fate of Jerusalem compelled him there to die, what if some John or Philip of his train, alive with all his life, glad with all his joy, had remained there! Think of fathers and mothers, brothers and sisters in the little town, every day more glad, more hearty, more manly, and more womanly. Social life becomes more broad, gossip dies, impurity is forgotten. The petty life of the village gives way to the large life of sons and daughters of God. It is not one raving maniac only who is clothed and in his right mind. It is that there are no drunkards at the wine-shop. Nay, there is no wine-shop; there is no lewdness in the street; there is no cheating in the market. Why, there is a new life at the theatre. There is new music at the concert-room. Men walk with a more manly step. The beauty of women is more true, and even the play of children more happy. This is what might have come, had Gadara welcomed the Saviour who had redeemed a man. But, alas! the butchers and pork-raisers of Gadara drove that very Saviour away.

It is easy enough to see that every village and town has the same choice to-day. Will it be distinguished only for its trade in pigs, as Gadara has become and other cities; or will it be distinguished for its men and women? Will it thrive in its trade in liquors, as Capua throve; or will it thrive in the lives and honor of its men and women! Will it be a place of gambling, like Baden or Hamburg or Monaco; or will it be known the world over as a place of true men and true women? Or, for a nation, shall its policy be a policy for bringing in gold and silver into its treasury, or shall the whole drift of its policy be the training of manly men and womanly women? Village, town, or nation, which determines on the nobler policy, not only admits this Saviour when he comes and knocks, but seeks for him, welcomes him, honors and obeys him. It is not as it teaches its boys to spell or to multiply that it succeeds. But it is as they see him and know him, as indeed a friend; as they do as they would be done by, as they bear each other's burdens. When they do welcome him, then their rags fall off, and they are clothed; their handcuffs drop, and they are free; the old selfish isolation ends, and there is society. Thus indeed do men know that they are his, when all men see that these people love one another.

Nor is it cities and villages chiefly who have this choice to make. You and I are making it every day. Is my first object to-morrow to build upon yesterday's foundation of things? Stones, land, clothes, cotton, woollen, hemp, iron, brass, or silver, or gold, — there are many of these things we have to deal with, just as these Gadarenes dealt in pigs, and thought they must deal in them. Have you and I come so far that, when to-morrow comes, we shall simply build on these same foundations, or have we pluck and manhood for something more? This Saviour will certainly come to us to-morrow. He is in town to-day. There are twenty proposals, even, which he will make to each one of us to-morrow morning. For the world is so far changed since this day of the madman, that he has his plans laid everywhere now, and he wants you and me to help him. Nay, we have received so much from him, that it is sheer dishonor, if we do not help his plans in turn. Can you lay down your pen and listen to the story of this boy, who wants your help that he may go to Colorado? Can you give up your afternoon drive, that you may help forward the Woman's Hospital? Can you give up the evening party, that you may spend the same hours with such-a-one, who is blind, or with so-and-so, who is bed-ridden? Can you set back, for a day, the contract for your own building, lest the service of the city suffer, and this matter be neglected, in which the interests of all of us are involved? Can you renounce the pleasure of the play to-morrow night, if the credit of the town require your absence from a degrading performance? All these questions are just the same question as the Gadarenes had before them, under which they broke down. It only simplifies the form a little to say, " Will you have a man saved,—well, and in his right mind? or, Will you have so many pigs sunk in the sea?" And these illustrations are only from outward things. The Saviour's own questions and demands are on a grade yet higher.

He bids you — yes, while you are caring for the swine, as those swine-herds were on the cliffs — to be looking on the clear blue of heaven, and thinking of the Father who made heaven and you, who makes heaven and you to-day, and is the wisdom and the tenderness which you call Nature. This Saviour asks you, as you add up the figures and as you write the letters, to use the ready help of your Father and his,—so to write and so to add as one who bears his brother's burdens. Your boy is at school, your husband is away, your daughter has gone out on the day's duties, and you are alone. But this gospel is everywhere now. Into your lonely room this Saviour comes, to every purpose. For it is his voice which asks you to be sure that home shall have its brightest greeting for all of these, when they shall return. It is he who says that home is God's present kingdom, and that we are to find God there, nor seek him on mountain or in temple. It is he who tells you that the very sacraments of religion are the sacraments of every morning's greeting. Now, in all these appeals of a Saviour, there is just the temptation before which the men of Gadara failed. You and I have their example. You and I know that he has word to speak which is life and strength to all who will listen. The more shame to you and me, if, at whatever moment we hear his voice or see his face, we ask him to leave our coasts, that we may plod on in our dirty, mean, and selfish way.

THESE THREE ABIDE.

"And now abideth Faith, Hope, Charity, these three."— I. Cor. xiii., 13.

WE observe every day that the great words of religion wear out, if it were only from too much use. Perhaps the use is reverent. Perhaps it is careless. Take these words. If I went into any reform meeting, as of temperance men, of independent voters, of friends of abused children, and told them they needed more Faith, they would take the phrase as professional. They would be glad to have me say it, so far as it added to the respectability of the meeting. Then they would want me to sit down, that some "practical man" might speak. All the same, the real thing, "Faith," is what they all need, and without which they fail. What they are tired of is a worn-out word. Our Latin word *Faith*, indeed, was but a poor word at the beginning. As for the word "Charity" used in this text, it was always a bad word for the purpose. It never really meant, to the common ear of Englishmen, what Paul meant. It owes its place here to a certain shyness of the translators,— first of the Greek into Latin, then from both languages into English. Paul, and the other, writers of the Testament, used the same word for God's love toward men and man's love to other men. To their mind, it was the same relation; the whole gospel, indeed, being founded on the identity of all spiritual essence. Man is of God's nature. God's love and man's love are therefore expressed in Gospels and Epistles by the same word. But, from the shyness of the translators, this word is sometimes rendered *love*, and sometimes *charity;* for they quailed before showing to us, who read English, the oneness of nature of God and man. The same pen, therefore, which writes, "God commends his love to us," and "the love of God which passeth knowledge," and "to know the love of Christ," or "the love of the Spirit," when it comes to apply the same word to the relations of men, speaks of "charity which abides; charity which suffers long, and is kind." I need not analyze this uneasiness of the translators. Perhaps they did not quite dare say that man's pure feelings are just like Christ's and God's, as in fact they are. Or perhaps they thought the word "love" was mixed up with human passion, with the love of man for woman, and did not well apply to the universal love which the Christian religion demands. Anyway, in these critical passages, they substituted the more technical word "charity" for the broader words "friendship" or "love." And to us this is a real misfortune. For, to Bible reading people, it lets down badly the whole plane of what is meant and needed. That plane should always be kept up to the level of what Jesus said, that the whole of life depends on two commandments: —

I. That one love God, and
II. That he love his neighbor as himself. In both these directions, the love spoken of is nothing less than such tender and all-embracing love as that in which God himself loves all his children.

As for the third of the great words, Hope, although Paul puts it midway between the other two, it has fared worse than either. For, between two schools of theologians, it has fallen to the ground. There is on one side the school of Luther, who insist on Faith; and, on the other, the school which cites St. James, and insists on Love. But Hope, which Paul places between the two, has as yet had no school and no sect. Yet Jesus Christ insists on what Paul means, — nay, he presupposes it. For what Paul means is that a man shall look outside time and beyond the world. He means that man shall live and move as an immortal, and Jesus Christ takes this for granted. It is not of Palestine that he states the laws. He states the laws of the universe for all children of God. It is not for to-day that he states them: it is for all life, for men and women who live beyond time, who are eternal. So is it that Paul, when he names the eternal elements of life, between faith in God and love of man places man's certainty of his own eternity. He bids man look beyond the line of time. That forward look is what the word "Hope" stands for, midway of the three.

And it is by another calamity — even worse, as I think — that the three have been spoken of as the "three Christian

Graces." Graces indeed they are, but they are only debased by that association, in either the modern or the ancient use of the word "Graces." For the three graces of the ancient literature were simply three adorners of life. They lend "the grace and beauty to everything that delights and elevates gods and men." Now, while it is perfectly true that Faith and Hope and Love do this, this is, by no means, all that they have to do. And when, therefore, a sentimental world, or an ignorant world, call Faith, Hope, and Love the three Christian Graces, and so mix them up with the three old Graces of Homer and Hesiod and the other Greek poets, they do great injustice to Faith, Hope, and Love. Poor Paul would have groaned in spirit,— indeed, he would have torn this immortal word to tatters, — had he supposed that the outcome of what he wrote was to be only a confusion of his three eternities with the gay and sportive Thalia, Aglia, and Euphrosyne, the three Greek Graces, whom you may still see in some alabaster mantel-ornament, clasping each other in amiable affection. What Paul says is that Faith, Hope, and Love are three eternal realities. He says that while all marbles and granites crumble, while all institutions are buried in sand-storms, while laws become obsolete, while idols fall from their thrones, and empires are ruined, there are three eternities. These three abide. They do not change. They cannot change. They are man's knowledge of God, man's love of man, and, midway, man's sense of eternity. To call these three rocks merely three "graces" of character is to confound the foundation of a palace with the sculptured playthings in its queen's boudoir.

This statement of the text is not Paul's statement only. It is his epigram, condensing into the fewest words the distinctive peculiarities of the Christian system. And, if any one care much for a scientific definition of Christianity, that definition would take its form from this epigram. For all religions involve faith, or man's sense of God. And all humane or altruistic philosophies involve man's care for man, or love. The distinctive character of Christ's religion is, that while he insists on these two as essential to each other, he compels man to regard himself and his brethen as eternal.

They are the immortal children of an eternal God, just as Christ is the immortal son of an eternal God. These three certainties all intertwisted together, so that each becomes a part of the other, make up the Christian system, if anybody care for a statement so abstract and dry. This, and no talk of decorative art, this statement of reality, and no upholstery of graceful adornment, is what Paul means when he says, of Faith, Hope, and Love, these three "abide." Prophecy fails, preaching fails, signs fail, miracles fail, tongues cease, and knowledge vanishes away; but these three abide, these are everlasting.

The late Ephraim Peabody, one of the wisest as he was one of the loveliest of those preachers who have led forward this city in a higher life, used to say of preaching that there are but eight possible subjects for sermons. He said that after a preacher had preached once on all of these eight, he had simply to do the same thing again, but to do it better than he did it before. I long since accepted the statement as being substantially true. And, in advising young preachers, I have sometimes gone so far as to tell them what the eight classes of sermons are. There are the three simple statements of God, of heaven, and of our relations to man. Then we want to know, and want to show, how faith quickens hope, how faith compels love, and how hope or the sense of heaven leads man up to his full duty to his fellow-men. Here are six of the subdivisions. The seventh would show what I call the intertwining of all these three elements of life with each other, and under the eighth head would come the immediate application of either of these themes in the formation of character or the improvement of the world. Under one or other of these heads, I believe you could classify every Christian sermon you have ever heard. Besides these there are heathen sermons, æsthetic sermons, sermons drawn from personal experience, or from the occasion of the moment, of which perhaps you have heard many; but those are not Christian sermons as such, nor is the memory of them important, or their classification.

I had occasion to speak here, last Sunday afternoon, on what are known among several thousand young people as the Four Mottoes.

They are the mottoes above the speaker's desk in our Sunday-school, where they were placed by the superintendent ten years ago. Around those mottoes, mostly through the agency of Miss Mary Lathbury and Miss Van Marten, has been formed a large organization in the Sunday-schools of the Methodist Church, called the "Look-up Legion," the name being taken from the first of the four. To this organization there now belong six or seven thousand young people, scattered in all parts of the world. These young people, let me say in passing, take their interest in the Legion wholly from their interest in the principles of the four mottoes. For, when Miss Lathbury founded the order, she had never heard of the book from which they are taken, nor of the young hero whose life inspired it. Now, those four mottoes are simply the translation into modern language of the central words of Paul and of Jesus. They state in the familiar words of our time these eternal principles of the Divine Life. Faith is the determination of man to "look up," — to look to a higher law than his own impulse. Hope is his determination to "look forward rather than backward." Love is his determination to "look out rather than in"; and, because Love must show itself in practice, Love is the determination also to "lend a hand."

The business of the Look-Up Legion, of any of the Wadsworth Clubs, as of every man who wants to live in the Christian or Divine order of human life, is to intertwine these principles in one life. That man is a fanatic, and he is sure to fail who rests on any one alone.

For an illustration of what Faith would be and is to any church or man tempted to rest on it alone, take the legend of Abraham's Faith; reported and preserved perhaps for this very purpose. To the venerable chieftain, in his old age, is born this only son. The craving wish of a lifetime is gratified. The authority, the wealth which he has achieved in this new land, shall now be transmitted to a descendant, as are those of other sheiks less powerful and less wise. Nothing is left indeed for the old man's heart to wish. But it is in this moment of happy pride — is it because of this happy pride? — that the temptation comes. I suppose the same false temptation or trial comes now, where any one-eyed Job's comforter tells you that you love your child too much. As if God were not best pleased when we love our children with that single love with which he loves his own! "Take thy son Isaac," says the voice, "and offer him for a burnt offering." And the poor old father obeys. He takes the wood of the burnt offering and binds it upon Isaac. He takes the fire in one hand, and the knife in another. "My father," says the boy. "My son," replies the father. "Behold the fire and the wood, but where is the lamb?" And Abraham said, "My son, God will provide." Till this moment, in this dreadful scene, you have a religion of Faith, without hope, without love. And it is only in the moment when the boy's life is spared, and Love comes in,— in the moment when Abraham looks down through the ages, even to a world made glad through the life of that child,— when Hope comes in, it is only when Hope and Love are intertwined with that crude Faith of the beginning, that there is even a foundation laid for the system of Christianity, which is Absolute and Positive Religion.

So you may see all by itself the habit of contemplating man's infinity,— the habit which looks beyond the veil, and is careless of place and time. This is that element of life, necessary to all true life, which Paul calls Hope. You find it all by itself, where Nathaniel sits in his garden. You find it in those orders of monks or nuns, for whose convenience Mr. Byrne wants us here to reconstruct the Christian law of poverty. A man sits on a pillar for fifty-six years, looking beyond the veil, and contemplating the infinite. Or, in a Carthusian convent, he takes a vow of silence, and lives his life through without speaking aloud either to God or to man. Far from striving to help his brethren, he retires from towns and from travel, builds himself a hut in the woods where no beggar even may find him, and there meditates on God and God's perfections. But this is no Christian meditation. This is not Paul's foundation. To any such muser, there ought to come the same word which spoke to Elijah in such solitude : " What dost thou here, Elijah. I have yet seven thousand left me who have not bowed the knee to Baal." Mere aspiration, mere culture, the mere contemplation of eternity, is imbecile and idle, unless it is knit in with the Love of God and the Love of Man.

Of Love, the third foundation, I doubt if it can be so often found alone. But there are instances here, which show you a like one-sidedness. In human passion, how often does the fanatic of love cry out, as Leonora to William in the ballad, " You are my only God, and you my only Heaven "! The French Revolution of 1848 was founded on the one foundation stone of Fraternity. " Liberty, Equality, and Fraternity," was the cry. But " Liberty " is merely negative : that only means that restriction is thrown off. " Equality " meant only that all men's rights are the same. " Fraternity " meant Love, — that each should stand by each, that each man should bear his brother's burdens,— Love without faith in God above, Love without the heaven of an infinite life. Yes. And I know nothing more pathetic than this effort to work out a religion as one-sided as Abraham's, as one-sided as any Mark's, in the midst of sceptical Paris herself, and in the very echoes of the ridicule of such austerity as Abraham's or such asceticism as Simeon's. Immense workshops were arranged in the spirit of fraternity, where brothers should work with brothers,— brothers, alas! who had no father. The success of these looms, the beauty of these stuffs, was to be the proof that better than the task-work rendered at the demand of greedy capital, is the free-will offering rendered by willing man to willing man. Alas for that experiment, if willing man be taught that he is only a beast that perishes, or a watch that can run down! Wretched the failure, unless willing man work as a child of God! Banners displayed on the walls and hanging from the ceiling taught spinner and weaver what is true, that "every shirk is a thief." Very true, very true. "And what if he is?" was the practical reply. The chaos come again of those workshops has never been fitly described. The trial balance of their failure has never been fitly struck. The shirks and thieves they assembled appeared next as the conspirators behind barricades; and the repetition of the lesson, a thousand times repeated, of the "whiff of grape-shot" in the streets of Paris, ended the experiment. So the experiment serves us as a memorial, like the others. You can make no system out of human love alone. For a system, for an institution, for something that abides, it must be knit in with the sense of God and the surety of eternity.

You remember the pretty story of the old age of St. John. Coming one day to a place which he had not visited for years, he asked for a certain boy whom he had watched with pleasure then, and whom he had led in the early steps of a manly life. They told him the boy had gone to the bad, had indeed joined a band of brigands in the mountains, whose plunderings and ravagings were the terror of the region where they were. The old apostle said, at once, that he must go and find him, and would not be deterred by any tale of danger. He laid his plans with his Master's own energy, found the band of robbers, and confronted the young chieftain. Nor had the flint lost its old fire. The old man, after his century of life, could still speak of life,— of what life demands, of duties and of pleasures, — nay, put it as this text puts it, he could speak of Faith and Hope and Love, so as to compel even these lawless young roughs of the Lydian mountains to listen to him; yes, and to obey and follow. For this is the last recorded miracle of the apostle's life : that he leads back his young friend, restored from crime, to the home he had deserted. Now that triumph tells the story of the union of the three powers in a life really manly or divine. It is not that John loved this young brigand. People enough who loved him who had never cared to go after him. It is not that John could look beyond the line of time, and believed, as our modern long words put it, in the infinite possibilities of human nature. Plenty of people who believed that, all the elders of the Church believed it; but that belief had not made them bold enough to go away into the mountains and find this sheep that was lost. No! And the courage which belongs to a child of God,— who believes that God is, and is here, — this courage alone is not enough, unless it be interblended with such spiritual insight and such perfect love. It is the union of Faith and Hope and Love which give to the old apostle the joy of his victory.

Yes, there are crowds of worshippers every Sunday in the churches of the world. But worship is not all. Under the vines and fig-trees of the world there are a thousand musing Nathaniels, thinking of a higher life. But aspiration is not all. And in the activities of the week there are, thank God, a thousand thousand kindnesses between man and man. But kindness is not all. It is when worship, aspiration, and kindness are united, when Faith, Hope, and Love all inspire one life, that you see the firmness as well as the grace of Christian living. These three abide, and are eternal.

CHRIST THE GIVER.

"He led captivity captive, and gave gifts unto men." — EPHESIANS iv., 8.

THE cant of our time is fond of saying that we can now go along very well without Jesus Christ. People ask: Why should we pray to God as Christians? Will he not hear us if we pray as his children? Why meet in church on Christ's day? Can we not meet any other day? Has not Jesus Christ himself said that we are all sons of God? Why single out with special honor The Son of God, Well-beloved? Such is one form of the cant of our time.

It is Christmas Day. Let me answer these questions by repeating a child's story, which I will extend a little further than the old English ballad takes it.

An English gentleman of Norfolk, dying, left his two children and their fortune to his brother's care. If they should die before they came to age, the uncle should possess their wealth. The boy was "a fine and pretty boy," the girl was younger than he, and "framed in beauty's mould." The uncle took them to his home, as he had promised. But, as the children grew, his passion for their fortune overmastered him, and

> "For their wealth he did devise
> To make them both away.
>
> "He bargained with two ruffians strong,
> Who were of furious mood,
> That they should take these children young,
> And slay them in the wood."

The ruffians took the children, as they promised. But so sweet was their prattle as they rode, that their pretty speech

> "Made murder's hand relent,
> And they that undertook the deed
> Full sore did now repent."

Rather than carry out his promise, the kinder of the two fights with his comrade and kills him. In the midst of the duel, the frightened children stray away into the wood and are lost. The night comes on,

> "As hand in hand
> They wander up and down,
> But never more could see the man
> Approaching from the town."

Darker and darker grows the forest. The little girl sobs herself to sleep, and the chivalrous boy tries to keep awake to protect her; but he, too, gives way as midnight comes, and he is only wakened at morning as he sees a great light. The level rays of the morning sun pierce between the bare tree-trunks, and shine full in the face of the boy who sat in darkness. And, just as he rouses his tired sister, help comes. A friend in need! A young man crossing through the forest paths, so strong, so cheerful, so kind, takes the little sister in his arms and leads the boy by the hand. Five words of sympathy, and hunger and night and sorrow are all forgotten. Hardly a minute, and the little fellow knows that here is a friend,— a friend not for a minute only, but for a day; nay, for all his boyhood; nay, for life. And, only to trace along the story, this new-found friend cares for both the orphans. It proves that he is himself a prince, — nay, the trusted son of the king, viceroy of all the land. With all a father's power and all a brother's tenderness, he trains both the little ones till they can care for themselves. Then he takes them back, youth and maiden, to their father's castle, which is renewed in beauty and splendor. They can just remember the sad parting from their father at his death-bed, but all is now alive and glad and wonderful. It is then that the orphan boy and the orphan girl, who have been thus rescued from abject misery, turn on this prince and saviour, who was light to them in outer darkness, to say: —

"We can do very well without you now. Possibly, indeed, we should have pulled through without you. This castle belongs to us; and, if you will go your way, we will go ours. We don't want to remember you, and we shall never think of you or speak of you any more."

The world of Herod's time and Cæsar's is the dark forest. The men and women of the world are the lost children. Thank God, the world of to-day does not know and cannot be made to understand what we mean when we say "Herod's

time and Cæsar's." The world of to-day is convulsed with
anger, if it thinks one of its rulers spends a week at a water-
ing-place when he should be in his capital. It cannot imagine a tyrant who would kill wife and child as carelessly as
the prince of to-day plays a game at tennis. To say "Herod's
time," therefore, means little or nothing now. It helps, perhaps, for the description of that dark forest, if we people it
with the assassins of Cæsar, if we renew the memories of the
lusts of Greece or the suicides of Rome. If we could read only
some one story of the agonies of some one tortured slave, dying in slow martyrdom, because he had placed a napkin of
the wrong color on his master's dinner-table, we should have
some notion of it. If we recollect that Claudius and Nero
and Caligula were bright particular stars in its darkness,
that will help our imaginations. The word "darkness" is
the best description, because, as Paul said, the people in
it had come so far that they did not like to retain God in
their knowledge. What way lust led, that way they followed.
What diversion the moment's whim suggested, that diversion
they secured. And blank, dead wretchedness was the out-
crop of that planting. There is literature enough to show
that. For these toys and follies of a moment, they had bar-
tered away everything which other times had valued. Civil
liberty was gone, which Greek heroes, and Roman and Jewish,
had died for in better days. The glories and greatness of
art were gone. Men looked on the work of Phidias only to
know that there was no such power left to them. The purity
and tenderness of home were gone. It was not in these
days that Cornelia showed her jewels so proudly. The simple pleasures of freemen were gone. Men's tired taste could
only be roused when they saw other men dying in the arena,
in the gripe of beasts of prey. Courage was forgotten,
honor and truth. It was the heyday of lust, of wretchedness,
and of suicide.

In that world, Jesus Christ lives and dies. In that world,
while the memory of his disgraceful execution was as fresh
as to us is the outbreak of the Rebellion, Paul wrote of him
these words, which he quoted from an old Psalm of Triumph,
"He took captivity captive, and gave gifts unto men."

He gave gifts unto men. It is no accidental custom of
Germans, nor a tradition of the Latin races, no habit of our
island ancestors transmitted to our times, which crowds the

streets with eager contrivers who want to celebrate a Saviour's birth by gifts of love. He is the great giver of history. And so Saint Paul commemorates him. For our lesson to-day, we will set in order a few of these gifts which he has been loading upon us, ever since he found his brothers and his sisters in that outer darkness of the forest; ever since that Rising Sun waked her from her cruel dreams, and him from his stupid rest. The first is that which Paul names. He led captivity captive; or, as we should say, he mastered slavery. Writing to poor wretches in Western Asia, whose least torture was the lash; writing to congregations of worshippers in which were slaves whose masters could put them on the rack, if they chose, for their amusement,— Paul says calmly, of one who was himself nailed to the cross within their memory, that he has put an end to captivity, he has abolished slavery. Years, generations, centuries, pass, and make it more certain and more that Paul is right. First, the master cannot strike the slave to whom this morning he passed the cup of communion. Surely, no slave can cheat the master who only last night watched by his dying father's bed. Such crude forms of service die away: serfdom dies away, and vassalage dies away. All men become equal before the law. Servant and master learn that they are needed, each by each: each bears his brother's burden. At the very last, since you and I can remember, the great nations of the world, bidden by that Nazarene peasant who hung upon a cross, crowd the ocean with their navies to suppress the slave-trade. They command; and, when they command, they are obeyed. They command the princes of Africa that they shall not trade in men. They command the sultan at Stamboul that he shall not trade in women. So that it is in our day that we see that victory now. Yes. And, when at last God's clock strikes, your brothers and your sons march even to battle at the same command, to free slaves who were born to slavery. They march and they die, obedient to Him of whom they know also that he led captivity captive, as his first gift to men.

I do not mean — and I must not say — that Paul confined himself to speaking of this single form of captivity. That Christ breaks every bond,— that is always at the bottom of Paul's thanksgivings; and the gifts Christ gives to men involve men's freedom from all restraint of whatever suffering. When Jesus himself cured the woman who had been bent and crippled by her infirmity, he said, "Should not this woman be 'loosed' on the Sabbath day, whom Satan hath 'bound,' lo, these eighteen years?" The promise is that, step by step, the Saviour shall loose us from disease. Life shall be better worth living till the end, when there shall be no more sickness and no pain. Here is another of his gifts to mankind.

I talked last Monday with the distinguished medical missionary* who opened the missionary hospital in Canton in China. He showed to me the terrible pictures of a few of the disfigured wretches whose sufferings it was his privilege to relieve. Monsters they seemed,— you can say nothing less,— with the shocking distortions which this and that abnormal growth, unchecked by science, had produced. I asked at once the question, "Are there more of these diseases in China than in the rest of the world?" And he answered at once, that this is what you would see in any street in New York and Washington and Boston, but for your Warrens and Jacksons and Motts, your Mays and Lindsays and Sewalls. Our freedom from such horrors is due to the work of Christian science in a Christian land. China calls herself the centre of civilization. China had done the best she could without this new life which Jesus Christ brought us. Of that life, we have no finer concrete representation than is given by medical science in its unselfish vigor. "An outside barbarian," my friend landed in "the Provincial City" of Canton, as a servant of Jesus Christ. He established his hospital as a servant of Jesus Christ. He was permitted to work among the abject beggars, who might have died, and no man would have cared. Well, he gave sight to the blind. He cut away these burdens of rotten flesh, beneath which men had staggered since they were children. Men saw in their own streets such marvels as we read of in the Testament. The woman who had been bound down by Satan for eighteen years stood up and walked before their eyes. Then the princes of the land came to beg his aid for their children. And, after twenty years of such service, he left the duty to younger hands, honored and blessed of the highest officials in the land. But he is most blessed in the remembrance that in those years fifty-three thousand men, women, and children came to him for relief, and that so often God permitted him to do his best for suf-

* Dr. Peter Parker.

fering man. Since he left that work, the hospital he established has received — and has ministered to — seven hundred thousand more of those who sat in that outer darkness. Such light have they seen. That is the gift of Jesus Christ to them, say in a quarter of a century. Now, I tell that story in that detail, because there is some chance that so we can take some notion of what one follower of Jesus Christ does, in his spirit and in his name, while it is hopeless to tell what all his followers do. I tell it as I once told here on Christmas morning the story of what Jean Waldo did for one dying girl in Lyons. But you shall not say this is romance, or that it happened centuries ago. This has happened since I was a man, and most of you. This is happening in this town to-day. "Greater things than these shall ye do," the Master says; and greater things do follow where he leads the way. There is not one of the prophetical images but is literally fulfilled. The blind see, the lepers are cleansed, the lame walk, and the deaf hear. And these are so many Christmas gifts which, from the cup of his suffering, he scatters over the world.

I remember, proudly and gratefully, — even in the very case I describe, — that these are not the victories of men of science only. I remember that this Missionary Hospital in Canton is endowed and maintained chiefly at the charge of the English and American merchants of that city. I am speaking to men who bore their share in such beneficence, and have perhaps forgotten it. This is a necessary part of my statement. What is modern commerce but a gift of Jesus Christ to mankind? It is the development in action — as man helps man — of the Golden Rule. No exchange or bank or insurance company could carve a better motto upon its walls than these words of Paul's, in which he says he defines the whole law of Christ : —

"Bear ye one another's burdens."

That is what trade is. That is what merchants do. Of modern trade, as distinguished from that of antiquity, the peculiarity is that it rests on honor. You cannot pass laws so intricate as to solve its problems or enforce its requisitions. It is impossible, unless your Rothschild, your Hope, your Baring, be a man whose word is as good as his bond. And this honor between men who only know each other's names — nor always know that — is the gift to us of Christian life. I do not say that you cannot now find it in the other religions. But I do say that you never found it before Christ lived and died. And I must say more. Let me hold to my illustration. In a land not Christian, among people who scorn them as outside barbarians, this colony of Christian merchants build up, in this one case, a hospital to relieve the beggars and the princes of that land where they are scorned. Do you find that Phœnician merchants did that for barbarous Britons? Did Jewish merchants do that, when they went down for gold and ivory to Sheba? Is there any hint of that eager and active benevolence, till the central word was spoken by Him who died on the cross, when he said, "One is your Father; and all ye are brethren?"

I cite such instances merely because they are small enough for us to study, and distinct enough for us to remember. Trace out any one of them in its results, and you have a Christmas present of Jesus Christ to mankind,— so magnificent that you cannot imagine what the world would have been without it. This prosperous America, for instance,— happy home this day of who shall say how many million of his brothers and sisters,— where it was, but for him and his, the cold lair of a few thousand starving savages. There is a Christmas present worth talking of and thinking of! For there is not a crisis in its history but bears Jesus Christ's trade mark. The discovery by Columbus gave meaning to his name of the Christ-bearer. Every settlement on these shores which gave impulse to true civilization was a settlement made by men eager to carry forward his gospel. The Declaration of Independence and the Constitutions of the United States were born in the Christ-blessed cabin of the "Mayflower." And, as General Sherman said on Tuesday evening, the old battle between civilization and barbarism is still going on. Where light and victory perch upon the banners of the right, it is, as he said, where such men as Miles Standish and such women as Rose Standish lead the way today. It is in the mines above Georgetown, it is in the cañons of the Arkansas, that are the true celebrations of the landing of the Pilgrims, amid snow-drifts which are deeper than theirs, in a December which is colder,— both endured by the eternal strength which comes to those who follow their Leader, as he brings light to those who sit in darkness.

For Jesus Christ has given law to the world in the place of anarchy. He has given freedom in the place of tyranny. He has taught men that they are their brothers' keepers.

And he spoke the text word of Democracy, when he said, he who is greatest among you shall be your brethren. I like to say, in passing, that the whole Civil Code on which all the institutions of Continental Europe are based, the gift and the only gift to mankind of the Roman Empire, is a Christian gift, a Christian present. It was a Christian Emperor who devised the Code; and it is inspired all the way through by the Christianity of his Court and of his time. Of that system of jurisprudence, our English ancestors were not fond. From their own customs and traditions, they built up our system of the common law. Through and through, this is interpenetrated by the gospel spirit, and in its axioms you can trace New Testament direction. So that, of the moral and legal science of the world, you may say what you say of the medical science,—that the new life, which the world needed, for the want of which it was dying, was the Life which was made manifest when Jesus Christ lived, and died, and was alive again.

The greatest gift of all is the gift to man of a loving God and a present heaven. In my little fable of the children of the wood, he led back the graceless boy and girl to their father's castle, beautified and restored. But the true Prince of Life, after he found you and me, has brought us to his Father's palace to tell us that this is our home. We may come and go as we will in it. We may read the books in the library; we may enjoy the pictures in the gallery; we may play with the children in the nursery; we may sing our songs in the music-room; we may amuse ourselves with the games in the play-rooms; we may revel in the flowers in the gardens; we may pluck any fruit we see in the orchard. Our Father's home is our home, and never is he so pleased as when we enjoy the wonders of his hand. It is no longer a judge who judges us. It is no longer a king who orders us. It is no longer a distant lord who sends to us. God makes his tent with men. They are his sons, and he is their father. From the tyrannies of old worships,—fringes, bells, tithes, and blood,—from the formalities of old creeds,—a string of beads, a string of words, a paper covenant, and a paper prayer,—we are set free.

"Son, thou art ever with me; and all that I have is thine."

So magnificent is the Saviour's gift to us on Christmas morning.

CHRIST THE FRIEND.

"And Jesus increased in wisdom and stature, and in favor with God and man." — LUKE ii., 52.

THIS is the statement of the very beginning, and with unconscious simplicity all the Gospels carry it out to the very end. The people hear him gladly. They cannot resist the grace with which he speaks. They throng together to hear him, and jealous priests are forced to confess that they can do nothing to resist this personal popularity. It is like what we call the magnetism of a man. None of the writers attempt any explanation. Not that it is beyond explanation, but it is enough for them to state the result. Matthew himself thinks it enough to say that Jesus saw Matthew sitting in his office, and said to him, "Follow me"; and he followed him. He does not pretend to say more. John gives the same account — neither less nor more — of what happened when he called Philip, Peter, Andrew, James, and John himself. Hardly more passed when he called Nathanael. Were this all we knew, we must be content with saying that this Saviour of men had an extraordinary personal command, such as we have no other illustration of,— that he commanded, and these men obeyed, could not help obeying. This, of course, would be all that we could say.

The world has perhaps been too willing to satisfy itself with this answer,— too willing; for, though the Gospels are but fragments, they are fragments all alive and quick with nature; and, in the midst of a hundred illustrations, we have many suggestions which explain the methods of his power.

I. Here is his complete self abnegation, self-surrender, forgetfulness of self. "He made himself of no reputation."

At the very beginning of his active life, when it was borne in upon him that the time had come at last which they had all been waiting for, that he must go down and be baptized by John, he saw heaven open. The story we have of his baptism comes to us in two forms,—from his own lips, very likely, to one of these writers, from John Baptist's perhaps to another. It is not very clear to us, but it was certainly very clear to him. What were his musings or determinations before this we can only guess, but we have no question as to what they were from this moment until he died. "I went down into the river," he said to Matthew or to Mark, who have written down for us this story: "I was determined to fulfil all righteousness; and so I told John, who would have held back; but I compelled him, and went with him into the water. And then and there I heard a voice from heaven, in which God himself said to me, 'Thou art my beloved son.' And then I knew that the Spirit of God came down upon me like a dove, hovering on its outspread wings." From that moment to the end, he never wavered nor faltered. It was no longer Jesus, the carpenter, the son of Mary: it was Jesus, the well-beloved, the Son of God. It was no longer Jesus of Nazareth, called to this home service or that: it was Jesus, the Saviour of the world, proclaiming the kingdom of God. This temptation or that or another came to him, as they come to you and me. But it was all one, whatever they were. Should he turn stones into bread, as you and I will be tempted to to-morrow? Should he make himself of reputation by some brilliant success, as you and I will be tempted to? Should he assume the lead of this troop or that troop, this nation or that nation? Not he! Not he! All that is settled and done with, in his life, once and forever. "Get thee behind me, Satan! Thou shalt worship the Lord thy God, and him only shalt thou serve."

We are to name this utter and complete forgetfulness of self as the first element discernible among the causes of his power. "He made himself of no reputation."

II. And, you see, this springs from the sense of God's presence and God's power, absolute and never flagging. "I saw the heavens open, Matthew. I saw the Spirit come and rest upon me." "So you shall see heaven open, Nathanael. You shall see the angels of God coming down on the Son of Man, and going back." "I am not alone; for my Father is with me." "Father, I know that thou hearest me always." Such phrases, coming in, of course, only in fragments,—

from the nature of the case, they cannot come in any other way, — reveal to us the perpetual method of his life. So that we can understand how these people who talked with him annoyed him — I had almost said, confused him — by their mechanical questions about his authority. "Authority! Why do you not try me by the same authority? Why do you not of yourselves judge what is right? Why have you so little of this inner sight which sees God? Faithless people, why are you faithless? Why have you so little faith? You might see him as I see him. You might hear him as I hear him." All along, he is disowning any individual or personal claims. "It is my Father who does the works. It is not I, but the Father who sent me. Blaspheme we say what you choose about me, but for God's own sake, for your own sake, do not blaspheme the Holy Spirit!" Well, you know what it is in little things. When a child of earth is possessed with the Holy Spirit only for an instant, only for an instant knows that God has given the appointment, and God has spoken the message, — when Joan of Arc feels this, you know what follows. When Saint Francis feels it, when George Fox feels it, when Toussaint feels it, you know how men follow them, and have to follow them. But you see how the Saviour's case goes beyond these. It is not with him a flash, which comes and goes. It is the calm, steady certainty of his life, — "God here and God now," — a certainty so calm and steady that he has given up his life to make all men and women come to the same certainty. "God here and now. The kingdom of God is at hand." This world shall know that. It shall believe it. It shall see it. Not that just now its Herods and Pilates and Cæsars, its Annases and Caiaphases, its Ananiases and Sapphiras, its Simon Magus, and its Elymas seem very likely to believe it, or to proclaim it. No matter for that. He is certain, and he will make the world certain. This world shall know and feel and see that God is here and God is now. "Go preach that, Peter and Andrew. Go preach that, James and John. Go preach that, Philip and Nathanael." And so when more of them come for work to do. There is no other work to do, nor any other word to say. Here is God, now is God. "Go preach that, all of you, everywhere, — that God's kingdom is at hand. The world shall know it one day; and, when the world knows it, why, the world will be a part of the kingdom of his heaven."

III. I do not believe that we take enough to heart the

social, kindly, friendly way in which he addressed himself to such enterprise. But, in his own day, it pointed all the sneers at him. "Drunkard and wine-bibber,"—that was the taunt these gentlefolks threw at him, whose selfish course he was traversing. How curious it is, by the way, that that same sneer is flung always upon any man of remarkable achievement by people who know nothing of him, who want to bring him down to their own level or lower: Swedenborg, John Bunyan, George Fox, all of whom have done so much to bring back to the world his word in its simplicity, were known to the men of their own time as drunkards and wine-bibbers. It is exactly as half the southern people had been taught to believe Abraham Lincoln a broken down sot, always in liquor, while in truth he was a total abstainer. Such men may have this cheer under such taunts,—that the same language was applied to the Saviour of mankind. And you can see where it comes from. It came from this,—that he was a friend of publicans and sinners. He sent nobody away. He believed in the people. He believed in human nature. He was of the people, and he relied upon the people. His work failed, when he tried to move their Nicodemuses and Alexanders. His work succeeded, when he went back into his own Galilee, when he flung himself among the fishermen of the lake and the marketmen of Capernaum. Nor did he put what he had to say in a scholastic way, formal or ex cathedra. Nor was there anything ascetic or hard in the message. Sufficient for the day is the evil thereof. Epicurus himself could not express more indifference as to future grief. But not sufficient for the day is the good thereof. There is where the Master of Life steps wholly in advance of Epicurus and his crew. For the Saviour knows that the future is in the hands of a kind Father who does foresee it, who does provide for it, so that we may look forward in hope, and may be certain that to-morrow will be brighter than today. The three Galilean Gospels are full of these suggestions of the cheerful, hearty, and sympathetic character of what he did to men. We lose sight of them — not unnaturally — in the age and of the tragedy which followed. But all the same are they there, and, all the same, they give color to the whole; and afterwards, all through history, the same thing has appeared. The little Christian communities won to themselves the attention of the heathen world, because these brethren were so happy as they were, because they took life's burdens so lightly. To this hour, indeed, you may fairly test the simplicity of a man's creed and the reality of his profession by the cheerfulness of his face and the steadfast serenity of his life.

IV. And this implies, perhaps it says, that the Saviour's movement and method were social and not separate. He did not trust, no, not to his own amazing power. Just so soon as he is well at work, he chooses these twelve disciples, now to be with him, and now to go forth to work as his messengers and ambassadors. He has no secrets from them. He tells them everything, and expects them to do what he does, is disappointed, indeed, that they do not do all that he does. "Heal the sick," he says to them, " cast out devils: freely ye have received, freely give." So he is glad to be in the midst of companies of people, small or great, unless those companies want to elevate him from themselves by making him king. Then he sends them away, or goes away to be alone. Wedding feast, stately dinner, groups of children, fishermen by the lake, travellers in the highway, formal company on the hillside, one gathering or another suits his purpose, so they are only together, so that life may quicken life in the glad sympathy and contagion of brothers and sisters, heirs of the same eternity, and children of the same God.

What follows is that we trace his life now, and find the results of it best worth our memory and study in the everyday careers, in happy homes, and in the conduct of active affairs. It is one of the mistakes of such a system as that of the Roman Church that it looks for its saints among those who separate themselves from mankind, and points out a life divorced from human sympathy as the life most Christian. Of which, you see, Jesus Christ knew nothing and said nothing. You see the true example of what he wanted in what, in fact, he has produced. You see it in such a life as that which has just closed in our little circle here, too soon for us,— the life of one, indeed, from whose hand many of you have taken the crumb of bread which is the memorial of a Saviour's love. Such a man as that has caught from his Master that simple mystery, by which he carries into everyday affairs the sweetness and the majesty of the higher life. To him, religion means cheerfulness, tenderness, justice, and honor, and means not the talking about these qualities, but the embodying them in familiar life. So it is that he makes home so cheerful, business so interesting, and makes every man glad to meet him, if he only catch a word from him in the street. I do not believe I ever met this dear friend of ours but that I made him stop to speak to me, from a feeling that there was a sort of benediction in one of his cheerful or brave words. And, if this were the place, I could not more intently interest you than by repeating to you, what I once made him tell me, of his personal dealings with those who had never seen him personally before, when he found the widow in her solitude, the orphan in his destitution, and found them in his errands of tenderness and relief. That sort of life is the applied Christianity which I was speaking of yesterday. Such habits of life are caught from the Master, who did his works of kindness " as he passed by " in the streets ; never had to be arranging occasions, but found them everywhere, because he found men and woman everywhere ; and who came not to make men dissatisfied with the world they live in, but to make that world for them the home of life eternal.

I hope the words *Son of Man* have not lost their essential meaning. They are words chosen by Jesus himself from the old prophetic literature, because he meant to show how he identified himself with the hopes and even the fears, the necessities and the triumphs of these people round him. He wanted to show that the Son of God can be and is Son of Man, that the Son of Man can be and is Son of God. Like all the words which we reverence, this phrase is losing its original value. But we ought not to surrender that without a struggle. To a limited extent, our phrase " child of the people " expresses what he meant, when he called himself " Son of Man." Expand that phrase, make sure that you see the confidence he expressed in human nature, his certainty that men could do what they would do, God helping them, and you will see that the phrase " Son of Man " meant everything, when he assumed it as his motto. Often and often, false prophets come to you, and try to persuade you that the country or the church or mankind are going to gain by trusting their destinies to the son of the grandson of the great-grandson of a hero, or to a class of rulers chosen by the accident of war or the accident of wealth, or any other accident of time. That is to say, such false prophets try to persuade you that you shall gain by an appeal from the manhood of the many to the ingenuity of the few. When you hear this chatter, remember that the Saviour of men, who knew he was Son of God, was willing to throw his whole cause on the divine longings and struggles of the whole human family, and asked for himself no better name than "The Son of Man."

V. You will trace all these elements of power in the deeds of mercy, where spirit rules over matter, which we call the miracles of the Saviour. Of course, such works called attention, were talked of from mouth to mouth, and made him known everywhere, even where people had not themselves seen and heard. With the same command with which he spoke to Matthew, so that Matthew obeyed,— had to obey, without "if" or "but," without excuse or loitering,— he spoke to the laggard spirit which had been caged in a paralyzed body, bade it use again this rusted machinery, and the spirit obeyed, had to obey. Nay, with that same certainty of gentle love, he spoke to the disembodied spirit of the widow's son, bade him return to his mother, to the body he had left behind; and the boy did as he was bidden. Take the miracles, on his own showing of them, as the acts of supreme tenderness of one who was supreme love, and they lose that miserable aspect of signs and wonders, which disgusted him as completely as it has always disgusted the thoughtful world.

Take with you, as you read any passage in the gospel, that quiet statement of the writer to the Hebrews, that the Saviour experienced all our infirmities, and was tried just as we are tried. Make real, in a fashion at least, some of these elements of his power, and the scene which passes, when he enters a village or talks to a group of the people, ceases to be magical and becomes utterly natural and real. As the afternoon comes on, in the course of one of those expeditions to Cesarea Philippi or to Syro-Phœnicia, journeys all made with a special motive which have left each its own result,— as afternoon closed in, the word ran through some village, where they knew him, that he had come again,— he, and a part of his company. Of course, the people pressed upon him. Easy to imagine how this publican makes hasty arrangement for a feast. Do you think the man forgets how cordial he was when he was here before, how he listened to every question, stepped over every prejudice, and gave him motive for his life? Here are the school-children rushing down the street to see if he will remember them. Here is a cousin of James, and a nephew of Andrew, proud to claim relationship with the suite. Here are women bringing their babies for a touch or a word. Here are beggars who know they shall get comfort, if they do not get alms. The feast goes on in that easy Syrian habit, the wayfarers peeping in under the folds of the awning, as the dogs might run in to pick up a crumb or a bone. And here is a woman, who is a sinner, anointing his feet from the box of her precious ointment. Ah, it is not to her only, it is to a group of those behind her and around her,— is it not to thousands upon thousands of those around them and behind them, to you and me in our sins and our repentances, that his words of comfort, of forgiveness, and of blessing, fall? Not words addressed from some stately pulpit to some abject throng, but the words of love and of life, which he can speak who is tried as we are tried, and who knows that we have God's own help, if we will struggle and be strong.

It is precisely because this is not a system of theology, precisely because here is one who is greater than a prophet, that the common people hear him gladly, that everybody presses upon him to hear the word of God, that the policemen of the temple say no man ever spoke like this man, and the centurion exclaims, "Surely this is a righteous man." Because he is one of us, who knows that God is with him, and who cares for us and cares for God, and for himself does not care,— for this is it that Matthew follows him, that John and James follow him, Peter and Andrew, all Galilee, and all Samaria, that the world follows him,— because the Son of God, who knows he is Son of God, shows frankly and simply that he is Son of Man, tried as we are tried, and suffering as we suffer. So much does the presence of the speaker, his character, his method, his life, enliven the word which the speaker has to bring. When we see him, then best we hear him, and then best we understand.

His life is our life. The bread he eats is the bread we eat. The table we sit at, morning, noon, and night, gathers together those we love, just as he was most glad to meet with his. Marriage feast, village welcome, Martha's supper, or this thanksgiving, how often he was known of them as they broke bread together! The common altar of daily affection is the place of the central sacrament of the Son of Man's religion. Each meal of daily life is made more glad and holy because at this table we break this bread; and the food which gives us strength for daily duty becomes divine now that he is willing to say of it, "Here is my body, which is broken for you." For a generation now, it has been our custom in this church to consecrate and make cheerful our hopes for the New Year by meeting on New Year's eve at this Supper of Commemoration. Of course, we bring the memories, sad or glad, of the old year. We bring as well the certainties and inspired hopes of the new. Memories and hopes, we lay them at our Father's feet, and ask his blessing on them. We shall meet in this service on Friday evening here. My young friends, who have waited for a fit season for their first communion, will find no time crowded more full with memories and hopes. Let me ask you, as the week goes by, to invite to the same gathering any of our old fellow-worshippers, not with us now, to join once more with us that evening in our communion.

ALL THINGS NEW.

"All things are become new." — II. Cor. v., 17.

We are accused by the cynics of discounting the future. By this, they mean that we borrow imprudently on the credit of its probabilities, and enjoy in advance the good which it has in store. I believe, on the other hand, that we do not study the future enough, nor look forward with that steady hopefulness to which we are entitled, or with that clear plan which is necessary for victory. There is, I suppose, a certain danger in living too much in the present,— a danger which the proverbs describe when they speak of a man as stuck in the mud, or fixed in a rut of convention. I suppose that a wise forecast, whether under the impulse of a prophet's frenzy or under the mathematical calculations of the statistics, is a very important element in the conduct of life. It is certainly the privilege, perhaps it is the duty, of the New Year.

In the face of all the ridicule of what is called "Hifalutin" and the "flap of the eagle's wings," it is to be observed that no prophet in our own country, who has commanded any respect in his own time, has ever aimed nearly high enough in his prophecies. In three or four years after the Revolution, George Washington devoted much time and money to the opening up of communication with the valley of the Ohio. If anybody was a prophet, Washington was. If anybody was an enthusiastic believer in the future of America, he was. But his prognostications, of which his letters are full, are simply absurd, when in their smallness they are compared with the reality of to-day. Where he hoped that a few canal-boats might deliver a little wheat and tobacco, there are two of six or eight great routes by which our Western empire feeds and warms the world. I should be safe in saying that in one day these two lines deliver at tide-water more freight than Washington expected in a year upon his system of navigation. And, of that produce, more than half, I suppose, comes from distant regions, of which he knew neither the geography nor the savage names.

I do not mean to dwell upon such instances; but there is a single detail in the history of near eighty years ago which is worth dragging from oblivion. We negotiated with France for the territory west of the Mississippi, by Robert Livingston, one of the ablest statesmen, clear headed and far-seeing, whom this country has ever employed. He agreed that the United States should pay $15,000,000 for the mouth of the Mississippi and all territory west of that river to the Rocky Mountains. The great object was the possession of New Orleans and the mouth of the river; and for this alone Livingston offered $3,000,000. Napoleon wanted money, and wanted to give England a rival; and he would not deal with us on these terms. He said he would sell the whole or nothing, so that Livingston was compelled against his will, without instructions, to agree to pay $15,000,000. The price was about ten cents a square mile for a region which proves itself to-day of matchless worth in agriculture; say one cent for sixty-four acres, or one-sixth of a mill for an acre. It is of this purchase that Livingston wrote home, "I know the price is enormous." But he said he had already agreed with a European power which would never interfere with us to take it off our hands for what we gave, and leave to us the mouth of the river and New Orleans, which was all he thought we wanted. "I have assured them," he writes, "that we shall not send an emigrant west of the Mississippi for one hundred years." Here was the halting forecast of one of the wisest men of his time,— the man to whose daring in acting and consenting to this enormous price, wholly without instructions, we owe our Western Empire of to-day.

Coming down to our own time, I remember myself the speech of my own father in Faneuil Hall, when he was urging the value of a railway west to Springfield. He was the fanatic of his day in that business, generally regarded in this community as insane on that subject. And he took for his starting-point the probability that there would be nine persons every day who wished to go from Boston to Springfield and Northampton, and nine persons who wished to come from those towns to Boston.

Now, I should not refer back to these halting and insufficient prophecies, nor to the real advance and success, if I supposed the advance and success depended on what people called physical laws. I do not suppose that they do. The same physical laws ruled the Mississippi Valley for ten centuries before 1803 as have ruled it for seventy-seven years since; and no change nor progress came of them. No. As we look forward on our New Year's Sunday, let us see how certainly all these improvements in our physical condition come from the new moral order which these texts announce. It is when you begin to see that man is God's child, it is when man is treated as God's child, that all things become new, and such miracles in society come in. In that particular case of the western half of the Valley of the Mississippi, it was that moral ingredient, which then began to handle physical laws, which has made that desert blossom with the rose. This moral element, the effect wrought by the courage and conduct of children of God, has wrought the miracle which wise men and prophets could only vaguely foresee. It is because man does work with the infinite power of a child of God, when he works with God, that these victories wait on his enterprise. And this power, because it is infinite, is wholly beyond the mathematical computation of men.

The truth is that neither Washington nor Livingston nor Jefferson himself had any adequate idea of the unmeasured power which they let loose upon society, when, in the American Revolution and the Constitutions which followed it, they gave to every man the right to do all he could do, as he chose to do it. Up to their time, and afterwards, every community had its leaders who did the thinking for it. I have lately looked over some diaries kept in a little town in Western Massachusetts at that time. The vote at the annual election was always unanimous on one side. The truth is that that town was almost a pocket-borough. One newspaper, or at most two, every week, sufficed for its reading, and the people all voted as the minister and the doctor bade them. Lawyers there were none. Now, you have only to contrast such a town, say of five hundred persons, with any village of the same size to-day, in which every man reads his own newspapers, chooses his own church, keeps up his own correspondence, and, in a word, forms his own opinion, to contrast a system of civilization where a thousand hands are worked by two pair of brains against one where a thousand hands are worked by five hundred pair of brains. The amount of ingenuity, of device, of new suggestion, of ambition and effort, is, in the latter case, a hundred times greater than in the former.

And the success is in the same proportion, with all the marvels of compound interest added to it as time goes by. It is to such steady emancipation of the American of the North from what was left of the aristocratic customs of feudal times,— a success due to the steady unfolding of the democratic principles which had been boldly enough stated in the "glittering generalities" of the Declaration of Independence,— it is to this development that the country owes what we call its preternatural advance. To this development, it owes the mechanical inventions which have aided that advance. To the same development, it owes the system of education and the system of simple jurisprudence, without which that advance would be wholly impossible.

In the year 1848, I met in Charleston, S.C., with the leading club of that city. Their subject for discussion was the question, "How shall we make Charleston a great city in face of the disadvantages of slavery and of the climate?" I observed that in their speculations they were studying the analogies of Lowell and Manchester and other cities, which had been built up by the influx of large capital. When it came my turn to speak, I said I thought they were following false analogies. I thought their real example was in such a town as Worcester, where I then lived. We had not there a single incorporated manufacturing company. But for every pair of hands we had a head to direct them. "You are trying," I said, "to find out how one head shall direct a hundred pair of hands, and I do not believe you can make a great city on that plan." They did not take my advice, which was perhaps not wonderful. But I observe, by the census returns published yesterday, that in thirty-two years, which have passed since, the population of Charleston has remained almost unchanged. Such increase as it has made has all been made since the civil war. The town of Worcester, in the same time, has increased from fifteen thousand to fifty thousand people, an increase of three hundred and thirty per cent. It is still true, I think, that there is no manufacturing corporation in that city. Almost every head of a family owns his own house and garden. For every pair of hands there is a set of brains to run them.* And what we

---

* It is pleasant to cite one of Abraham Lincoln's speeches : —
"I say that, whereas God Almighty has given every man one mouth to be fed, and

call physical prosperity is due wholly to this absolute recognition of the rights of men, and the fact that every man has a chance to do the best he knows.

We dwell with natural pride and interest on the amazing inventions of our time. They emancipate for us latent power. They make the water, the electricity of the air, and the heat of the sun do our bidding. Nay, they even set to work for us the sunshine of old prehistoric days, which God has stored up for us in the coal mines of the world. These work for us while we sit easy and luxurious. These inventions are indeed amazing. But we owe all these, in the first instance, to a moral change,— a change due to the steady power of this gospel. You say of your own countrymen, and say truly, that there is, particularly in New England, a remarkable inventive genius. Where did this genius come from? All of it came from that same moral triumph, the triumph of the Christian religion when it made for America the democratic statement of the rights of every man. Up till 1776 there is hardly a trace of this inventive genius. So long as men lived in the aristocratic systems of provincial life, it had little chance to show itself. For all that appears, the cannon that were served at Bunker Hill were of the same pattern and structure as those imported by Winthrop when the settlement began. The identical musket of Queen Anne's reign was actually levelled over the breastworks at the soldiers of King George. The buff leather clothing of the minute-men was cut on the same patterns and sewed with the same stitches as the clothing of the Pilgrims. Their linen shirts were woven on looms and spun on spinning-wheels which had no essential improvements upon those which came over in the "Mayflower." And their newspapers were printed with worse ink, worse paper, and worse type than the broadsides which Winthrop and Dudley read in England before their emigration. The marvellous inventive genius of America has appeared since then. You owe its development to the opening to every man the stimulus for invention. In other countries where there is such advance, you owe it to a like liberality. And you do not have any such inventions in

---

one pair of hands adapted to furnish food for that mouth, if anything can be proved to be the will of Heaven, it is proved by this fact, that that mouth is to be fed by those hands without being interfered with by any other man who has also his mouth to feed and his hands to labor with. I hold, if the Almighty had ever made a set of men that should do all of the eating and none of the work, he would have made them with mouths only, and no hands; and, if he had ever made another class that he had intended should do all the work and none of the eating, he would have made them without mouths, and with all hands."

such countries as Spain and Turkey and the old States of Rome, so long as men are kept in leading-strings. The truth is that the government there really orders them not to be inventors. They once forbade an Italian nobleman to place the Latin word *Spes*, the motto of his house, on the gate of his castle, because it meant *hope;* and no subject of the Emperor of Austria ought to be dissatisfied with to-day. You have poor chance for invention in any country so handicapped.

But, if you leave every man free to do his best, if you then educate him to the best you know, and, which is equally important, if you encourage him to combine with others, you set loose, far more largely than you dreamed, a set of wholly new physical possibilities. Inventions help each other. An English writer of the first authority says truly that, in an American machine-shop, every person employed, from the head of the works down to the boy who sweeps up the iron-filings, is interested when the model of a new invention comes in, and wants to have it succeed. And he says that every workman in an English shop hates a new invention. Now, in the great watchword " Together," you find another secret of the successes of to-day. Each new invention smooths the ways for projects which have been faltering ; and, from each single step up the mountain, we gain a better view and an enlargement of the whole horizon.

In the time we have, I must not attempt to illustrate such advances. They are all due to the infinite range of man's faculties; to the truth that man is really child of God, and, when he goes to work rightly, is a partaker of his powers. This is my reason for speaking of these things here. In what is called physical success there are other pulpits and platforms which will tell the story. Our business to day is to see that all such success has hinged, and must hinge, on moral powers ; and, if I can, I want to state, for the thousand thousandth time, why these prophets here, why Jesus Christ himself, proclaimed, so certainly and absolutely as they did, the complete newness of the life before us, and the unending enlargement of prosperity and blessedness in the future. It is not simply man's inventive faculties which are enlarged when you give all men their fair place. But that is a convenient example. One man alone, rightly fed, can lift, say, a hundred pounds from the ground. But twenty men, who are taught how, combine ; and they build a steam-engine which can lift a million pounds from the ground. One of the twenty men attends the engine. The other nineteen look on till their turn to attend it comes. And, while they look on, they do with the engine, united, five hundred times what they could do alone. This additional power to the world is gained as soon as the moral powers have sway, which induce and permit them to work together. There is, I say, a handy example. Now, what Jesus Christ and all the prophets mean, when they talk of new life and of the blessed future, is that such moral powers, the infinite powers of a child of God, shall have such scope and sway that not in steam-engines merely, but in every wish of man's heart and in every fancy of his spirit. He shall mount thus into a higher life, and work those miracles which only yesterday you said were impossible. Jesus Christ means, first, that everybody shall want to work the miracles. Thus, every living man shall want to see Ireland established in comfort. Every living man shall want to see every such nest of wretchedness destroyed. Every living man shall want to see purity where there is lust, temperance where there is vice, happiness where there is misery. And then, as every man and every woman has this wish, they shall certainly, and without hindrance, so come "together" that from the wish may be born the germ, and from the germ the stem shall grow, and from the stem the buds shall bourgeon, and from the buds shall spring the flowers, from which shall ripen the perfect fruit of the blessedness and victory of mankind.

Now, to discredit this declaration, because thus far this thing has not happened, is to say a steam-engine will not work because the wooden model in the patent-office stands still. When has the world taken Jesus Christ at his word? Here is his model and plan. When has the world tried squarely to build upon it, and to set it in action? Who has ever struck the match, which was to light the kindlings, which should fire the coal, which should boil the water, which should dilate into steam to drive the piston to turn the shaft, which should compel the machinery of the world to move in his divine order? "The greatest among you shall be your servants." Here is one of his directions. When has this been recognized as a truth in politics till within fifty years? "One is your Master, and all ye are brethren." What trial did you give to this statement in this country, so long as you had four million slaves beneath the lash of one hundred thousand masters? "Bear ye one another's burdens." What has been the practical answer of the Christian world to this direction, so long as taxes were intentionally thrown on the laborer for the benefit of the landlord, or on the layman for the benefit of the Church? Nay: in matters which you called specially religious, you did no better. He sent his disciples to preach glad tidings. But, till this century came, by far the greater part of Christian preaching was pitilessly bad tidings,— the tidings of damnation and despair. "Ye are all kings and all priests." What sort of an echo has been made to that statement in a world where, from Constantine's day to the third Napoleon's, a close corporation of priests, meaning to keep themselves in office, has been trying to keep Christendom under the sway of a handful of kings? "God's temple is holy, which temple ye are." How far has a world expressed its practical belief that each man is the temple of God,— every beggar's brat, every harlot, and every slave,— which has parcelled out its education for the rich, and has left the rest to "get their living in that state of life to which it has pleased God to call them"? "They that take the sword shall perish with the sword." How far do Christian lands show their belief in that moral axiom, when, as Mr. Evarts said the other day, "every peasant working on the farm has to carry a soldier on his back"? Such are only seven instances of central assertions of Jesus Christ, and of the contempt with which, in the eighteen centuries, they have been regarded.

Now, I do not say that in this country, or in our time, by one great leap, we have crossed the faithless gulf before which the world has shivered in eighteen centuries. But I do say that, with the sincere wish to carry out the Christian plan, this nation has professed, in form, its allegiance to these injunctions of Jesus Christ. I grant terrible exceptions. That corporation of priests is trying to persuade this country to go backwards, and trust to its control again. The great unincorporated body of manufacturers and dealers in liquor would be glad to have us believe that man's body is not holy, and need not be kept pure. So there are cliques and knots of men, who would be glad to arrest universal education. But the general drift is the other way. The laws and the constitutions acknowledge what no laws and no constitutions squarely acknowledged before 1776; that "the greatest among you shall be the servant of the others"; that "we are all brethren," that therefore we must "bear one another's burdens"; that we are all "kings and priests," that every man is child of God, and must have the best possible in education; and that international peace is not only desirable, but profitable. Side by side with this political change is the change in theology, in which the gospel becomes "glad tidings" to every child of man, and is no longer a tale of predestined horror and despair.

I say, therefore, that we have chance and right to look for the fulfilment of prophecy, such as our fathers never had. And the improvement of the future will come directly and visibly in the lines which Jesus suggests. It will be in happy homes, it will be in life not bent by hateful toil, it will be as pure love binds heart to heart, it will be as aspiring man listens to God's voice, and in glad society, in easy intercourse, in music and other fine art, in letters and other mutual advance, man enjoys God's matchless gifts. It will be as a happy world grows happier and happier, as a free world tastes the real blessings of freedom. So will men begin to know what they say,— what they now scarcely conceive,— when Jesus bids us pray to God, "May thy kingdom come."

THE ABOLITION OF PAUPERISM.

"The poor have glad tidings proclaimed to them."—MATT. xi, 5.

AT the annual meeting of the "Associated Charities" in November last, the Vicar-General of the Roman Catholic Church made a careful plea for the preservation of poverty, as an essential element in society. Indeed, he seemed to take it for granted, and I think did take it for granted, that his audience at heart agreed that poverty was a necessity, and that, in all our devisings, we must leave it as one of the foundation-stones of our whole social edifice. The argument limped. So far as there was any argument, it amounted to this: Many of the orders of the Roman Church are sworn to poverty in their vows. So far, then, you must have poverty, or you cannot have these orders of beggars. But I do not think he meant to rest on this argument. I think he meant to appeal to an undefined feeling in his hearers' minds that, of course, there must be poverty in the world, as there must be midnight or pestilence or tempest. He certainly said that there were such great advantages connected with the institution that we must take care never to be rid of it.

Now, in fact, this sort of talk belongs to just the class of protest with which, in 1721, the older physicians in Boston pleaded for the preservation of the small-pox, in face of the eager clergy of the town, who wanted to introduce inoculation. These doctors then said that small-pox was ordained of God, and that men must not fly in his face. They said there always had been small-pox, and therefore there always must be. They had some success in enlisting on their side the most ignorant people in the town and those who would profit most by the proposed improvement. All the same, they were in the wrong, as the conservative eulogists of poverty are in the wrong; and they had to give way to God's purposes in making an old world new.

I am quite sure, however, that Dr. Byrne, in his speech,

appealed to a latent feeling which is widely spread, though probably ill-defined everywhere. You see it trickling out in commonplace stories for children on the last pages of religious newspapers, in which the impression is given that the poor children are little saints, and the rich children or grown people are badly tainted with sin. Of course, if it is true that poverty is the best school of righteousness, we ought to encourage poverty. Then there are the words of Moses, " You will always have the poor with you," — words which Jesus cited once, which people remember as dully as they remember most Scripture texts, which they write as a phylactery or talisman, and then idolatrously worship.

Nothing is more certain than what Jesus Christ did mean when he said this. Of that, I will speak before I have done. He did not mean at that time, or at any time, to fix the seal of poverty on the social system of the New World which he was founding. On the other hand, he meant that it should be a New World. As he abolished slavery, as he abolished tyranny, and meant to abolish disease of the body, he meant to abolish that poverty which makes slaves of those who suffer under it. Wherever his principles have had their way, his intention has been carried out. There are towns in all parts of the Christian world where such pauperism as curses unchristian society is wholly unknown. And, as the social order improves, such pauperism becomes less and less, till it ceases to be.

The abolition of pauperism now is, therefore, an object just as definite as was once the abolition of the small-pox or of slavery. If we will relieve ourselves from the false sentiment of the goodyish stories of which I have spoken, and the false logic of that Catholic Church which has always wanted to keep nine-tenths of the world under the spiritual dominion of the other tenth, we shall devote ourselves with courage and hope to this abolition enterprise. And as the Board of Health three years ago abolished small-pox for the time in this community, as the steady growth of a conviction in two generations of men abolished slavery, in a long endeavor of near fifty years, so is it in the power of any Christian community, which carries out in fact the central and eternal Christian principles, to abolish pauperism. That is to say, it can abolish it with those of whom it has the permanent care. You would not say that the Health Commissioners had failed, because, after the city was free from small-pox, a ship-load of people sick of it arrived at the pier. That is no fault of theirs. You do not say that Mr. Garrison and his friends have failed, because slavery still exists in Brazil. That is out of their range. It is in the power of a Christian community to extinguish pauperism within its own sphere. Let unchristian communities, or let the Pope of Rome, speak for themselves, or speak for Rome. I say to extinguish pauperism. The distinction is to be carefully drawn between pauperism and poverty, as we shall see. But I do not mean to press this distinction to a fine point. I mean that it is in the power of a Christian Church and a Christian State, working in harmony and with energy, to give to every man, woman, and child, who is not disabled by disease, a life of reasonable comfort and happiness, not meanly dependent on the alms of others. So far we abolish pauperism, and, in the ordinary sense of words, we abolish poverty.

It is not so much my business to-day to show in detail how this is to be done. If that were necessary in this place, it would only be because I had wholly failed in the preaching of five-and-twenty years here; and it would now be quite too late for me to repair such damages. I will state very briefly the requisitions made on State and Church in this matter, if we mean to have the kingdom of God come; and then I will pass on to look at the fallacy of which I have spoken.

1. A Christian State does for all what it does for one. And in no case is it satisfied with that supervision which may be merely accidental, which a father or other guardian gives to the children under his care. Thus, in matters of education, every child shall learn to read and write, and shall have a reasonable knowledge of arithmetic. This shall be done, whether the father knows these things or not, whether he cares for them or not. So boys and girls shall be taught to swim, and trained in other physical exercises which look to health of body and health of mind,— shall be, whether the parents are or are not careless about these things. And their education in both these directions, mental and physical, shall be carried so far that each child, on coming to manhood, shall be able to make a fit beginning in one or other of the industries of that community. A sea-faring community shall fit its boys to be seamen; a manufacturing community, to be machinists and manufacturers. And in every community those who are born to be Mozarts or to be Raphaels shall

have their chances as well. And all this is vain, unless the training of every boy and girl rests from the beginning on the Three Eternities, on Faith and Hope and Love. The old phrase of Queen Elizabeth's time was not a bad one. In those times, they did not teach the children to spell. Even Shakespeare and Sidney spelled very much as they chose. They taught them no geography till they learned it from the mast-head; and, as for their arithmetic, it may be that Raleigh and Lord Bacon could not have worked out a modern sum in vulgar fractions. Still, their theory of education was rightly centred. They said every boy must learn, even while he was a boy, "to speak the truth, to serve the Queen, and to fight the Spaniard." In this concrete form, they stated the eternal necessities more distinctly, perhaps, than if they had veiled them in more abstract expressions. To be true enough to speak the truth is at the bottom of all practical education. In this matter which engages us to-day, all pauperism, if you carry back its genealogy far enough, descends from a liar somewhere; and it is one of the crowd of evils which vanish in proportion as men and women and children are all true.

II. A Christian State re-enforces its system of education by the whole drift of its legislation. For it is merely a trick of sixpenny sophists to speak of education as if it were only an affair of books or of the schools. In a Christian State, all the legislation is guided by the same certainty,— that, if one member suffer, all the members suffer,— and by the same determination,— that no single member shall suffer. The whole theory is that the whole ship may be lost, if there is one rotten tree-nail. That is the interpretation in politics of the Christian instruction, "Honor all men." So the State provides that industries shall be varied. If Robert Stephenson be born to be a great inventor, he shall not be predestined by any accursed Calvinism to spend his life in fishing for codfish or in harvesting grain. Again, a Christian State provides for the purity of its boys and girls. Even supposing that grown men and women have a right to risk or throw away their lives, a Christian State screens its boys and girls from the seductions of the liquor-shop. Till they are men and women, they shall not be led into temptation. Once more, a Christian State is absolutely just to the weakest classes in its taxation. Of course, States must use money but there are those writers — and I think they are right — who say that it is wise for a State so to adjust its taxation that, until a man have somewhat advanced from the nakedness to which he is born, till he have made some accumulation of visible property, he should not be compelled to make a contribution to the State. Of course, if he wish to vote, he must pay properly for that privilege. Of course, too, wherever the burden were fixed, he would indirectly bear his share. But the theory supposes that it is well for the State to bend over, beyond the line of strict justice, in its effort to encourage beginners: so to speak, to tempt every one to take a share in the commonwealth. That we have not failed in this business here appears in the Governor's statement on Thursday that, of the population of Massachusetts, men, women, and children, including even new-comers from foreign lands and little babies, who cannot tell their right hands from their left, nearly one-half now have deposits in the savings banks. All legislation which looks in this direction is genuine. It proceeds on the true hypothesis of a Christian State, that pauperism is only an accident, and never a permanent element in its affairs.

III. When you apply the immense latent forces of republican government to carry out these principles, you find that comfort is indeed the rule, and pauperism, or what people call poverty, is the exception. This is a great point gained over that sentimental theory of the Kingdom of Heaven, fostered by the Saint Dominics and Saint Francises and other apostles of beggary, in which poverty is the rule for the great mass of men, and comfort the exception for the rulers, whether in State or Church. Let no man say that I am talking of a mere ideal. I had occasion, eleven years ago, to study the social condition of Vineland, a town then seven years old, in New Jersey. The population of this town was ten thousand. Its pauper expenses in the year 1869 were four dollars, and its police expenses fifty, the salary of one constable. The town had been founded with certain peculiarities of organization, chief among which was the certainty that there should be no retail liquor traffic. A letter from Vineland informs me that now, after eleven years, all the expenses for the poor are seven hundred dollars a year. As for crime and its repression, the charge, for a year, is one hundred and four dollars.* Nor do the expenses of crime,

---

* When I delivered this sermon, I had misunderstood the letter I cited from Vineland, and accidentally confused the expenses for pauperism and for crime. They are correctly stated in the printed text above.

such as they are, seem to belong to the population proper. It is only on Saturday night, when certain railroad trains expose them to a sort of invasion, that they keep a constable on duty to care for criminals and beggars. His wages — of two dollars a week — make the charge for the care of criminals. That is the sort of standard we are to aim at. And, as you all know, this is by no means a single case. We all remember county jails, where the keepers take summer boarders because they have no other inmates, and town poor-houses which are vacant through the whole year. If there were any necessity, I would furnish a thousand cases in this country as satisfactory as this of Vineland.* I certainly do not say that in a city like Boston, which has not been permitted to train its own people, you can expect such results in an hour or a year. We have a population, half of whom were trained under the sky of the most miserable country in Europe. They are under the dominion of a Church which has never squarely tried to prevent poverty, but has always apologized for it and retained it, as a part of its ecclesiastical policy. We are, so far, in just the same position that the Board of Health would be, in my illustration, if a thousand vessels, with small-pox on board, came up together to the wharves. But this unfortunate and temporary accident does not change our duty, nor does it affect the certainty of our ultimate victory. In the long run, it is Comfort which triumphs, and Poverty which comes to an end. It is Health which in the end triumphs, and Disease which gives way.

IV. The promise of the Sermon on the Mount is that, if we will seek first the kingdom of God and his righteousness, such clothing and food as we need shall be ours. It is the fashion, even among Christian critics, to explain the Sermon on the Mount away, as a compound of "Orientalisms," or "glittering generalities." That has been the interpretation of a Church which is a close corporation, which believes in poverty, and for its purposes wants to maintain the class of beggars. It is more fair to the Saviour of men to take his words as if he meant what he said. Compare them with what he said all along, and you will come out on the certainty that he gave this promise: If a man will care for the good of mankind, — which Jesus calls the kingdom of God, —

---

* Thus, in Alfred, N.Y., as a letter from a well-informed correspondent tells me, there has been no pauper for twenty years. Greeley, Colorado, reports no expenses for police and nothing for the poor.

if he will live a righteous life, pure, temperate, honorable, and industrious, he shall not want either for clothing or for bread. Try that experiment fairly, and see if it does not come true. Let your man start, not handicapped by ignorance, by the burdens of low caste, by outrageous taxes, or by drunkenness. Start him on a free world, with a freeman's energy, and with the purity and courage of a son of God, and he does have garments sufficient and food sufficient added to his endeavor. In the one case in a thousand, where he is disabled by a bullet from his country's enemy, or by a shipwreck in some tempest which he did not brew, it is not in vain for him that the Christian commonwealth has been founded. Garments and bread surely come to him; and you feel that these are not alms, but are his due. As the disabled soldier is honored and not disgraced by the traces of the wound he carries, the man or the woman who, in the discharge of duty, has become incapacitated for farther effort, is honorably entitled to the help of the community he has fairly served. That exception is clearly an exception. Poverty is no longer the groundwork of your State. Poverty is the unintentional accident, and comfort is the rule.

Note carefully the central and real statement of Jesus Christ, far beneath all that superficial drivel in which men justify the poverty which is really only an inheritance from barbarism. "Together" is his great watchword. His "Kingdom of God" is a "*Common*wealth." "Ye are all brethren," that is his encouragement and his direction. Born from the womb of the same mother, we all partake the nature of the same Father, God. So we are all bound to each other in a tie we cannot shake off. It is a fellowship as real, if as mysterious, as the attraction which binds the atoms of matter to each other. It is true, then, that each from each other needs something. No man can live alone. In a convict's cell or on a desert island, he slowly dies. You need the tenderness, the counsel, the sympathy of the brothers and sisters whom you meet in daily life. And they need yours. This life is all a broken wreck, indeed, unless you can rely on their intelligence and skill. You cannot make sails, unless he makes masts. Nay, both of you are useless, unless those yonder will freight your ships. I cannot read, unless some one will write the books. And they write in vain, unless others will print them and bind them. Every man is his brother's keeper, as Cain found out to his sorrow, and as the followers of Cain, in the selfish schools of to-day, will find out to theirs. In this sense of mutual dependence, and in this only, is it true that the poor are always with us. It is mutual dependence. But it is not one-sided dependence, which makes abject dependence. It is the dependence of brother upon brother. It is not the dependence of vassal upon chief, of subject upon king, of penitent upon priest. All that abject dependence is done away in the new life of the kingdom of God.

And you and I, trusting ourselves to that goodness of God which feeds and clothes those who try to obey him in this common life, have the other duty of trampling out what are left of the sparks of the old fires. We are to put an end, where we can, to the contagion of the old disease. These are our marching orders. We are to open the eyes of those it blinded and the ears of those it deafened. We are to set its lame to walking and its mourners to rejoicing. In our intelligent philanthropy, we are to proclaim glad tidings to those whom the worldliness of the world and the corruptions of the Church would have left forever poor.

THINGS ABOVE.

"Set your affection on things above, not on things on the earth."—
Col. iii., 1.

I lately met with the following passage in the Life of one of the leaders of our time, as written by himself:—
"I suffered in my early life great anxieties about religious experiences and about doctrinal truth. These I conquered by a habit of prayer, which I formed with great difficulty and obstinate persistence,— led to it by reading the biographies of the saints, Brainerd among others, and by gradually acquiring a sense of God, which set aside the childish images of a form and put me into the possession of my spiritual senses. I can recall the day and hour when I first felt a reliance upon the witness of the Spirit with my spirit. It is like my memory of the first time I trusted to the buoyancy of the water, and, after two years of being in it without faith, suddenly found it, and so could swim."

This illustration from the experience of a young swimmer is perfect, and states perfectly the case of what I always call "the great experiment"; the experiment, namely, of prayer. I am afraid that the statement from the biography may seem to some young people unintelligible, because outside of their experience in that form. But there are others, as young as they, to whom such communion with God is so entirely a thing of course that to them the unintelligible thing is that anybody should make this confession in his biography. To older people, the experience will recall experiences of their own. The older they are, the more certain is it that they will sympathize with the writer. There is no way in which we demonstrate the being of God to another. I might just as well demonstrate to a frightened child on the beach that salt water will certainly float him. Nobody proves God's being. But, all of a sudden, one finds God is here. One speaks, and God answers. And thereafter all is sure. Afterward, you wonder that you did not see it before. You cannot help seeing it now. It is like one of those hidden forms in the amusing puzzle-pictures. Before you see it, nobody can help you to make it out. Of a sudden, the shape flashes upon you; and then you cannot understand why you did not find it before.

This has always been as true as it is now; and it is the great central truth which found expression so long ago,— as long ago as Moses' farewell to Israel,— in words which are to me among the dearest words of what I sometimes call our " South Congregational Liturgy,"—

"If ye seek me, surely ye shall find me, if ye seek for me with all your hearts."

If, in life, we try to draw with any precision the line between people who succeed and those who fail, we shall find that those who succeed are those who "fix their affections on things above, and not on things on the earth." The words stare out from the Epistle, as some of these epigrams of Paul's do; and one feels for the moment that there need be nothing else in the whole Bible, that this is the whole story. Everything follows, Paul would have said, where one thus begins. This writer, whom I have cited, started with this fixing his affection on something higher than himself. He had not heard God with the ear,— no. He had not seen him with the eye,— no. But he thanked him. He honored him. So far, he loved him. He fixed his affection on him. And so the time came when he did see God, as the pure in heart see him; heard him as one hears him who needs his consolations; and trusted him, as a loving swimmer trusts the loyal waves. On the other hand, how clearly you see what follows, where the affection has been placed, as Paul says, "on things on the earth." This poor tramp, who comes in to you to beg, bringing the very atmosphere and smell of dirt and disease with him, is clearly enough a man who has put his affection on things below. He cannot look you square in the face as he makes his appeal. He wants first a quarter-dollar. If you will not give that, he wants a coat; if that fails, a pair of shoes. You turn the conversation to the chance of finding work, and he is not interested. You try to rouse his sympathies by asking about wife or child, and he has neither. No, for the man is what he is, because very early in life he put his affection on some very earthly things. It was liquor, or it was cards, or it was something to eat. What higher tastes he had, he blunted. What lowest tastes he had, he encouraged. There is element of beast in us all. He made the most of this element. There is element of angel in us all. He made nothing of that element. It is a pity that the vulgar phrase has become vulgar; for it expresses, under the old symbolic language of the dark ages, the precise truth. Vulgar people say of such a man, in their coarse phrase, that he has "gone to the devil." That is, in symbolic language, just what he has done. He has not turned his affection on God, nor on heaven, nor on anything beautiful; not on anything above him, not on anything large or grand; not on any master whom he obeyed, not on any woman whom he loved, not on any friend whom he respected. On the other hand, he has placed his affection on the taste of food or of drink. He has tried to have a soft bed or an easy day. He has tried not to work. He has tried to live as a hog lives. He has placed his affection on things below. He has tested that statement, which I quoted the other day, which Lord Byron puts into the mouth of Satan, where Satan says,—

"He that bows not to God has bowed to me."

And the poor tramp finds, alas! that the statement is true.

Now there are a great many people who would disown the name of being "religious," who would say they could make little of religious books, and that they were themselves quite outside the religious line, who ought to take real comfort in knowing that all any teacher asks of them is that they will place their affections above, and not on things on the earth. I remember a man came to me once, and said he could make nothing of religion because he did not believe that the first chapter of the Book of Genesis was literally true. I had to tell him that it was of very little consequence in comparison what anybody believed about the first chapter of Genesis; but that the important thing is whether I am setting my affection on things above my present self, or whether I am setting it on myself, or whether I am setting it on things below myself. There are saints in heaven who never heard of the Book of Genesis. But if I, by any machination or magic spell, should elevate myself or anybody else into any sphere which all angels of light might agree in calling heaven, it would be no heaven for me or for any one, while we had our affections fixed on things below,— fixed on our pretty selves, or fixed upon the food we ate or the drink we drank, or fixed upon the chirping of crickets or the flattery of fools.

Here is the basis of the advice I am always giving to young people,— to make the most of such chances as they have to see aged people intimately, to coax them to talk of life, and to take the impression life has given them. And the other practical rule belongs with this, which directs us to seek every day the society of some one whom we know to be a superior. To start squarely on an accomplishment, or only a hobby, which turns your affection to some thing or some power higher than yourself, is another application of the same principle. "The undevout astronomer is mad," Dr. Young says. And, in truth, you will not long collect your flowers and arrange them, or dry your ferns, your colored leaves, and your other specimens, or work out the laws of creation under which they are classified, and become familiar with Nature in her secret haunts,— you will not long fix your affection in this way on things quite above your logic or your comprehension without growing yourself into a higher life. A man of science once told me that one of the two great religious crises of his life was in the moment when he first put his eye to the eye-piece of a compound microscope. The truth was he then saw with his own eye the process of creation. It was as if he stood by when God set Orion in order, and started him on his journey through our winter sky. I have known another man of science who did all this, and yet fancied he was not religious. But, for me, all I could say to him was that he was profoundly religious, only he would not take the comfort of his religion. And, in truth, you will always find that, as men or women do fairly and steadily place their affection on things above them, their own lives enlarge, they tread under feet temptation, they know more the joy of living, and real success waits upon their endeavors.

Carry the same principle to explain the suggestion of the author with whom I began, as to reading biographies of the men who are allied with God. He speaks of the Life of Brainerd, a man, I am afraid, not now often cited or remembered. Brainerd was a man who did not know what fear was. He went among the Indians of the then savage valleys of the Susquehanna and the Ohio, with the first lesson of love and light that was ever carried to them. Such a life as his, gaining its real strength from God, communicates that strength, long after Brainerd is dead and forgotten, to other lives. For, as you read, you cannot escape the conviction that, unless this daring pioneer was a fool, he knew where his power came from. Well, clearly he was no fool. I must then trust him, when he says he sought almighty strength and found it, asked for it and received it. So you read Milton's Life, and you find that he believed that he had strength higher than his own, and light outside his own, for such work as the serving of his country or the composition of *Paradise Lost*. You read Luther's Life, and you find the same steadfast reliance on the Holy Spirit. You find St. Bernard civilizing Western Europe by his reliance on Almighty God as his daily helper. Now, you know these men are not simpletons. You know that the world has pivoted upon them, and they did not give way. It would not be the world it is, had they not served it. You read their lives to look for their secret. And they all say that they could not do these things themselves. They say that they put their affection on things above. They sought help from the Infinite Power, which moves the world, from which men are born, which makes right conquer and makes wrong fail. They say they sought him, and that they found him. You cannot help placing some degree of credence in their assertion. When you find it backed by the experience of the successful world, you cannot but wish to try the same experiment. You set your affection on things above; and you ask for God's partnership in your endeavor, just as they have done.

For, if you set your affection on things above, you escape from the smallness of the narrow horizon of your little separate life. One does not wonder if you sicken of that. It is monotonous, and it is petty. It would be queer, if you did like it always. Outside of this little life, so petty and alone so tedious, there is the larger movement: it is the infinite movement of the universe. It is the movement in which Good conquers Evil, in which Truth sets foot on Falsehood. Now, if you choose, you may gnaw out of the bands which shut you dead in your close cocoon, you may mount on angel-wings, may enter into the courses of this unending life, and be a partner in the universe. You may confide with God, and he may confide with you. Yes! I understand that this seems too great to believe, but certainly not too great to try, certainly worth trying if one be tired of that imprisonment, as a chrysalis in its bandages. The grub in the cocoon has a perfect right to say that his imprisonment cannot end. But the grub is not such a fool as to say that. He tries. He gnaws out, and, lo! he soars on purple wing. You, too, might say it was your nature to be always hedged and cabined and confined. But you, too, are no fool. You hear the voice of your fathers, and your fathers' fathers, testifying that those who try succeed, that those who ask are answered, that those who pray receive an answer to their prayers. Nay, so full is this answer, and so certain, that prophets have written down the word which they have heard from God himself.

"If ye seek me, surely ye shall find me, if ye seek for me with all your hearts."

To all which, I can hear my young friends replying that these Lives of Milton and Cromwell, of Heber and Brainerd, of Mrs. Tait and Mrs. Ware, may not prove entertaining,— may prove dull or even slow, may prove hard reading, and dry. I have not said otherwise. True, I will say that the development of character, and that of noble and pure and successful character, is the highest theme with which even romance can deal, whose business it is to be entertaining. And I will say that the noblest biographies stand well by the side even of the noblest romances, merely in the matter of interest. But that is not the thing which concerns us here. I have not asked you to read these lives of true men and women because they are entertaining. I urge it because it is an important and well-nigh necessary part of training for life. I dare say that when you first went to dancing-school you did not want to go, and it was necessary to compel you. Still, I do not see that you dislike the dancing party to-day, because of that disagreeable beginning. And so you did not like your French teacher, and "hated French," if I may use the spirited vocabulary of childhood. Still, I see that now you like a good French novel, when one is found for you. Set aside in a much larger matter this miserable business of likes and dislikes, and choose the reading, dry or entertaining, which shall bring you into report with the men and women who have blessed and helped mankind.

Step by step, you find how it is that life is enlarged and inspired, so that it is no longer petty and material. You find what it is that lifts a man above this narrow thought of what he likes and what he does not like, into that larger current of the infinite motive of the universe. You have a glimpse of the way in which other men have risen from the poor little code of personal morals,— a code hardly larger than the etiquette in which a man trims his nails or smooths his hair,— and you have entered into the movement of the religious life in which a man does what angels do, because he is an angel; nay, does what God wishes him to do, because he is a child of God. This is what the old books, perhaps too mechanically, called the experiencing of religion. This is the enlargement of separate or atomic life, so that one becomes a partner in God's concerns, and a partaker of his nature. I do not wonder that he whose experience I read you found his guides into this life in the biographies of the saints, or men of success who had gone there before him. They taught him, you see, their talisman. They made him look outside himself and above himself. They compelled him to fix his affection on things above. And so he learned to pray.

In a fashion, and a very noble and elevating fashion, we learn to pray at our mother's knees. And there is many and many a noble man and saintly woman who has never needed to learn more of prayer than was there taught them. To say, "Our Father, who art in heaven"; to say, " Now I lay me down to sleep," with the confidence and eagerness with which a child asks and receives,— may well open up the whole habit of personal prayer, so that one shall '' experience religion " in infancy, nor ever find the lesson in any sort new. Only let child or man be sure that intercourse with this Power who makes for righteousness, and who is always eager to make for righteousness, shall be frequent, simple, personal, and never dependent on a form. Let child or man be sure that in conscious thought,— in spoken words, if he choose, but that is indifferent,— in conscious thought he open to God all his wishes, all his hopes, and all his fears. Child or man, let us come to God, not as if we were asking the conundrum whether he is or what he is, but with the loyal confidence of those who thank him for life, want to enter his life, and want him to enter ours. It is not to ask him for gold or silver, it is not to ask him that after death we may enter a bower of roses and myrtle, it is not to ask him that our ship may float, while in the tempest another ship goes down. It is to tell him of to-day's success or of its failure; it is to turn over with him the plan for to-morrow's adventure or amusement; it is to lay out in order this perplexity and that misfortune, and gain light from higher life as to the solution of the puzzle or redemption from the failure.

For us who are hot-tempered, it is calmly to cool passion

in the infinite ether; for those who are indolent, it is to feel the thrill and glow of the great line of battle, as the knight most lazy would surely put his lance in rest, and charge with the others, if some Richard led the way. For him who is downcast, because he is alone, prayer is to find that he is not alone. No! Here are all men and women, all angels and archangels, all cherubim, seraphim, and the host of heaven are on our side: nay, God himself, the present power of present love, is here, strength and companionship. Prayer quits the humdrum of my own separate life, and introduces me thus into the society of the universe. It lifts me above the dust and malaria of the things around me into the high, clear air, where I see as I am seen.

It is to this contemplation that the apostle invites me, when he asks me to fix my affection on things above. As Jesus had done before him, when he asked me to place my treasure where moth would not eat and rust would not gnaw.

"For where your treasure is, there will your heart be also."

NOT LESS, BUT MORE.

"What I do, thou knowest not now; but thou shalt know hereafter." — JOHN xiii., 7.

"I have many things to say unto you; but ye cannot hear them now." — JOHN xvi., 12.

THE managers of the Church have looked with suspicion on such statements of Christ, and naturally enough like to keep them in the background. The Roman Catholic Church, for instance, really lives only by looking backward. It rests on tradition. Luther and the Protestants inherited its habits. And, so far from believing that time explains Christ's work and makes it more clear, there is a superstition in Protestant Churches, and in the great Catholic and Greek Churches, that, if you only knew more exactly what Christian men did in Thessalonica and in Ephesus in the times of Paul, you would be safer and better than you are, if you would imitate them. This is, in truth, just as if we should say that, if we could find out what sort of a mud hovel Governor Winthrop lived in, the first year after he landed here, we should all live in mud hovels like it, to show our respect for his memory.

Now, this superstition not only runs counter to the whole order of history in every other matter, but it contradicts every statement of Jesus Christ himself, of Paul, and of the others. They all knew that they had a very great thing in hand, nothing less than the absolute reign of God in the hearts of all men. To bring that about, they were injecting into the veins of a dying world the quickening spirit of its new life. Never was enginery so slight for a cause so great. If they knew anything, if they felt and believed anything, it was that the first new struggles and plunges of the dying man, into whose veins this new spirit of life flowed, bore only a faint resemblance to his energy and simplicity when he had recovered from disease, and the new life had full chance with him. And just what they did not believe was that the social life then, or the daily habits of handfuls of persecuted outcasts, hiding in caves and dens of the earth, could exhibit the true method of life of the perfect kingdom, or of the conquered world. Nay, they did not pretend to prophesy the detail of its coming. Not even prophets can do that. Why, in our time, Mr. Cobden could not tell in England, the day free trade began, how free trade would affect England after fifty years. Henry Clay could not tell in America, when the American system began, the detail of the effect of protection in America. Mr. Chase could not tell in 1861, when national banking began, how that system would affect the United States. A new principle trickles into the world's life; and, literally, all things are begun new, on a scale which no prophet can foretell. To bring into the outskirts of Thessalonica the gospel principle, in talk with a few women praying by the river on the Sabbath, is no test of what the gospel principle will work, when codes of law acknowledge it, when judges and kings are sworn to carry it out, when marriage, servitude, commerce, and all social arrangements are swayed by it, and all the world, in its heart and life, espouses it. These men did not prophesy the detail, because, even in vision, it was beyond them.

Their language, therefore, was always on the key of this text, "What I do thou knowest not now." Paul borrows from an older writer * the great words, "Eye hath not seen, nor ear heard, not hath it entered into the mind of man to conceive the things God hath prepared." They had no thought of keeping the new world looking backward and therefore walking backward. They always referred it to the present Spirit, and bade it trust to the infinite certainty that the infinite life of this Spirit would work out infinite victories.

In the opening of Paul's letter to the Romans,— a most impressive and instructive study of the progress of religion, — he shows with eager interest how from "faith to faith" the absolute perfectness of God had been revealed; how, in this great joy of knowing God better and better,

> "Nature always gives us more
> Than all she ever takes away." †

---

* Now lost. The title of the book was *The Revelation of Elias*. For this statement the authority is Origen and Jerome.

† From one of John Sterling's hymns, poems which have not so many readers as they deserve.

And, in truth, as every sincere Christian must have expected, that has come to pass which these prophets foretold. With every step, the world has stepped forward and upward in its religion. Jesus Christ himself is better understood and more widely honored than the day he was crucified: that is always confessed. But not only is this so, he is known better and honored more than he was when that century went out, or the next or the next. So men know what you mean by the inspiration of a holy spirit, as they did not know then. And their knowledge of God, slight though it may be and small, compared with what shall be or might be, were the fetters of time and space broken, is still infinitely beyond that poor knowledge of Pharisee or Sadducee,— though it were the best of that time,— who thought of God as sitting somewhere on his sapphire throne, or going to this place, or resting in that upon a journey.

You have only to open any book of history at two places, say six hundred years apart, and you can see this in the concrete, without attempting any abstract discussion of the causes of the intervening change. Thus, Richard, the Lionhearted, would have been called one of the most religious monarchs of his day by any Christian writer of his day. Well, he showed his religion by taking his life in his hands, risking it fearlessly in miasma and in battle, by causing the death of hundreds of thousands of Saracens, and taking the responsibility of the deaths of hundreds of thousands of Christians. Turn the page six hundred years, and read the life of such a ruler as Mr. Lincoln or of Mr. Gladstone. See what has come upon the world in a larger interpretation of religion. See how a Christian ruler — in the midst of battle, if you please, struggling for the right, praying for it, nay, dying for it — has as his distinct object to make other men happier, freer, and better, to bring mankind nearer God. So far has the world's ideal enlarged and improved.

But it is not my business to-day to make historical contrasts or to compare principles in the abstract. I want to relieve one anxiety of faith, which shivers in the fear that, with the changes in civilization which are admitted to be necessary, with the advent of more light and more truth, this world may be left, alas! to less religion. Wretched, indeed, if it were so. As if the traveller at the north, midway in that midnight which is measured by months of winter, should see the northern aurora blazing up more brightly and with richer color in its rosy arches, but should find at the same moment that the mine of coal on which he is depending for his life is only worthless slate, and that in the new glory all around him he must freeze and die. But the truth is that every step mankind has taken has been spirit-led. Every new discovery has been God's revelation of himself. With every new blaze of light, man comes closer to the central Power of the world. What follows is that God seems nearer to him. The child knows his Father, and therefore the Father knows his child.

With a catholic desire to join with all reverent people in their worship, whatever may be its form, I always repeat the Apostles' Creed whenever I find myself in an Episcopal church. I repeat it, I need not say, sincerely and earnestly. And, in fact, I suppose that the more thoughtful of the men who used it when it came into common use, about four hundred years after the apostles died, used the words with the same significance which I give to them. I mean, that to symbolical phrases, in what was virtually a hymn, they gave a broad or poetical interpretation, and did not tie themselves down, as so many people do now, in the hard fetters of the letter. But it is impossible for any person, however reverent or free, who has been trained as we have in the religion of the nineteenth century, to use this ancient symbol without exultation that we see so much more, know so much more, and believe so much more than did the men who composed it. That, in good faith, Jesus Christ, the Son of God, is brother of our brotherhood, strength of our lives, and that we may come to God, just as he came, for a Father's help and sympathy, nowhere appears in this creed. That God himself is here now, the Companion and Inspirer of my life, to help me when I am weak, to lead me when I wander, to rejoice with me when I am glad, nowhere appears in it. That with every day this world is to grow brighter and better, that the sparks shall run through the tinder till the whole is in a blaze, that this world shall become in truth the blessed kingdom of a loving God,—this nowhere appears in it. That man with man must live as brother should live with brother, in life common and not isolated; that man must bear his brother's burdens,—this is hardly hinted at. Worst of all, that man may come to God in prayer, may ask him everything and receive everything, is nowhere suggested in it. For all that the Apostles' Creed says, the heavens are still, as they were to the Jews, a firmament of brass over our heads;

and, except for an occasional messenger coming and returning, there is no sort of intercourse between God and man. And so I might go on. But I name these points, because I think these are the points which we should first think of, say in the training of our own children ; or if, for instance, an intelligent Japanese asked us, in brief, what are the essentials of Christianity. I think we should say that they are these: that God reveals himself to man in a being of perfect manhood,— that all men are really God's children and God really their Father,— that their life is a common life in which each must help each,— that it is an everlasting life, and that for this life we have the constant help and blessing of prayer. Of these essentials,— of these five points, shall I say,— the Apostles' Creed only mentions everlasting life. The other four it does not even suggest in any language that would be understood even by an intelligent reader. One or two of them can be forced upon it perhaps by a person resolved to find them there. But others, as I said, cannot, by any ingenuity, be tortured out of its symbols. Yet here is a statement which wrought itself well into use thirteen hundred years ago, as a brief statement, in symbolic or poetic form, of the Christianity of the time.

Let no one say that I am speaking thus with the natural prejudice of one who was born into the Unitarian Church. The truth is that I have been led to this train of remark by a series of confidences which I have received, most of them within a few months, from persons who have had to fight their way out from the jumble of the creeds into the clearer atmosphere of freedom. Their testimony is of one accord, that now first do they know what religion means, so much larger is it than what they had been taught. I met such a man in travelling lately, who had been an eager preacher in the Methodist Church. He said to me: "The Evangelical Church talks of Saviour and Bible. Why, I never knew what the worth of the Bible was till I read it in the new light of our time. The Gospels were never so near my heart as now, when I know I have a right to interpret them for myself and to read them with all my heart and mind and soul and strength." "And as for the Saviour," he said, with intense feeling, "I never knew what the word 'Saviour' meant till I found Jesus Christ was really human, really lived as I live, and died as I die." "Religion!" said another gentleman to me, who had been a very eloquent and true preacher in an Orthodox Church,—"religion! I never knew what the word 'religion' meant, while I was expected to pick up in a life-boat a few stragglers who were saved from this drowning hulk of a world. I can give you no idea of the sense of enlargement that comes to me now that I begin to preach to all men with the certainty that no one is opposed to God, and that all may work together to his glory." "Tell me," said another, " how my little girl may grow up so that she shall not lose an hour of her childhood in the notion that Jesus is her king or her judge, but that she may always know him as her elder brother and her best friend." "You know," said another preacher, "what was my theological training in the Baptist schools. You know how long I tried to cling to those standards. Well, I cannot undertake to tell you how the range of my religious life has widened since I read Renan's *Life of Jesus*, and the body of biographical literature which it has started into being. You who were born to such freedom cannot conceive of the enlargement of life for us to whom it is new." You will remember similar statements in the recent declarations of Stopford Brooke in London. If these men know anything of themselves, if they can tell to us their own experience, they are not less religious, but more. The step they have taken is forward and upward. They leave thought of visible things to float with the tide of the spirit which controls and orders things. They rise from doctrine, which is at best but the statement of the intellectual result of the studies of the past, to try what they can add to the rush of life which is to sway and bless the ages that are before.

I have been reading, with entire sympathy and respect, the story of the recent imprisonment of the ritualistic clergymen in England. They seem to me to be martyrs for conscience' sake, as truly as was Stephen. But what is the cause for which they make the sacrifice? It is for their oath's sake. In their ordination vows, they promised to obey the rubric in the Prayer-Book. As they interpret that rubric, they think it binds them to wear certain colored dresses, which were in use in the reign of Queen Elizabeth. Other men, equally conscientious, think the same rubric binds them to wear the simple black and white dresses which were in use in 1663, after twenty years of Puritan administration. There can be little doubt that this would be the view of unprejudiced persons. Certainly, these martyrs for principle command our respectful sympathy. But they do not regard the form for which they suffer as in itself essential. They all say that, if a convocation of their Church would relieve them, they would wear whatever garments it would prescribe. In the most precise manner, they avow that they suffer for their wish to obey exactly the literal direction of a verbal statement, vaguely made in a fear of revolution. It is the loyal service of the letter.

Such is a fair illustration of one of the martyrdoms of the religion of the Middle Ages,— of the religion which looks backward rather than forward. What might not such resolution achieve, were it emancipated from this thraldom of the letter; if, instead of counting the jots and tittles of a statute of Charles II., it might conscientiously spend every throb of its energy on mending the sufferings of to day and bringing in the hopes of to-morrow! Here is a private letter from a martyr of the nineteenth century. She is a woman, not learned, and never what the world calls prosperous. In a happy moment, she was startled into the new life of a spiritual religion. I mean, she found out, in some blessed inspiration, that God is with her always, and that she is God's child. She found out that rituals are nothing and dogmas nothing, if one live and move and have one's being in one's God. How shall she show her gratitude to God? How shall she use this priceless treasure of his indwelling spirit? She will build up the lives of those who are not so happy. She takes into her own home, at the very crisis of their wretchedness, the poor girls who have been deserted by the men who have ruined them. In her own humble house, with the work of her own hands, and what she can earn by a lecture here or a reading there, she will carry them through sickness and restore them to the world which has cast them off. But they shall not go, if she can help it, till they have found out the love of a Saviour who was willing to die for them, or of the God who has never forgotten them. Now, the martyrdoms of this woman are not of the dungeon or the stake. Hers are the sufferings of one who sees a baby without its milk; of one who sees a recovering patient without a fire; of one who has sent her parlor furniture to the pawnbrokers; of one, in short, always asking how she shall keep the wolf from the door. It is not what you would call romance, though I think the romancers lead us to nothing more pathetic. It is what comes to one who is willing to forget herself, and make herself of no reputation, so only she can lift up those who have fallen down and preach glad tidings to the poor.

Now, mark me, I do not deprecate in the least the conscientious rigor of the English martyrs of this hour. I only say that when it shall happen, in the steady progress of pure religion, that such courage and faith as theirs work for the real thing itself, and are not wasted for the forms which surround the thing, it will be better for the preacher, and better for those whom he would serve. It will be better for the cause, and better for the martyr. And, to go back to that anxiety of faith with which I began, I want to ask those timid ones who feel it, to look behind the shell, and to find the substance. The elegant processional at St. Alban's, or at St. Vedast's, with boys chanting hymns and bearing banners, the cloud of incense, and the awe-struck priest in worship, do present religion to the sense, to the eye, and to the ear. Perhaps there were times when men had to be satisfied with such symbols of religion. But no man claims that these are religion. True religion and undefiled is something else. What God requires of us is something more for which the banners and the incense and the procession are but a preparation. For the reality, there is not one of us but would rather knock at the humble door of this working woman and find her reading with the women whom she is trying to save, or sewing with the little girls whom her kindness has seduced from the wretched hovels which are their homes. There is not one of us but would say that, in her emancipation from all anxiety about ritual or dogma, this martyr of the nineteenth century, as I called her, had found not less religion, but more.

"When the Spirit of Truth shall come, he shall lead you into all truth."

"Many things I have to say to you, but ye cannot bear them now."

"What I do thou knowest not now. But thou shalt know hereafter."

CHRISTIAN REALISM.

"The Life was manifested, and we have seen it." — I. JOHN i., 2.

OUR puzzles with these transcendental chapters which begin the Gospel and first Epistle of John come from the use of language which we have wholly forgotten. Really, the injunctions or directions apply to us quite as much as they applied in their own time. For, in the first chapters, both of the Gospel and of the Epistles, there are two more efforts to do what religious teachers are always trying for; namely, to bring the life of heaven into the life of earth. They are both efforts in the direct line of the Lord's Prayer that "thy kingdom may come, and thy will be done on earth as in heaven." Mr. Gibbon illustrates the difficulty in his cynical and cold-blooded way. He says, "The preacher, who is illustrating with the eloquence of a Bourdaloue the necessity of a virtuous life, will dismiss his assembly, full of emotions, which a variety of other objects, the coldness of our northern constitutions, and no immediate opportunity of exerting their good resolutions, will dissipate in a few moments." This is to say that the temptations of earth in a few moments overcome the resolutions of heaven. And Gibbon's remark only covers behavior. The truth is that we find it much easier, in whatever line of life, to obey our infinite longings, separately or by themselves, or our earthly habits, separately or by themselves, than we find it to mingle the two, and so to set earthly powers to carry forward heavenly longings. Mr. Gibbon talks of behavior, but the same is true of other aspirations. I sit entranced by divine music, and am in that stage of rapture which Paul so well describes, "whether in the body or out of the body, I cannot tell"; and I do not want to. The concert ends. I am in Tremont Street, waiting for my car; and then I scold the conductor, or jostle a competitor for a seat, in the same mood with which one dog competes with another, as if no ray of the angelic effulgence had ever beamed upon me. Just so, these dreamy philosophers of Egypt, for whom St. John writes, could separate themselves from forum, from market, from senate, and from workshop, could write and read, and talk and sing, about "The Life," "The Infinite," "The Glory," or "The Light." But when there was a mob in the street, or when the Nile failed to rise, or when the price of bread doubled because a Roman speculator had made a corner in wheat, the philosopher was just where the butcher or the beggar was. His philosophy was one thing, and his daily life was another. And we — I do not think we are so far removed from St. John and Alexandria but what we understand that experience.

St. John meets this difficulty with a central Christian statement. True, he uses words outside our common language; and to us they sound unreal. But, to those for whom he wrote, the words were only too hard and brutal. "Talk of 'the Life,'" John says, "this ideal 'Life,' this 'infinite Life,' the 'Life of the universe,'— why, I tell you 'the Life' was made manifest. I have seen 'the Life.' All these people round me saw it. I handled it. They handled it." All Egyptian bubbles of vapory fantasy were pricked, and burst by so square a statement of a fact. For once, he said, God's will had been done on earth as in heaven. He had seen with his eyes the person who did it, and handled him with his hands. The statement seemed hard and brutal; but John had to make it in that form, because it was true.

What is called the realism of our time is trying to do the same thing again for Jesus Christ,— and, really, for very much the same purpose. The people who need the lesson are not dreamy philosophers in Alexandria. Some of them are Christians "in good and regular standing," who have so long bowed their heads at the name of Jesus, and worshipped him as the unseen maker of heaven and earth, that they have lost all the reality, and all the sincerity, indeed, of the gospel narrative.* Others are enthusiastic votaries of nineteenth century learning,— who are so sure that they are themselves inspired, and are so delighted with the revelations made to-day, as to be quite indifferent as to anything which happened or transpired eighteen hundred years ago. It is for the real benefit of both classes that the hearty, affectionate common-sense of the world has undertaken in the last fifty years, to find out and to show what manner of life

---

* As when as sensible a man as Dr. Thomson talks of Jesus as walking about Nazareth, and enjoying the prospect from the hills he has himself made!

this was which Jesus of Nazareth led among his people,—what he did and why he did it, how he lived and why he died. To this, we owe the countless biographies which half a century has produced, and other studies in the same line, which have not taken the form of biography. To give any color or sense to these efforts, the "isolation theory," as Mr. Tiffany well calls it, had to be swept away. Palestine had to become a part of this world again, and not a secret or separate world by itself. Men and women there must come and go, like other men and women; and the Saviour must make plans and execute them,— nay, must take his chances of their failure, if a conceited Nicodemus stood in his way, or a crafty Caiaphas. In this study, which tries to make his life a reality instead of an exquisite fancy, men have gone every length. They make paintings of wayside flowers, that you may be sure you know what lily was more gorgeous than Solomon. And they troll and drag in Genesareth, that you may know what fish rewarded the work of St. Peter. When Bida published his magnificent New Testament in Paris a few years ago,— the most costly book which has ever been printed,— he knew that our time would not be satisfied, unless the most competent artists had been sent to Palestine that they might figure precisely mountain, rock, and river, mustard and mint, cedar and olive trees, for the illustration of the record which was to be so sumptuously clad.

From this resolute effort for a real study of Christ's life has sprung a literature distinct from anything which existed before. In this country, it was born with Dr. Furness's *Studies of the Four Gospels*, printed in 1836; and, in Europe, by Strauss's *Life of Jesus*, published the year before,— two books conceived irrespectively of each other, and differing widely in their view, but both leading to a study more genuine than the fanciful habit of former years, in which the truth of history was always made subservient to some moral lesson which the truth was to convey. In the remarkable series of books which have followed in this resolute effort, the three most valuable have been Furness's *Jesus and his Biographers*, a fascinating book for every reader; Renan's wonderfully picturesque life,— so picturesque, however, that it has been said to be the life of Jesus with Jesus omitted,— and Professor Seeley's *Ecce Homo*. The last was written by an Englishman for English feeling, and probably has had the largest influence in England of any of the books of the kind. I think that these two last books owe their great success in attaining their object very largely to the fact that the authors are not preachers. We preachers, for our office' sake, must try to improve people. We must point a moral. That is our duty. When, therefore, a clergyman writes a life of Christ, he is forever showing the moral purpose of this or that, or the valuable lesson to be drawn. It is very hard for him to read or to write as an historian. He reads or writes as an ethical narrator. St. John himself did this; and there are passages in his Gospel where you cannot tell whether the words are his or are those of Jesus whom he describes. Matthew does not do it; and the business-like character of his Gospel arrests the most careless attention. M. Renan and Mr. Seeley have been able to approach the work without making a text for a sermon out of every sentence. One consequence is the vivid reality which attends the celebrated biography of the one, and the treatise of the other.

The determination to see with the eyes of those who looked on has gone beyond the work of fine art and of biography. It has been taken up by one and another author, who have attempted works of imagination, of which the scene is laid in Palestine, in Christ's time; and the actors see and report to us his work, as so many evangelists might do, each from a new point of view. The effort is quite legitimate, and has many advantages which do not belong either to a sermon or to a set biography. This very week, our friend, Mr. Freeman Clarke, publishes such a study, which we shall all welcome. Thomas, called Didymus, is the centre of his story. The remarkable book *Philochristus*, published two or three years ago here and in London, was one of the most successful of such attempts. Governor Wallace has just now published another called *Ben-Hur*, which has some curious studies and vivid scenes. I have brought here a poem where the life of Mary Magdalene is studied so, and I am going to read some passages from it. The merit of such a book, as you will see, is that precisely because Jesus is not the centre in this case, because Mary Magdalene is the centre, you are able to imagine how his power appeared in act and fact. You are not asking the vain question where it came from or what it was. You are only accepting the reality that it was. And all the more are you able to ask, at least in imagination, what might he do for me?

This new poem is by our townswoman, Mrs. Greenough, now living in Rome. It is in three parts. The first describes Mary Magdalene in her splendid palace in Jerusalem, with her troop of flatterers and admirers around her, as a novelist might describe Aspasia in Athens. The second describes Christ's entry into Jerusalem at some visit, when Mary Magdalene waits for him at the wayside, and sees him for the first time. Afterwards she sees him again at the feast, where she anoints his feet and wipes them with her hair. The third part describes the crucifixion and the resurrection. But all this is not from an evangelist's point of view, nor as if one were writing Jesus' life, but with her life the centre. Here is, for instance, the first time she hears of the Saviour: —

> "Now, as she listless dreamed, her ear was caught
> By sudden harshness in the tones of one
> Who seldom spoke, a swarthy, gray-haired Jew: —
> 'A beggarly impostor, nothing more;
> One of the spawn of ignorance and craft
> That swarms upon us in these latter days,
> Leading the stupid multitude astray:
> Soon to be smitten by the very hands
> That now applaud.'"

In answer to this Jew: —

> "A youthful Roman knight, a stranger there,
> Who was in act of raising to his lips
> A rubied nectarine from the broad vase
> Of fretted gold that stood beside his arm,
> Turned his calm look upon the hoary Jew,
> And quiet answered: 'I have yet to learn
> What crime may lurk in teachings such as those.
> Last week, as I was travelling hither, near
> The hostel where I tarried for the night,
> This cunning villain, as thou call'st him, stood
> And taught the wondering multitude his faith.
> As in the hostel not a soul was left,
> But all had crowded thither, I too went
> To see what novel folly moved them thus.
> I stood and listened. Cavil as thou wilt,
> He spoke as never mortal spoke before.'"

They laugh at the young Roman, and ask him to tell them more: —

> "He slow replied, 'I doubt me if the words
> This peasant spoke could find an entrance here.
> He told of truth and purity and good.
> He taught God is a spirit, and as such
> Must worshipped be in spirit and in life

>   Of noble deeds, of love from man to man,
>   Counting no cost too great to win that pearl
>   Of price, the spirit's holiness.' He paused,
>   And looked around upon the silent throng."

This description of Jesus of Nazareth is enough to awaken Mary Magdalene's interest; and she compels young Probus, fairly against his will, to give up all talk either of compliment or of passion, and to tell her more. She sends her own slaves to bring her such tidings as can be had of the peasant prophet; and, when Jesus next enters Jerusalem, she makes an opportunity to see him.

>   "At last, the Nubian, from the hillock where
>   He stood and watched, came hurrying to her side.
>   'Behold, he comes!' And, moving hastily,
>   She knelt upon her litter, raised above
>   The surging crowd, amid the tossing boughs
>   Of feathery palms. Her eager eyes
>   She bent upon the coming form. Her hands she clasped
>   Above her bosom, seeking to hold down
>   Its quick, tumultuous throbbings. And he saw—
>   Jesus of Nazareth saw the Magdalene!
>   The eye that loved the beauty of the flowers
>   Rested upon that flower-like face. His look,
>   Piercing and puissant, clove that pearly breast,
>   And saw the struggling human soul within,
>   That blindly yearned for purity and love.
>   He saw her past, he knew her as she was;
>   And a divine compassion stirred his heart.
>   A look of mournful pity gave response
>   To her imploring eyes. So passed he on;
>   And the great multitude closed round his form,
>   And followed him toward the city gate.
>
>   "She did not weep, she did not cowering hide
>   Her face within her hands, as she had feared
>   To do, remembering Probus' cruel words,
>   Beneath the Prophet's look of stern rebuke.
>   A strength undreamed of from the Saviour's gaze
>   Flowed in upon her heart. She felt a new
>   Transforming power move within her soul,
>   That drew her on, she knew not how, yet felt
>   That she must follow the great Prophet's steps.
>   There was the answer to her questionings."

And this is the answer to her questionings.

>   "And ever from that day, where Jesus taught,
>   In the still coolness of the early dawn,
>   Standing within the crowded market-place
>   Amid the simple country-folk who brought
>   The bright-hued products of their narrow lands;
>   The hardy fishermen who, from the shores

Of deep blue lakes, had borne their glistering spoils;
The shepherds who the younglings of the flock
Reluctantly had led from dewy meads;—
While all, close gathered, reverently heard
Wise speech of gentle counsel from his lips;—
There, standing on the farthest verge, was seen
A youthful figure, wrapt in shrouding veil
And sweeping robes of dark and shadowy fold,
Still followed by a swarthy Nubian slave
Who in a silver leash a leopard led."

Of such occasions, as you know, only one is described in the Gospels. Mrs. Greenough accepts the supposition that it was Mary of Magdala who anointed the Saviour's feet at the house of Simon the leper.

"Jesus sate
At meat within the high-born ruler's house.
And, as they stood and watched, a youthful form,
Shrouded and veiled, passed slow athwart the throng,
Bearing a vase of alabaster, carved
And set with stones of price. She neared the gate
And asked for entrance; and the servants looked
Upon the precious vase, and passage made
For her who came with such resplendent gift.

"Awhile that shrouded form stood motionless
Within the portal of the long-roofed hall,
Trembling and silent. Then she forward moved
With faltering steps, until she reached the couch
Where Jesus lay reclined. Upon her knees
She sank beside his feet: her veil fell back,
And all beheld the golden, waving hair,
The lovely face of Mary Magdalene.
She oped the vase: its costly perfume filled
The spacious room. She bent above those feet
Fevered with loving toil. Her lips she pressed
With timid touch upon them, and the while
She bathed them with her warm, fast flowing tears,
Then wiped them with the gold of her long hair.
Then from the open vase she ointment poured,
Of priceless worth, upon them, sobbing deep,
As one whose heart is breaking in its pain."

And then it is, after Jesus has extorted from the Pharisee the unwilling and unwonted lesson of forgiveness, which you heard me read from the Gospel, he continues:—

"Wherefore, do I say
'Her sins, and they are many, are forgiven,
For she has loved much.' He turned and looked
On her that was a sinner, as she knelt;
... and in a voice

Of tender, yearning pity, Jesus said:
'Woman, thou art forgiven. Go in peace.'"

It is in the garden on Easter morning, after Mary Magdalene has seen him killed on Calvary, after she has helped to bear him to burial, that Mary Magdalene is represented in the statue by Mr. Greenough, which has suggested this poem:—

"Deserted by all else, one mourner there
Beside that rifled couch of stone kept watch,
Weeping, while in her clasping hand she held
The crown of thorns, the all that now remained
To her of him. 'Twas Mary Magdalene.
Sobbing, she prest her shuddering lips to those
Keen points stained cruel crimson with his blood;
She held them to her quivering breast, nor thought
To heed the sharp pain of their pointed darts:
'Twas all she had of him, and he was dead."

"And, while she wept, upon her consciousness
A form dawned slowly, standing near to her.
Mist-veiled by tears, her blinded eyes she turned
Upon that form, nor knew whom she beheld;
And the Lord spoke to her thus mourning soul.
'Woman, why weepest thou?' he gently said,
'Whom seekest thou?' And still her ears the while,
Throbbing in cadence with her sobs, knew not
The voice of him who spoke.
            And Jesus looked upon
That loving, lovely face, and said to her,
'Mary!'
Her soul sent up its worship in the cry,
'Master, my Master.'...
            ...'Touch me not; for I
Am not ascended to my Father's home:
Thee have I chosen for my messenger.
Thy lips shall be the first to tell mankind
That I, Christ Jesus crucified, still live.
Go thou from me unto my brethren: say
Unto them, I ascend unto my God,
And to my Father. To your God I rise,
And to your Father. Go and bear my words!'

"And she fulfilled that sacred last behest:
His messenger, appointed to proclaim
His resurrection to the waiting world.
She bore unto the sad, remorseful band
Of those who had forsaken him, their Lord,
His greeting of forgiving love sublime,
Ere he ascended to his God and theirs;
And then we know no more. We know but this:
When Jesus Christ was risen from the dead,
He first appeared to Mary Magdalene."

I read those passages, and I would gladly read more, that I may ask if it is not better thus to consider what Christ did for the people who knew him than to ask what his nature was, or what we shall call it, or how he did what he did. It is clear enough that somehow he moved the world. He set the apostles to their work, their followers to theirs. They overturned thrones, they remade all social order. Now, when you go back to the history, you find that they were under the power of this person who sent them. His name was Jesus, and they called him Christ. The world is in the habit of disputing his nature, how he came here and what he was. But the world is of one accord, that he was; and, as to what he did, is it not better for a man to ask what he would have done himself, if Jesus Christ had appealed to him?

Occasionally, some young preacher sends me a sermon in which he pleases himself by proving that it is all a mistake to apply the Hebrew word "Messiah" to him, that that was a bad piece of nomenclature. What if it was? Or another sends me a sermon in which he says Jesus was not infallible, — he did not know about the calculus, or the law of eclipses: he shared the error of the Jews about devils and possessions. Granting he did,—though there is no evidence of it,— this is the real question: If you or I had been at Simon's feast or at Martha's table, if Jesus had told us what God wanted us to be and to do, if he had addressed to us the parable or the appeal, should we have obeyed or resisted? Well! if you had had the fortune to be there, you would never have discussed details. You would never have asked him to define his terms. You would never say, "I do not acknowledge that you are an infallible teacher." You would have known that that great heart was beating for you, that great mind planning for you, that great life controlling you; and, with the same enthusiasm which swept them away, you would have obeyed. "Follow me." "Yes, Master." You would follow.

Can it be a matter of much import what name we give to this person? People try to make me think so; but I do not think so. One set of people tell me it is his divinity. I assent at once, and I say: "I also am divine, then. I also am child of God." Then another eager set says that is all wrong: it is his exceeding and perfect humanity. Have it your own way. Call it what you will. I like to think it is his humanity; for I know I also am a man. Surely, the power of his personality makes clearer what he meant, when he said we are not creatures of God, but his children. It shows what he means, when he says God's spirit shall inspire us. And we, if we will look at him more and repine about him less, if we will obey him more and question less, if we will follow,— that is, his word,— we shall be more sure to find the worth of the lead and the certainty of the power of him who goes before.

THOMAS CARLYLE.

It is not yet a year since we were all trying to review the effect on the religious life of half a century which had been wrought by one man,— William Ellery Channing,— in a life not long. The death of Thomas Carlyle, in England, sets one again on a like review, because at one period he so swayed the education of thoughtful persons, as to advance largely that revolution in religion which has made the last fifty years to be almost another Reformation in the progress of Christianity. This sway has not extended, perhaps, beyond England and America. But for those nations it has been very powerful, and that means for a hundred million people, the leaders still of the civilized world; a sway to be remarked, indeed, when exercised by a man without place in government, not attached to any university or other organism of power. It is the most remarkable exhibition in our time of what he would have called The Hero as Scholar.

Mr. Carlyle is now, perhaps, most often spoken of as a political writer. I am afraid that in this country he is most often remembered as a writer who has said unkind things of America. It is, indeed, true that he is a monarchist: he believes in power, in holding a firm hand over people,— in telling them what is right, and compelling them to do it. Such a man of course traverses the opinions and the feelings of Republicans, who know the good of maintaining the least government possible, in leaving promotion open to every person, and in letting those lead who can lead, wherever they may be. But, because of this utter divergence between our political principles and his, we should not neglect to see that in his younger life he was the most efficient moral teacher whom England has known in this century. His moral teachings crossed the ocean. They were welcomed here before they were welcomed at home. They became the staple of the new thought and the new resolve of the young people

who came upon the stage here forty and fifty years ago. In
this way, he has moved the religious action and the education
of both England and America. Just at the moment when
the Oxford movement, what is now called the Ritualistic
movement, began to impel many of the members of the
Church of England toward a renewal of forms of worship
which had been long abandoned, there started up this Presbyterian school-master, this hearty admirer of Cromwell and
the Puritans, who proclaimed that all forms were rags,
whether in politics, in society, or in religion. With the
"Old-Clothes Philosophy," in which by a satirical irony he
pretended to justify the world's worship of its dress, he set
the world of England and America laughing at all its customs, and probing them to the bottom. Do not understand
me that the Old-Clothes Philosophy was suggested by the
Oxford movement in particular. *Sartor Resartus* was in advance of it in time of composition, though not of publication.
Nor was this work specially aimed at that set of formalities.
It hit every conventional custom, — thrones, crowns, and
sceptres, the judge on his bench, the soldier in his uniform,
Parliament and its rules, æsthetic teas, and professors' humdrum, — all the white lies of society were ridiculed. It struck
all these as squarely as it hit any ecclesiastical formalities.
And where Carlyle hit he left a mark. I shall best describe
the moral influence of Carlyle in those years when I quote
what the poet Arthur Clough said of him in 1849. He said,
"Carlyle has led us all out from the Egypt of shams into the
desert." By "us," Arthur Clough meant the educated young
men of England, the thinking men, conscientious and serious. He had led them out from a comfortable Egypt, where,
if they did serve taskmasters, they still had lentils and meat
to eat. He had led them into the desert, where, instead of
vassalage, they had open air and fresh adventure. But they
had to rely for their food on the flocks of quails or on the
collection of desert manna. And Arthur Clough added
sadly, "He has taken us into the desert, and he has left us
there."

This remark of the young poet, whose early promise was
dashed by his early death, was repeated to me by an American traveller to whom Clough spoke. Thirty years have
passed since then; and they have proved, even painfully, that
Arthur Clough was exactly right in his estimate of the position. In fifteen years, — between 1832 and 1847, — Mr. Car-

lyle's power as a moralist had been very great in compelling men and women, by argument, by ridicule, by vivid illustration in present fact, by the pitiless verdict of history, to strip off this form and that, to disregard this or that convention, to go out into the cold, as we say. Those were the days of "Come-outers," and for this John the Baptist life in deserts no man was so much responsible as Mr. Carlyle. But, when they had made their protests, when, on the whole, most thinking men said "Amen" to their protests, and asked what was to come next, this Moses, who had brought them into the desert, could not lead them into the Promised Land. So far, there was a precise parallel with the old Moses; but this Moses could point to no Joshua. He could not lead them himself, and he could not tell them who should lead them. Worse than this, he did not seem to care for those he had led. He retained a certain interest in his old work, but it was no longer the craving interest of his life. He was much more interested in finding fault with this effort or that in the world of politics than in organizing or leading the hordes or tribes of those who had followed him. They were all in the desert, and they found sadly that he left them to shift for themselves.*

It is hardly possible to read in *Sartor Resartus* his sensitive biography of his double, Herr Teufelsdröckh, without being sure that he tells his own story between these lines. He thus represents himself as in babyhood: "A still infant that kept his mind much to himself; above all, that seldom or never cried. He already felt that time was precious, that he had other work cut out for him than whimpering." In his childhood, in the old Scotch farm-house, it would seem that "everywhere the strait bond of *Obedience* held me down. Thus already Free-will came in painful collision with Necessity." And describing the church-going of his parents: "The highest whom I knew on Earth here bowed down with awe unspeakable before a Higher in Heaven. Such things, especially in fancy, reach inward to the very core of your being. Mysteriously does a Holy of Holies build itself into visibility in the mysterious deeps."

He goes to the high school and college, and learns nothing from his teachers; but at the university he does pass

* I had forgotten, till after I wrote these words, that Carlyle himself compares his double, Herr Teufelsdröckh, to John the Baptist: "In our wild seer, shaggy, unkempt, like a Baptist living on locusts and wild honey, there is an untutored energy, a silent, as it were unconscious strength, which, except in the higher walks of literature, must be rare."

through fever paroxysms of doubt, and he tells how he cast himself before the All-seeing, and with audible prayers cries vehemently for light, for deliverance from death and the grave.

Then, when he leaves the university, there come the inevitable experiences of "getting under way," of young love and sorrow, and the questions which since that time have been always called the questions of the "Everlasting No." It is in *Hell Street* in Paris that the answer comes to him,— in the *Rue St. Thomas de l' Enfer:* —

"All at once a thought arose in me. I asked myself,—

"What art thou afraid of? What is the sum total of the worst that lies before thee? Death? Well, death; and say the pangs of Tophet, too, and all that the Devil and man may, will, or can do against thee. Hast thou not a heart? Canst thou not suffer whatsoever it be, and as a Child of Freedom, though outcast, trample Tophet itself under thy feet while it consumes thee? Let it come then! I will meet it and defy it. And, as I thought, there rushed like a stream of fire over my whole soul, and I shook base fear away from me forever....

"The Everlasting No had said, 'Behold thou art Fatherless, outcast; and the universe is mine,— the Devil's,'— to which my whole Me now made answer, 'I am not thine, but Free, and forever hate thee.'"

It is when from the Everlasting No he makes his hero pass into the Everlasting Yes that Carlyle establishes himself as the moral teacher of the Englishman of his time. That the spirit of man is superior to things,— sways them, if it will,— this is the gospel. Twenty or thirty pages in that part of the book contain that gospel. Of those pages there are fragments which young men and women could repeat in those days as oracles, which have indeed passed as proverbs into the language. Goethe's assertion, that "you should do the duty that comes next you," then first appealed to Englishmen as a solution of a religious problem. That "there is no act of legislature that you should be happy," that "blessedness is better than happiness," were lessons, strange to say, that even "the Religious World" needed. The depths to which even thoughtful people had then sunk in their sentimentalisms can now be scarcely sounded. It was in such depths that this John Baptist startled them by the cry, "Lay down your Byron, and take up your Goethe." "The Fraction of Life," he said, "can be increased in value not so much by increasing your Numerator as by lessening your Denominator." That is, if a man will not so much try to enlarge his estimate of his own deserts as to diminish the amount of his claims or expectations, it will be well for him.

"Fancy thou deservest to be hanged, as is most likely, thou wilt feel it happiness to be only shot. Fancy that thou deservest to be hanged in a hair halter, it will be a luxury to die in hemp."

"Make thy claim of wages Zero, and thou hast the world under thy feet."

Side by side with these oracles were his words on the dignity of labor,— words which quickened the manhood of every workman, whether he used hand or brain, or both :—

"Two men I honor, and no third. First, the toil-worn Craftsman, that with earth-made Implement laboriously conquers the Earth, and makes her man's. Venerable to me is the hard Hand, crooked, coarse, wherein notwithstanding lies a cunning virtue, indefeasibly royal, as of the Sceptre of this Planet. Venerable, too, is the rugged face, all weather-tanned, besoiled, with its rude intelligence ; for it is the face of a Man living manlike. Oh, but the more venerable for thy rudeness, and even because we must pity as well as love thee ! Hardly-entreated Brother ! For us was thy back so bent, for us were thy straight limbs and fingers so deformed : thou wert our Conscript, on whom the lot fell, and, fighting our battles, wert so marred. For in thee, too, lay a god-created form, but it was not to be unfolded. Encrusted must it stand, with the thick adhesions and defacements of Labor ; and thy body, like thy soul, was not to know freedom. Yet toil on, toil on. Thou art in thy duty, be out of it who may. Thou toilest for the altogether indispensable, for daily bread.

"A second man I honor, and still more highly,— him who is seen toiling for the spiritually indispensable ; not daily bread, but the bread of Life. Is he not, too, in his duty, endeavoring toward inward Harmony, revealing this, by act or by word, through all his outward endeavors, be they high or low ? Highest of all, when his outward and his inward endeavor are one : when we can name him Artist ; not earthly Craftsman only, but inspired Thinker, who, with his heaven-made Implement, conquers Heaven for us. If the poor and humble toil that we have Food, must not the high and glorious toil for him in return, that he have Light, have Guidance, Freedom, Immortality ? These two, in all their degrees, I honor : all else is chaff and dust, which let the wind blow whither it listeth.

"Unspeakably touching is it, however, when I find both dignities united; and he that must toil outwardly for the lowest of man's wants is also toiling inwardly for the highest. Sublimer in this world know I nothing than a Peasant Saint, could such now anywhere be met with. Such a one will take thee back to Nazareth itself: thou wilt see the splendor of Heaven spring forth from the humblest depths of Earth, like a light shining in great darkness."

It is to the last degree pathetic to see the stolid way in which such oracles were received by the established critics of the time, even when they were accomplished men. There seems to be a fatality brooding over the post of the established literary critic.

There was then, and there is now. But, for all the short-sightedness of the critics, and the grotesqueness of the dress it wore, Carlyle's rugged gospel made its way directly to the hearts of thoughtful men and women. We have reason to be proud here that the value of *Sartor Resartus* was at once comprehended here, so that the first collected edition of these papers is a Boston edition. Carlyle himself afterward cited the book, as a "New England book," because this edition preceded by two years the London edition. Such pride of ours is due to the happiness that we had here our own prophet, Mr. Emerson, who saw from the first the depth and the worth of these papers, and, with the author's permission, collected and published them. Carlyle himself says that two Americans joined in this work. I do not know who the second was, for there are and well may be many claimants for that honor. That New England should have appreciated it is almost a matter of course. Its religious doctrine is stern Puritanism. The Puritan here learned, long before Goethe whispered it, that renunciation is the highest victory of man. In the Puritan Bible, he read of "blessedness" at the same texts where Bible-readers in France were chattering about "happiness." While Carlyle was pronouncing this eulogy on the craftsman, Channing, who was the fine flower of Puritanism, was bidding us "honor all men," with an iteration which fools thought wearisome. And the centre of the whole proclamation of the *Sartor Resartus*, the statement of the Everlasting Yea,— the statement, namely, that man, because he is man, may reign supreme over all things and circumstances, may tread the Devil under foot, and rise superior, even to the pangs of hell,— was but the statement in another form of Emmons's statement, that he was willing to be damned for the glory of God, or of Channing's fundamental of the Divinity and Infinity of the nature of man.

A like welcome for like reasons attended this John Baptist gospel among the best thinkers of England. This, too, was of course; for the heart of England is Puritan. That is, it believes in purity, and at bottom it wishes to push principles to their ultimate consequences. It has been so since the days of Pelagius, and before; since Roman emperors said sadly, what Roman pontiffs have said ever since, that England was a "nation of rebels." Whether the regular critics of England saw, or did not see, that here was a new proclamation of some essential features of the everlasting gospel, the young men and women of England saw it. New schools of criticism, of history, of art,— nay, of manufacture and of decoration,— and, of course, new schools of philosophy and religion, sprung into being. Carlyle taught them to tear down all shams, precisely as two hundred years before Pym and Prynne had taught them to pull down the wooden images of saints that never existed. And young England took him at his word. When Mr. Ruskin attacked conventionality in art,— nay, when Stanley and Arnold built up a realistic school in history,— when the Crystal Palace and Kensington made men study a real morning-glory before they even modelled the handle to a poker, when Drury Lane would not mount "Hamlet" without a correct painting of the Castle at Elsinore, these were so many recognitions of that hatred of shams, of that holy quest for the real blood of the thing, which had been exacted in the desert cry of this Jordan prophet, in his girdle of hair-cloth. And these are but visible illustrations. Who shall say how profoundly this hatred of shams has descended, or what miracles this spirit has wrought in building barriers to Imperial arrogance, in resisting the babbling of infallible popes, and on our side the ocean in abolishing the slavery of man by man?

What now were the limitations to this extraordinary power? Why is it that Carlyle left without a leader those whom he had led into the desert? He had a Promised Land. He was on his feet, and sure. Why could he not be the Joshua as well as the Moses? I know it seems presumption for me to answer. It is like Gulliver measuring the giant with his angles and foot-rule. But every religious teacher ought to have his answer to this question, or to abandon the duty for which he is not fitted. Whether presumptuous or not, I ought not to stand here, if I had not my suggestion.

It would seem, if we looked at method alone, as if Mr. Carlyle neglected — from accident perhaps, or perhaps a certain wilfulness — some duties necessary to a great religious leader. Thus, he never lost for himself the habits or convictions of his childhood in the Scotch village: he always had the child's sense of God's present power and his present love. He came to God in his own weakness, and for God's strength in duty he sought God's alliance. Now, he seems to have taken it for granted that other people would do the same. He seems to think that it is idle to teach other men to do so. It is like telling a voyager on Lake Erie that, if he wants water, he must throw a bucket into the lake by his side, and draw it. But that sort of teaching is necessary. There are all degrees of dulness. When, in 1812, the English Navy-board sent out to Canada the fittings for their fleet, they sent out, with the rest, the water-casks which the sailors on Lake Erie and Lake Champlain and Lake Ontario were to fill before they started on a cruise. Just like that ignorance is the ignorance of many a man to-day, who thirsts and grows faint for want of the infinite supply and help which would come from his real abandonment to the present God. The weakness and grief of the young England of to-day come from just that ignorance. Yet Mr. Carlyle could not condescend, it would seem, to meet it. Evidently a religious man himself, through and through, he takes it for granted that the strength and cheer of prayer and a religious life will come to others, — as a thing of course, — because it came to him, from all the careful training of his boyhood's years.

But this is simply a matter of method. Far deeper down, and fatal to Mr. Carlyle's power in the long run as a leader, is a defect in the whole basis of his religious philosophy. He is eager to show each man his own power, — that he can smite down the devil, and hold him down. True. But, all the same, man is not alone. With man, man must live; and with man he must work and conquer. Mr. Carlyle does not recognize this "together," which is the centre of successful life. His recruits, therefore, do not make an army. They are all so many come-outers, fighting each man "on his own hook." Now, because we are men, because we are gregarious animals, as much as horses in their herds, as birds in their flight, as the fishes of the sea in their wanderings, the teacher who is to lead us must lead us together. The great Leader of leaders would have had every excuse, had he kept himself apart from men. His apostles must have galled him on every side, duller than hounds in taking his meaning. But all the same he chose them, kept them by him, explained to them, bore with them, loved them. He sent them forth, and sent them two by two, that courage might quicken terror, and sense get the better of dulness. Every successful teacher of his Word, every Paul or Luther or Ignatius or Wesley has thus bound his hearers and followers together, has inspired them with a common enthusiasm for a common victory. It is as an army that they march, and not as so many separate travellers. They move to conquer, and to conquer they combine. It seems to me that Mr. Carlyle failed, on the very brink of Jordan, to achieve the greatest victory of this century, because he did not feel or recognize this necessity. He repelled all those who came to him. He sought and of course found the points of opposition with them. He resented their admiration. Because he could stand alone, he made them stand alone. So he never knew for himself the joys, nor gave to those he led from Egypt the victory of that common cause in which each man bears his brother's burdens.

All the same have the England and America of to-day their debt of gratitude to the man who for one generation tore off the disguises of the world's follies and disclosed them, tore away the screens from its true nobility, and disclosed that as well. We must not ask too much from our heroes. If Moses leads us out from Egypt, we will find some Saviour who will lead us into our Promised Land. The men of my time — the men who have been for a generation in public life — are what we are, say what we say, and do what we do, because fifty years ago the last of the prophets summoned us into the wilderness. We should be graceless, indeed, if we did not always remember that call, and at his grave express our gratitude.

GOD IS A SPIRIT.

"God is a spirit."— JOHN iv., 24.

IN this statement to the woman of what she herself felt and tried to understand, Jesus met, and for the time overthrew, all her anxiety about temple or place. Whether the temple shall be on one hill or another is an absurd thing to discuss, if God is a spirit. This is not a hard thing for the woman to receive for the time. Even to untaught minds or simple, it is not inconceivable. Even the American Indian, whose range of language is very narrow, and whose metaphysical practice is inconsiderable, always spoke of God as a spirit. We have no better name for God than the "Good Spirit." And the American savage came so far toward meeting us that he called him the "Great Spirit." The theory does not hold which supposes that simple worshippers are merely fetich worshippers, or idolaters. The Ashantee negro may go to a temple to leave his offering before an idol; but, as he travels home in the darkness,— miles away from the shrine,— he fears or he hopes that his god sees him there. That is, he fears or he hopes that this power outside himself, with which he would connect himself in prayer or by sacrifice, is close to him in that darkness. This is to fear or to hope that this power is a spiritual power, is a spirit outside of place and outside of time.

As the world, growing older and wiser, grows more religious and more, one evident reason for this improvement is the greater readiness with which men take this idea of spirit as they come to see more and more of its ways. Language has now a thousand images by which to illustrate the spiritual reign of God, which it had not in the days of David and of Homer. So much the easier is it for us to avoid errors of thinking of God in this place or in that, which made the hazard for Jeroboam and Jezebel. It is indeed pathetic to see how simple people and ignorant then, seized on the very best they had to illustrate the range and extent of the power of their gods. Thus, a flash of lightning, because it was instant and everywhere, because it came from no one knew where and acted no man knew how, was the natural image for the sceptre of Jupiter or of Jehovah,— whether a Greek poet or a Hebrew poet wrote the hymn. Jesus himself is glad to seize the image to illustrate the universality and instantaneous power of God's empire. As the whole land, he says,— from the sea to the desert, from Dan to Beersheba,— is in a blaze at one instant when the lightning flashes, so shall the Son of man come, not in this place, not in that place, but everywhere and in a moment. That illustration was the best they had: it stood almost alone in their faltering science. And eagerly they accepted it. But every step of advancing wisdom teaches us more, and so gives us other and new parables. Newton weighs the worlds, and he finds a power unseen, invisible, unheard, inaudible, untasted, not to be tasted, not to be handled, not to be fettered, but all the same it binds the different worlds in one system. Its work is stated by the same simple formulæ which Newton calls the laws of attraction, whether it work when a bit of paper flutters in its fall, or whether it direct the movements of planets round the sun, or of the sun round his centre. So that, from Newton's time to this time, it has been easier than it was before for men to conceive of power acting without form, without time, and unfettered by space. The world gained a new illustration of God's power in that discovery.

If one believed, what even intelligent Greeks in the early days of Greece really believed, regarding their own land and the seas around it, it would not be hard to believe as those Greeks did about their gods. If the whole world, or all that was of any account, were the islands and peninsulas of Greece, while no ships came from a distance, and no traveller ever went to other lands, it was not hard to suppose that high on Olympus or other mountain ranges lived gods large enough and strong enough to order the winds and the lightnings, the plagues and famines, the fortunes and misfortunes of a world so small. The ancient religions began with such tokens of local worship and limited power. When commerce began and travel began, when the world grew larger, of necessity all this localizing of religion fell away. But Greece and Rome did not lose in religious sentiment. They gained infinitely, just as soon as their gods ceased to be so many local princes, and when men began to worship, not an unseen neighbor a little stronger than themselves, but the Lord of the whole world.

A similar step, but infinitely greater, was made when Copernicus made his great discovery of the true solar system. Next to the revelations made by Jesus Christ in his life and work, men have had no such help for their true conception of their God and Father as they gained in this unmeasured enlargement of their knowledge of his works. Up till that time, the solid earth, as men chose to call it, was the centre, indeed it was the foundation of all things. To begin with, it was the largest of all created things. Here it was, the central, solid foundation. Around it moved every day the sun, for the purpose of warming it and lighting it. One of the Greek philosophers incurred the ridicule of generations, supposing the sun to be enormously large. He said it was as large as the province of Attica, say fifty miles across. Whoever looked at the little thing saw it was no bigger than a wagon-wheel, and felt sure that the astronomer was a fool. When the sun went down at night, certain lesser lights, the moon and the stars, gave such help as they could to relieve the darkness. Although learned men knew better, such was the opinion of the common world when Shakspere wrote his plays, when the Pilgrims landed on Plymouth Rock. Now, for such a world as this, the theology of the Dark Ages might be made to answer. Thus, you could just fancy the God of such a world as that taking the form of a man for a while, walking by Lake Gennesareth, and permitting men to kill him upon Calvary. You could imagine a hell beneath your feet, and on the other side the mountain of Paradise, as Dante described it. But so soon as Copernicus showed what Galileo proved, so soon as men of thought knew that of one system the sun was the centre, all this was changed. It was not philosophy, so called: it was the common-sense below all philosophies, which saw and knew now that God was infinitely greater in power and in wisdom than the Church had ever called him. If Jesus Christ had not long before told them the truth, in words they had never understood, if he had not said God was a spirit and was everywhere, if the statement of the Roman Church had been the only statement, the new revelation as to the truth of the solar system would have been the end of the religion promulgated by the Church at Rome. As it was, the Pope fought Galileo, as well he might, with rack and thumb-screw. And, of course, Galileo conquered him.

In that victory, religion did not lose. It gained immeasurably. It made the longest single stride it had made since the days of Christ himself. Christianity did not lose. Christianity is positive religion. And by every new transparency, by every stripping off of a veil, Christianity gains new life and credence. Men see that their astronomy would have been better, and their view of everything more grand, if, long before they did, they had bravely taken home Jesus Christ's announcement that God is a spirit, and is everywhere where spirit is or can be. This spirit will not shut himself up in any man's form though that man wear three crowns and sit on seven hills. He does not reign at Rome alone, more than he reigned at Gerizim or on Zion.

The enlargement of the old system showed that the world was only as a dust speck in the solar system. But the same discovery, as Tycho Brahe and Kepler and Newton carried it further, showed that for this immense system there is one law. The farthest comet obeys just the same attractions as the apple in the orchard, and moves obedient to the same will. Astronomy pushed its vantage ground. And to-day, while we know that comets, planets, and all make only a dust speck in the universal system, still we know that the farthest dim nebula of that system obeys the same will, follows the same order. Unity, and not diversity, harmony, and not discord, reign in the universe. So far, apace by steps so magnificent, do men enlarge their conception of the nature and power of their God.

The theology of the world has been adapting itself to this knowledge, slowly, it sullenly, for two hundred years. In our own times, kos and prism, chemistry and astronomy, patient observer and clearheaded mathematician have added their untold contributions to this great revelation. They teach us that the most distant worlds which they can reach obey not only the same law of gravitation as our world, but the same laws of heat and light. They show that crystals form and fuse there as here — ay, that the things there are made of the same matter — carbon, hydrogen, nitrogen, and the rest, the names by which they choose to designate the elements of the things we handle. Nay, they guess, and guess successfully, to terms by which all these laws as they have called them — laws of motion, laws of heat, laws of light, — may be stated as one law. Law is all correlated. It is one law, and it speaks one will. After three thousand years of its separate gropings, science finds, in the heavens above and in the depths beneath, One Power. It finds, what David proclaimed three thousand years ago, that

"If I ascend into heaven thou art there.
If I descend into the deeps, thou art there.
If I take the wings of the morning, and fly into the uttermost parts of the sea.
Even there shall thy hand lead me, and thy right hand guide me."

What is this but to say, as a poet says it, that the almighty Power that sways the universe is everywhere one and the same? They say what David said, but they illustrate it with a wealth of illustration of which not even David nor Homer was capable.

It is perfectly true that, as we find God to be a sovereign infinitely greater than David or Moses dreamed, we lose some of the human figure, by which they expressed his power. When we sing that "he holds the seas in the hollow of his hand," we know we use a figure of speech. But did not they know this also? When we say, "He smiles in the sunbeam and frowns in the storm," these are such figures. When we say, "He looks forward to the future, and looks back upon the past," there are such figures. Or when in prayer we ask him to draw near to us, that is such a figure. Or when we ask him to blot out the memory of our sins, that is such a figure. Spoken prayer itself would be absurd, if anybody were such an idolater as to suppose that God had ears with which to hear our words, precisely as David and Isaiah showed that it was madness to suppose that God cared for the sheep or the oxen of sacrifice. All that anybody can say we lose, is we learn that God is not a form who lives here or goes there, that he is a spirit, to be worshipped in spirit, is lost in some such shreds of language which never really helped us. What we gain, as new knowledge tells us more and more of God's majesty, is what all language falters in expressing, all wisdom falters in conceiving. Words fall short. As the writer says from whom I have been reading, "Wherefore in sum he is all."*

All this time, while all new knowledge and all quickened

wisdom teach us more of the agency of the spirit we call God, man who is learning of that spirit is learning more of himself. Chief of all, he learns that he is a spirit also. He is in a physical body, and he uses it for his tool. So God uses sunbeams and rain-drops. But man is lord of that body, and uses it for infinite purposes. The astronomer finds the law of God in the farthest corner of the universe. He says that the nebula there is not so far away but that God forms it, "nor so far away but I see the work of its formation." "In the beginning," he says, "God created the heavens and the earth, and I — I can forget time between, and I go back in my imagination to that work of creation." Nay, man penetrates to some untrodden section of this globe. He mounts some peak where no man ever stood before. He looks over valley and range, range and valley, which no eye ever looked upon. He did not make it. No! But he finds the prospect exquisite in beauty, it satisfies every yearning of his curiosity. It was set in order by power outside himself, by infinite power; but this is power with which he can sympathize, whose work he enjoys and can begin to comprehend. God is a spirit, and man can give to him a spirit's reverence, homage, and praise. It is not the terrified obedience of a beast, nor his dumb fawning. It is what Jesus called it, the love and reverence of a child. God is a spirit, and he is the father of our spirits, too. So is it that, as the world's knowledge of other worlds and of the unending work of God increases, man's knowledge of himself and of the possible greatness of his own life increases also. On both sides, the divine side and the human, his religion is **not** less, but more.

As man traces the history of his own race in his own world, he finds there also is law. Certain courses have insured permanence and success, have fitted in with other courses in harmony: certain other courses have jarred and grated in discord with other courses, and in the end have come to nothing. Man finds that the Infinite Power outside himself, of which Jesus Christ says man is child and not creature, is a Power which makes for righteousness. People who do right, work with others who do right, and what they do in the end succeeds. People who do wrong jar against all other workers, and in the end their work fails. So Herod the Great is a sovereign of immense power; but what he does is wrong, and after 1800 years no trace of Herod the Great is left upon the world. Jesus Christ, you said, is a peasant without one faithful follower. But what he says is true, and what he does is right ; and, at the end of 1800 years, he rules the world. Such moral victories prove to be as certain as that, in a country like Egypt rocked with earthquakes, a pyramid will stand five thousand years ; but a column will not stand, it will fall. So certainly, indeed, does right prove itself to be might, so certainly do nations succeed, and men, in proportion as they do right and eschew wrong, that speculators are now beginning to say that this is where our idea of right is born. They say that men could now afford to sweep away all gospels but statistics, and live and move and have their being, not to please any God, but to satisfy the provisions which social economy makes for them. It is not so that, in fact, men have begun. They have believed God spoke to them: they have believed God spoke to others holier than they. What he said they have tried to do ; and, as they tried loyally and in faith, he has given them the victory.

"If ye seek him, surely ye shall find him, if ye seek for him with all your hearts." This was the promise of the Good Spirit, as one of his eager children made it, now well nigh four thousand years ago. Year by year, since he wrote it down, the men of his race, nay, the men of every race, have sought and sought, have sought with all their hearts indeed, to know more of God, to make all screens transparent that they might see, to break down all barriers that they might hear,— yes, to quicken their own minds and language that they might understand their God. And the answer has been returned, which that seer promised.

It is true that no man, as he muses now before his fire at midnight, fancies that, by any blessed chance, the door may open and the God of Heaven enter in human form, as Jupiter was supposed to enter the cabin of Deucalion, or as Buddha was supposed to ask for help in some Indian shed. It is true that no man supposes that God is hiding behind a cloud, and that the arrows of his wrath may strike the irreverent, as they thought the arrows of Apollo smote Niobe and her children. It is true that no man supposes that one prayer more or less recalls God's distracted or forgetful attention, now to a battle-field by Nazareth, or now to a shipwreck by Cyprus, as men supposed in the days of the crusaders. Nor should any man now suppose that God loved Hezekiah and Josiah with other love than that with which he loved Themistocles and Miltiades. Yet John Winthrop supposed this, and other good men among our fathers. It is true that no man supposes that at any moment God stands in need of the perfume of a cloud of incense, or longs for the perfume of a wreath of flowers. Yet there were times when men brought him such offerings,— as if he did not have them already! — as my boy might bring me a bunch of violets when I had none. So far, it is true that with the world's advancing knowledge, as men's eyes see further, and their minds understand more, the old language of worship, of reverence, of love and wonder, has fallen away or is changed, as men know, more and more, that God is a spirit, and that they, his children, who are spirits too, must worship him in spirit. This they might have known eighteen hundred years ago. They know it now better than they knew it then. That they are of his nature, and in his likeness, this they know as they never knew before. That, in this world, he relies on them to carry out his purposes, this they see, cannot help seeing, as they read their history. That they work with him, when they seek the right, this is every day more sure and more. So all veils are rent. Every man becomes his own high priest, and stands face to face with God in the Holy of Holies,— Spirit with spirit. Life with life, child with Father. So much nearer is the child to the answer to the question of questions: "Will my Father hear me, if I call to him? I know his power, as no age till this has known it. I know its infinite sweep, as men never suspected it before. I know its harmony and unity. I know its beauty. I know its wisdom, and I suspect its love. He must hear me, the child. as I whisper, or, without whispering, grope for him. Will he, the Father, answer?"

Dear child, for the answer, you must do what Moses did, and David and Isaiah; nay, what Jesus did, and bade you do. If you would find, you must seek. If he is to answer, you must ask. They sought, and they found. Because they found, they trusted. When they needed strength, they asked for strength, and, lo! the strength came. When they needed light, they asked for light, and, lo! the light came,— came because there is identity of essence in all spiritual being and all spiritual life; came because God is Father, and they are children; came because he is a spirit, and they worshipped him in spirit and in truth.

Such worship is easier to-day than it ever was, because temples are worth less, because altars are less needed, because creeds are crumbling and forms are dying away, because men know as they never knew what that word "spirit" means, and seek God neither at Jerusalem nor at Gerizim nor at Rome. All the more simply and easily does the child seek the Father, all the more closely does the Father bless the child.

SEND ME.

"Here am I: send me."—ISAIAH vi., 8.

A THOUGHTFUL man, ten years my senior, was so kind as to give me his early experience as to the power of preaching. "I followed," he said, "with many of my young friends who were at the bar and in business, with a thoughtful company who listened to the most promising preacher of our time. With passionate oratory, he asked us if we were satisfied with the mechanical and conventional lives we led. We were all eager to say that we were not satisfied. 'Did we not see,' he asked, 'that society might be set on a higher plane, and God's law be more universally honored?' We all hoped for it and longed for it. 'Why would we not join shoulder to shoulder to bring in this higher life?' he cried. Well, in substance we said we would join shoulder to shoulder, if he would show us how. But, when we met Sunday after Sunday to learn how,— what we were to do, where and how we were to cross Jordan, and when and how we were to storm Jericho,— we always heard merely the same appeal again: 'Dear friends, will you not leave this outside life that you are leading, and mount higher to something that is more true?' I am now sixty-five," said my friend. "I was then twenty-five. I am not so hopeful as to my own ability as I was then. But my eloquent preacher has never come beyond that stage of exhortation. In these forty years when I would have gladly followed, he has never shown me the particular thing he wanted me to do at that particular hour."

If I were lecturing to a company of young clergymen, I could not have a better text than this story. I should improve it, to show what is, I am afraid, the special danger of prophecy or of the pulpit,— the danger, namely, of dealing with abstract propositions, and the failure in specific statement of immediate and definite duty. But such is not my purpose now. I am not speaking to many persons who propose to become preachers; and I want to try to state a larger lesson, and warn against a danger of far wider range than any pulpit difficulty.

You have anticipated me in the advice which we should have given to this clergyman. We should say to him, "Take one step forward on the earth in the midst of all your prophecy about soaring on wings like angels." "Teach your hearers," we should say, " to walk, or at least to creep, while they are getting ready to fly." Even a caterpillar crawls before he becomes a butterfly. And, in the special instance, this eloquent prophet would really have met the requisition, had he done this,— had he said to these young aides who rallied round him, " We do not know exactly how the kingdom of God shall come in, but we can at least teach jig-sawing to three or four of these street-boys "; or, "We can take an orphan out of the almshouse, and place him in a cheerful home on a western prairie " ; or, "We can go into our village canvass, and rip up the ring that nominates the county supervisors, and so take one step toward clearing out the mad-house in the county town "; or, " We can start the neighborhood on a system of sewerage which shall relieve us from the risk of fever and ague." And if my prophet of a heavenly kingdom had in any such way ballasted the flight of his winged words even by lumps of lead, no matter how petty the thing, not one of his pupils would charge upon him to-day the burden of their failure, as, perhaps, they do.

This is all I say about preaching. My business to-day is not with preachers, but with other conscientious men, and with women as well, whatever be their calling. Are we not all tempted as this prophet was tempted? The danger is that in reading the Bible, in making our religious resolutions, in looking into the infinite range of life, in trying for as great a reality as communion with an infinite God, we shall set on one side, as if it belonged to a different effort and a special resolution, the immediate business to which somebody must attend to-day,— as if indeed that were petty, worldly, common, or unclean.

The mathematicians do not calculate the flight of a comet simply by observing its place at one end of that flight and at the other. This they can seldom do, if ever. They calculate it by the study of the "infinitely small difference between the two successive states or places of the comet." Here is a good practical suggestion for our achievements in heavenly or religious life. We want to see God and know him. We want to make heaven real, that we may not fear death. We want to live as immortals live. Yes. And this is a great effort. Because we want to know this and to do it, we must begin as these astronomers begin, with a very little part of this infinite orbit: we must study well and manage rightly the infinitely small difference between one minute of life and the next minute. We must attend perfectly to some one detail to-day, if we would rightly project the orbit or the life which is to run through eternity.

So falsely has religion been taught, however, that this lesson is neglected, and is unpopular. Naaman wanted to be cured of his leprosy, and he was told to wash himself. He did not like the injunction. People seldom like such lessons, which imply that the infinitely small teaches the way to the infinitely great. Here is Lent coming upon us now. It is the season when, in our northern zones, man's body is more or less reduced by the absence of the sun in winter. The Catholic Church, with its accustomed wisdom, has seized the occasion for a season of religious reflection and communion; and we all follow the suggestion in one way or another. I can imagine that you see the reason for giving up the theatre for a while; for dancing less for six weeks to come; for reading more, and more thoughtfully; for serious and devout attendance on some special course of religious instruction. You wish you were nearer God, and thought of him more often. You knock at the doors of the Madame Guyon and the Thomas à Kempis, the Bernard and the Bonaventura, who have sung with most rapture and have prayed with most certainty. "Oh! if only I could see as clearly as they see, or hear such ravishing accents as they hear." This is your cry, and it is a very noble cry. Now, in truth, if Madame Guyon or St. Bernard come to your help, if, when you knock, either one of them opens the door and looks out far enough to answer, it is to give the perfectly commonplace direction. It is to say: "If you mean to travel to the Holy City of God, you must begin by sweeping off your own front doorstep. And, when you have swept it, you must keep it clean." People hate to hear this answer. Most prophets hate to make the statement. But it must be made. Jesus was making it all the time: "Why do ye call me Lord, Lord, when you will not do the meanest thing I tell you to do? How will you enter the kingdom of God, unless you repent of this or that petty habit which debases you, and unless you keep it under? It is idle to talk of eternity and heaven, unless you can attend to the things of earth and of time."

Now, when people shrink from this injunction, the difficulty is not the simple difficulty which the pupil feels who is told to do a little thing instead of a great one. Thus, a boy comes to me to learn how to paint historical pictures, and I tell him to begin by copying a mug. He does not like that; but he sees some reason in it, for the drawing the mug and the painting the picture seem to be in the same line. The religious difficulty is far deeper, for the religious aspirant does not believe that the little thing demanded is in the same line with the great thing he seeks. He seeks to begin to be an archangel, and he does not choose to begin with being a street-sweeper; for, at bottom, he does not believe that archangels sweep streets or that street-sweepers develop into archangels. He wants to know God, to see him and hear him, to pray to him and receive from him; and he does not believe that he gains this knowledge or this insight by knowing man, or by converse or intimacy with the things of man. He wants to enter eternal life; to "accept the Universe," as Margaret Fuller says; to live in infinite relations, as the philosophers say. He does not believe that any intimacy or relationship with time can train to that eternal affair. Such disbelief sends men into hermitages or puts them on the top of pillars for their devotions. Such disbelief gives point to all the stories of hypocrites, as they are called, who offer loud prayers at the corners of the street, while at home they abuse their families and cheat their customers. The familiar Southern story tells of a prayer-meeting of negroes, where a man proposed that the worshippers should pledge themselves not to rob hen-roosts, and was told he disturbed the harmony of the meeting. We laugh at that absurdity. But it really reveals, in its droll way, this doubt, which lingers low down in people's minds, whether their demeanor here or their conduct here, in what they please to call the little things of time and of the earth, is an essential and integral affair in their aspirations and struggles toward the life with God or the life in heaven.

It is therefore, as I have said, to this precise point that our Saviour addresses himself; and so do all his successful apostles. He undertakes to show us, when he deals with the beggar in the gutter, with the outcast leper, who shrieks to him far away, that he is dealing with a child of God, who really, and not in metaphor, partakes of the divine nature. So, when he welcomes the little children, who cannot even speak perhaps, but who have, all the same, their own ways of expressing faith, hope, and love,— which are the only eternal attributes we know of, whether in babies or in archangels,— Christ's whole injunction is: "If you would come nearer to God, come nearer to the children of God. If you would understand God better, see that you understand his children better; and, if you would gain keener sense of his constant and present help, gain it by extending that help yourself, in your own ways, to those in need from you." It is, all through, spark from his fire. If you would learn what spiritual power is, try the effect of spiritual power. If you would know that love rules the universe, find out by experiment how far love will go in the management of your own household. Such is the key to Jesus' somewhat blunt refusal, made more than once, to discuss what I may call the transcendentalisms of a religious life. He will not do it. He turns attention to something quite commonplace in their immediate surroundings. Wash this leper, and you draw closer to God. Stop this baby's crying, and make the little darling laugh again, and you have worked one of the infinite miracles; for you have shown the power of a loving spirit over the things of time. This is the explanation of the steady "Follow me!" to those who wanted to enter the inconceivable kingdom of an infinite heaven. It is in dusty travel in the by-ways of Galilee that they are to begin to walk with cherubim and seraphim in a world without measure and without time.

Duty — square, solid duty — is one essential step to the noblest or highest communion with the Infinite. Let a man remember that. Nor let him be confused by the fallacies of "small" and "great." "I am so small," a man says, "my work for God or with him is so petty, that God cannot stop to think of me or of it." All this belongs to the old heathen notions of God, as if he were a giant-man, larger than we are. And all this vanishes when a man learns that spirit and the power of spirit cannot be weighed on scales, counted by figures, or measured by tape. For myself, as I have already said, I received one of the greatest lessons in the science of Eternal Life, when, in the study of mathematics, I came upon that law which I have cited, by which the infinite hyperbola of a comet's flight is calculated from the differential, infinitely small, which marks its motion in an infinitely brief period of time. Since then, I have needed no other parable to show me that, with God, nothing is small and nothing great. I have heard men who use the microscope say that they had learned the same lesson, when they found the perfect organization of a tuft of mould which the naked eye cannot see, but which shows symmetry, beauty, and law, as perfectly as nebulæ in the void or the perfect constellation. Always man, though he be a pigmy with giants, finds he is a giant with pigmies, as Gulliver, who thought himself a mite in Brobdignag, found he was a monster in Liliput. And this law may be traced out in all forms of service. The boy who shod the field-marshal's horse was necessary to the field-marshal. The blear-eyed beldame who taught Milton his letters was necessary to Milton. The mouse who gnawed the net was necessary to the lion. When once we know that it is not as separate creatures that we are working, for separate purposes, but as those who work in one great organism with God and for God, why, it will be with us as it was in the conservatory with Mendelssohn,—you will strike the infrequent drum-beat, or play on the disagreeable trombone, with pride and eagerness as if you led the violins, if only the Great Master asks you, and you carry out the harmony of his great design.

I am not now addressing myself to men and women to whom the Higher Life seems a delusion and folly, who are satisfied with this earth and what it can do for them. The statement I make, and such argument or illustration as I have tried, is nothing to them. I speak now to men and women who really wish they felt God's presence more real, and were sure of it more often. I suppose them eager to feel heaven more a reality, and those whom they love there still loving them. I suppose them willing to work with God, if only the certainty could come to them that he cares for them.

You have come to day to church, to join in prayer and hymn, seeking this higher life. You will seek for books of devotion, written by those who have bathed in this ocean; and you hope they will teach you to swim in it. You curiously inquire if this or that ritual, nay, if fasting, self-denial, or penance, will bring you and God any closer to each other. For which experiment and inquiry, I offer my tenderest hopes and sympathies. But do not rest on them alone. With them and a part of them, a step toward quicker faith and deeper insight, is this square and simple discharge of some bit of present duty. There is your service for Lent. There is the first step, which must come before you take a second. Let no man resolve that he will enter on the eternal life and measure himself with angels and archangels, unless he determine on the specific task which shall begin that course to-day. Thus, he will read an hour to a blind man, or he will walk to the jail and counsel a prisoner. He will find his way into the hospital, and lighten the long Sunday of a sick child. He will give strength to the failing resolution of a drunkard. He will encourage the aspiration of his own child by coming down to his level. He will speak to the beggar-boy who is wondering at the treasures of a shop-window, will walk home with the little fellow, and become his friend. He will read in the newspaper, and will heed the imploring appeal of the Associated Charities. He will courteously welcome his busy neighbor, and will assent when he calls to urge him to attend a hearing at the City Hall or at the State House. In one of these ways, or in some way, he will find how he can enter into the common life and do his share in the common work. This is to act as a child of God, and to act with other children of God. And this, in the success of one distinct experiment, is to find that spirit rules flesh, that the eternal law is stronger than time,— a discovery which, when once made, is never disproved or forgotten.

It is only the first step which costs. And it does cost. It costs resolve and determination. I renounce my separate will, and I accept the will of God. And, on the other hand, who can take the first step can take all steps. He can mount on wings as eagles. He can walk, and not faint. He can run, and not be weary. That man enters into the infinite life, who seeks and finds a place where he can work with God. The train of the angels of the Eternal filled the heaven. The gigantic seraphim, the archangels, and all the host were in presence. The earth was filled with the glory of the Lord, and at his voice the pillars of the temple trembled. Least of all, you would say, in the unnumbered assemblage was this fearful man, so weak and faint, who describes it all. But, when the moment of crisis comes, when the Lord of Hosts needs a messenger, when he asks, " Whom shall we send ? " then this trembling listener becomes peer of the noblest in that great hierarchy of God's children, simply because in that service he volunteers.

"Then said I, Here am I : send me."

THE RELIGION OF AMERICA.

"When he had come near to Jerusalem he beheld the city, and said, 'Oh, if thou hadst known, in this thy day, the things which belong to thy peace! But now are they hid from thine eyes.'"— LUKE xix., 42.

WE can look back and see what the leaders of Israel could not see. Jesus Christ himself had appealed to them. With his marvellous command of men, he had tried Annas and Caiaphas and Nicodemus and Alexander and the rest, and to all visible purposes he had failed. He had been forced to take other measures, which have in nineteen centuries largely succeeded.

What was possible, so far as we can see, was this.

Here was the whole Roman Empire at the very acme of its power. And all through Roman Europe was an eager craving for the mystery, the secret of the East. Men were looking eastward, in their crude Western power and wealth, for Asiatic art, Asiatic learning, Asiatic culture, Asiatic religion. It was just as to-day a bonanza king of Nevada or California sends his son eastward to Harvard College, his daughter to Paris, buys his pictures in Rome, and in his own steamboat sails up the Nile. At that moment, the Lord of Life comes to Jerusalem. To the rulers of Jerusalem, he offers the keys of a new kingdom. He urges them to throw overboard the local formulas of a local religion. He asks them to announce to the world a God not peculiar to Zion or to Judah. He shows them, in terse epigram and in picturesque parable, that all the world is God's family, and that this is not true merely of one handful of Abrahamites. And they will not hear him. They stone him. They excommunicate him. Once more, he goes to make a last appeal; and then it is that he says so sadly: "If thou hadst known in this thy day, the things which belong unto thy peace. But now they are hid from thine eyes."

They refuse him again. Nay, they seize him and kill him.

And, before that generation passes, the Pharisee pride is forever broken, which would keep Judah separate from the world. The Roman legions close about Jerusalem. The mounds and battering-rams of Titus rise against it. The mad soldiery storms at last the wretched city, torn by quarrel and faint with famine. A torch is thrown into the midst of the gorgeous temple carvings. The flame runs from curtain to gallery, from gallery to roof; and our lovely Zion, the glory of the world, becomes a ruin and a desolation.

There is a double lesson : *first*, of the vanity of local pride ; *second*, of the supremacy of spiritual forces over material forces, the lesson of the eternal empire of truth and right. It is to this last that Jesus himself appeals. That nation prospers which understands the spiritual law of its own prosperity. That nation fails which does not accept the principle of its greatness, but is resting on some incident external, and therefore transitory. If Annas or Caiaphas or the rest of the Jew rulers could have been made to see that the power of Israel was all in her recognition of God as a spirit, the unseen God, well for Israel. Victory over the world for Israel, victory going forth from this very Jerusalem! But if Annas or Caiaphas or the rest try to keep up that gorgeous temple, those particular rites, this tribute to the high priest, and that etiquette by which the circumcised are higher than the uncircumcised, woe to them all! The besom will sweep, the threshing-mill will winnow, and such chaff will all be burned with unquenchable fire.

It is impossible, when we transfer this critical appeal to our own country, in this day of her glory and success,— it is impossible not to see that the same temptations seduce her, under which poor Israel stumbled, fell, and was trampled to death. For there are on every side to-day, as there were on one side then, those who conscientiously substitute ecclesiastical method for the intensity of religion in the nation's life, and in the forecast of her history. Annas and Caiaphas, then, believed in an unseen God. Yes : in their fashion, they prayed to him. But, all the same, they had this professional notion,— that he must be worshipped with this incense and that sacrifice, this procession and that liturgy, this feast day and that fast day. And when the great Reformer would have swept all this away, would have made the world to be the temple, and all honest speech a liturgy, they nailed him to the cross. Well, what is the aspect of the religious life of

America to-day? A hundred years ago, the country unconsciously settled the basis of its religion. In its political constitutions, it virtually declared that each man is child of God, and one man as much child of God as another. For it staked everything on a suffrage which at once became universal. It trusted its destiny to the weakest and meanest, as much as to the highest and strongest. Since that time, in the civil war and in the fourteenth and fifteenth amendments, the country has ratified that determination; nay, has sealed it with its best blood. It proclaims the "honor all men" as the central principle of its existence. Though those men be black or red, it honors them. It admits that they are all children of God. And this childlike relation of all to God,— God's fatherly care of each and all, and their consequent mutual dependence as brothers in one God-born family,— this is the basis of the country's religion. Now, it is to such a country as this that an Italian prince, crowned with three crowns and sitting on seven hills, comes with the most amiable and affectionate accent, and says: "The Virgin Mary gave you all to me. God speaks to my heart as he will never speak to yours. Give up this phantom of an unseen Father, and obey the directions of a present father, whom you can see and handle, who lives only four or five thousand miles away, and who thinks of you as often as once a week, when his attention happens to be directed across the ocean."

And this Latin-speaking imitator of the dark ages is only a little larger and a little more absurd than twenty other popes, who, in their way, are cooing or sighing, scolding or cajoling, as they would seduce this free-born people from its enthusiasm for freedom. For, whenever any ecclesiastical machinery pushes forward any ecclesiastical puppet to make his dumb, wooden gestures in some little play-house, before this free-born people, in the hope of persuading it to substitute the judgment of others for the personal conscience, or to pray by proxy or by machinery where God seeks personal communion, the managers of those ecclesiastical puppet-shows are only so many lesser popes, trying to beckon us back to the lethargy of the past. One sometimes sees, in our time, one of the miracles. You can see one, in the start of glad surprise with which a man, trained for half his life to believe that machinery and organization and doctrine are religion, wakes all of a sudden to find that religion is life. I have seen such a man, who for twenty years had painfully assisted in carrying on the mechanism of the Presbyterian Church. He had contributed for this mission and that college, he had voted for this and that delegate, and had commissioned this and that elder. He had fasted in this fast, and given thanks in that thanksgiving; nay, had bound his conscience as he was directed, by this or that article of this or that creed. I say I have seen such a person, when the great miracle of God was worked upon him,— when he saw, almost of a sudden, that all this was not itself religion, but only a sort of hemp and matting by which timid men had protected religion from sun and air. The Saviour speaks to such a man, and says, "Awake, arise!" And you see his eyelids slowly open, you see the color flush his marble cheek, you see his lips gasp for fresh air, and then the smile of heaven itself lightens up the man as he knows and first feels that this is pure religion,— for man to seek God, and for God to bless man.

Particular attention is called at this moment to the tyranny of the Mormon ecclesiasticism in Utah. An admirable instance this is, for it is visible and tangible, of the tyranny which an organized priesthood can wield as against even a large number of unorganized men and women. But that tyranny in Utah is not a whit worse than the tyranny with which the Jesuit fraternity rules the territory of New Mexico, or the tyranny with which the Roman Catholic Church wants to sway the education of the whole country, or with which in practice it often does govern the city of New York. And there are a dozen other little ecclesiasticisms in the country, which gladly exercise the same sort of power on some petty sphere, whenever, by bad luck, they have the opportunity.

Thank God that all these efforts do seem to us puny. For, among a thousand blessings which surrounded the birth of this nation, one was that the infallible Church of Rome was fortunately at that moment in one of its paroxysms of inefficient lethargy, and for half a century could not mix nor meddle in our affairs. Other ecclesiastical organizations were as weak; and to this happiness we owe it that the constitutions of the country, as I said, are based on each man's separate right to come to God alone, without the bolsterings or promptings of any priest or priesthood. Such efforts of the sects, therefore, as I describe, whether of the great sect of Rome or any of her petty imitators, are but the puny attacks of outsiders who assail an establishment, now well assured by the triumphs of one hundred years. Well for the country that this is so. The conservatism of this country is thus on the side of freedom. And, when you appeal to the American to maintain the American system of religion, you appeal to him to maintain the absolute freedom in which child comes to Father, and Father to child, with never man or rag or dusty form between. This freedom in religion is the central truth on which rest the glory of the country and its strength. And if Jesus were to look upon this nation, in this day of its power, it would be to pray and to hope that this central glory of its glories might not be hid from its eyes.

For it is to be observed all along that the country is profoundly religious. It believes in right, and it wants to have right done. The Puritans did not cross the ocean for nothing, nor the Huguenots. Such men as Asbury and Brainerd did not preach for nothing. Such lessons as the Revolution taught, of great made from small, by the mere power of faith, were not neglected. And that eternal experience, by which people who live much in the open air, in hourly presence of nature, become thoughtful and religious people, has made a religious race from the pioneers and settlers of the frontier. The leader of Americans, who may wish to lead them forward in the line of the destiny which has triumphed thus far, leads a religious race in the methods of personal and spontaneous worship, with constant reference to the eternal laws. He does not appeal to this man's selfishness or to the greed of that community. He does not teach the wretched doctrine of a bald economy, to induce them to pile up gold or iron or brass. He appeals to the highest motive men can grasp, and cites the noblest law he knows. This law is a law outside themselves: it is the infinite law of an infinite God, because this people is at its very heart religious.

I have lately been asked to prepare a short memoir on the Religion of America in 1880, for the reading of those who may live in Boston in 1980. It is to be enclosed in a copper box, with many other memoirs of the present condition of the city, not to be opened till the centennial celebration a hundred years from this time. I have never found any literary task so difficult. Whenever I approach it, I ask for a little more time; and the first word of it is as yet unwritten. It seems well-nigh certain that no large ecclesiastical organization now existing will exist then without serious changes. In those changes, it is very likely that the methods of men's worship may largely change. It is difficult, therefore, to say what features of the religion of to-day will have most interest for a reader then. One dreads a reader of whom he knows so little. So far the memoir is hard to write. But this is easy: to say that, on the whole, the men of this time are seeking to do the right thing, and eager to find what it is. Some of them ask priests to tell of them, some of them ask poets, some of them ask chemists, and some ask mediums or seers, some try their own experiments, and make their own study of history; but, on the whole, people want to have the right thing done. And, if they shall be misled, they will be misled by those who pretend to lead them rightly. This is to say that they are, on the whole and at heart, a religious people.

If they know the thing that belongs to their peace, in these the days of their glory, they will hold to this simple love of right and determination to win it, each man for himself, without submission to external authority. Dr. Furness has said — and I think the remark is true — that outside a republic no critics seem to understand what Jesus Christ means, when he speaks of the Kingdom of Heaven. Outside a republic, even learned men cannot be trained to understand how there can be a kingdom with no king but God. Inside a republic,— praise God! — men can understand this. Inside a republic, men understand how the least man is essential to the greatest, and the greatest to the least. They understand how he that would be first of all shall be servant of all. They ought to understand the whole law of Christ, which is that man shall "bear his brother's burdens." And to understand that law is one step toward fulfilling it. The man who leads this people will keep it true to this great law of mutual service. The rich will help the poor, and the poor the rich. The East will help the West, and the West the East. The carpenter will help the goldsmith, and the goldsmith the carpenter. No man will live for himself. No man will talk much about his own things; for all men will be seeking the common-weal of the commonwealth, and be eager for the prosperity of the trade, the mining, the manufacture, the farming, the education, and the worship of the whole.

One of the wisest and one of the most instructive of the great men of our time has put on record his dread of this common life and common interest in America. It is tha pure man, that clear thinker, Stuart Mill, who points out the danger that, with equal rights to all, with the same training in the same circumstance to all, we shall all grow to be like each other. If we go to the same schools, study the same books, have each a homestead farm of one hundred and sixty acres, in a land without mountain horizon, or any desert of clay or gravel, how can we fail to lose our individuality? he asks. Is there not danger that we shall become as like as the pegs cut by the same machine? Well, it is not enough to say in reply that we do not yet see this. Mr. Longfellow is not like Dr. Wayland, Dr. Wayland is not like Mr. Edison, Mr. Edison is not like Mr. Tilden, Mr. Tilden is not like Bishop Simpson, Bishop Simpson is not like Jay Cooke, Jay Cooke is not like Frederick Douglass, Mr. Douglass is not like Mr. Garrison, and Mr. Garrison is not like Mr. Longfellow. We must not say this in reply to Mr. Mill, because it is conceded that these men were trained by the past, and that there is not yet time for the destruction of individuality by the life in common. What is the future to show of individual power among men who have confessedly been bearing each other's burdens?

Well, let us say frankly that it is very clear that great individuality has not been an unmixed blessing. The individuality of Napoleon the Great was a curse to Europe for fifty years, and hardly works any benefit up to this hour. The individuality of Dominic in his conduct of the Albigensian crusade set back the civilization of Europe for three centuries. If we here have hit on any device by which the tyranny of one man shall be held in check by the steady, united force of fifty million, the loss of individuality is more than compensated. Is there any danger that, if another Shakspere should be born here, another Goethe, or another Stuart Mill, we should lose the advantage which the individuality of those men has given to the world? I do not see it. Such lives will assert themselves. And if, while we secure such blessing, the whole theory and drift of our social order is to make man stand by man and be his brother's keeper, there is hope—shall I say for the first time?—that here the real genius of mankind shall have perfect chance. Man is God's child. Therefore, man is man's brother. Till the world gives this chance for brother to work with brother, each brother on each other depending, the world does not fully know what man is, or what man is good for. If any man believe that Jesus Christ knew what man is, that man must see that man has no full chance for his full being, till he live thus in mutual relationship with his fellow-man, and that on an even plane. The prayer of Jesus Christ and his injunction are that none shall be our master, but that we shall be all brethren. The plan of Jesus Christ and his prophecy are for a commonwealth, where we shall all give thus, and all share,— not in any stupid communism, not in the surrender of one's own rights or one's own life, but in that noble love in which the lord of the feast asks to the feast even the halt and the lame, in that loyal benevolence in which the Good Samaritan chooses his brother where he finds a traveller stripped and bleeding by the highway. That man truly advances the American idea who governs his life by this Christian idea, in which a man learns, not for his own amusement, but that he may teach others. He educates the beggar's child, not simply for the child's good, but for the good of the community. He plants and reaps, not that he may feed himself, but that he may feed the rest. He spins and weaves, not that he may wrap himself in his own cocoon, but that he may do his share to clothe mankind. He lives, not for himself, but for the commonwealth of his brethren.

"I have given you an example that ye should do as I have done unto you."

"A new commandment I give unto you, that ye love one another. By this shall all men know that ye are my disciples, if ye have love one to another."

"This bread is broken for each and all of you."

"This cup is the token of my blood, which is shed for each and all of you."

PARABLE AND BIBLE.

"Without a parable spake he not unto them, as they were able to hear it."—MARK iv., 33.

THIS is the severe condensation in Mark's Gospel of a statement made more at length in all three of the Galilean Gospels of Jesus' method. He justifies it or shows its principle in two recorded conversations. The people who hear are stupid, he says. They will not understand much. Perhaps some of them will understand nothing. But they will remember, if what is told is told in a picturesque or dramatic way. Therefore, he uses the method of teaching by example or illustration, that hearing they may hear, even if they do not understand. That phrase has become a proverb. And it may be observed that long before his time, and ever since, this is the method adopted by all moral teachers who have to do with the people generally, with what we call the rank and file. It was the method of Jotham in Judah and Æsop in Phrygia hundreds of years before Christ, as it is to-day the method of every stump-speaker addressing the populace in a public meeting. "I will tell you a little story," he says, if he thinks their attention flags. It is to be noticed that in St. John's narratives of what passed in Jerusalem between the Saviour and Nicodemus, or between him and the priests and Pilate, there are no parables. This is one of the points urged with great eagerness by those who would prove that this Gospel was not written by one who was an eye-witness. But it does not prove much. We should not argue that Abraham Lincoln was not a story-teller because we found no "little stories" in his public messages, or in some one record of his conversations with Lord Lyons or with the chiefs of his cabinet.

What Jesus Christ means by a parable is a presentation to the eye or the imagination, or both, of some moral or spiritual principle. The representation may be imaginary, as in the parable of the wedding feast, or it may be something passing under their sight, like the growing of mustard-seed or the spark running through tinder. And it has been thought also that sometimes he took some incident well known in his own time, as, that the story of the dishonest steward was a real experience known to his hearers, or even the story of the good Samaritan. This is certain, that when he said, "What king, going to make war against another king, sitteth not down first to consider whether he be able with ten thousand to meet him that cometh against him with twenty thousand?" he used an historical parable taken from King Herod's position just at that time. War was brewing on the frontier between Herod, King of Galilee, and Aretas, the King of Arabia. Herod eventually lost his throne in the result; and he had on his mind much this question, when Christ spoke. Thus, a parable may be the description of a natural process, of an event in history, or of an imagined event. If it be a dramatic representation of the result of some moral principle, it is a "parable," in the use these writers make of that word.

The world's instinct for story-telling and story-hearing is thus distinctly recognized and approved by the greatest of teachers. The instinct which makes all people delight in the drama is a part of it. Some of you heard Miss La Flesche here on Friday, when she avouched the eagerness of our Indian tribes for such legends as those which Mr. Longfellow has made familiar to us in "Hiawatha." And the same eagerness appears almost everywhere. Oddly enough, the only considerable permanent opposition to this instinct has appeared among the professed theologians of this very Christian Church, which was itself built on a corner-stone of parable. The standard theologians, and the preachers most in formal ecclesiastical repute of the Church, have always presented the moral which they had in hand, with a dry or dull, decorous omission of any parable to illustrate it. It is thus that the phrase "dull as a sermon" is a proverb now. And another proverb might be made, which should say that people forget the average sermon as they forget nothing else in literature. I remember that I have myself been condemned, by what is called "a leading religious journal" of this country, for one of my own poor efforts in parable or fiction with a moral purpose, as being "a forger and counterfeiter."* This decorous habit resem-

---

* Since I preached this sermon, I have heard of a church, not three hundred miles from Boston, where some advanced reformers bought a Sunday-school library from an establishment which might have been thought safe,—the Baptist Sunday School Society. When the books arrived, the trustees of the church sequestered them simply because the stories in them were fictitious.

bles that of some dried-up old school-mistress, trying to teach a child to repeat from Æsop's Fables the "moral" of the story of the Fox and Grapes. The child knows the story, but cannot repeat the moral. In face of this habit, the in-formal prophets of the Church, the unecclesiastical re-formers, delight in parable. Luther, Wesley, Whitefield, were never afraid to preach as their Master preached. And, in the Catholic Church, the same is true of Fénelon, of St. Francis of Bernard, and of Savonarola.

At the present moment, this method of teaching is condemned in similar fashion by quite another set of moral re-formers and advisers. They are men who are very tired of churches and preachers and old-fashioned gospels. They are indeed indisposed to worship, though, by a certain figure of speech, they are disposed " to worship truth." It seems to me very curious that all this school — the extreme agnostic, the more doubtful sceptic, and, in general, the utilitarian moralist — seem to propose to dispense with the parable in the teaching of the world with exactly the same hatred with which high and dry Orthodoxy hates it. Dr. Emmons or Jonathan Edwards would have put into the fire a play of Shakspere or Fénelon's *Télémachus*. The advanced moralist of to-day seems to hate dramatic illustration as bitterly. He proposes to us, if we assemble people for instruction, to give up from the Bible its wealth of historical illustration, and to satisfy ourselves with the Book of Proverbs and Ecclesiastes. He asks us to introduce into the place of Isaiah and the Book of Samuel select passages from the Veda, from Zoroaster, and Confucius, driest of the dry. Macaulay said of the Puritans that they disliked bear-baiting, not because it hurt the bear, but because it amused the people. It seems to me, as I read the modern ghastly suggestions for improved worship, that the central purpose is a like desire to strike out of religious training everything that is imaginative or entertaining.

The forefathers of this school, in the French Revolution, tried just the same experiment, — may I not say committed the same folly? Thus, they made a calendar to take the place of the Roman Catholic calendar. The madness of that day was to instruct people in physics, or what they called " natural philosophy" and " natural history." So the new calendar assigned to each day a specific subject for study and contemplation. Thus, where the Church had called men's attention, say, to the faith and martyrdom of St. Sebastian, the new calendar would ask them to give the day, say, to learning the culture and qualities of pepper. Or, where the Church set aside All Souls' Day or All Saints' Day, for the memory of all unnamed souls and saints who had set the King's work forward, the new calendar suggested the chemical formula of the proportions of common salt as the subject for that day's contemplation. In this particular form, this absurdity belongs to the folly of that time, in which people mistook the laboratory, which is one beautiful porch of God's temple, for the Holy of Holies itself. The present drift seems to be just as absurd. It supposes ethical science, which is another porch of the temple, to be the Holy of Holies. When any one asks me to give up reading from this pulpit the story of Joseph, and to substitute for it the most accurate and what seems to me the most true statement of intuitive morals, even by the best writer of our time, he seems to be committing this same absurdity. As matter of history, the Buddhists, who are at this moment quite in fashion among Christians, have tried this long ago. They have temples in Japan, of which the walls are adorned with ethical texts from their best writers. The worship consists in the reading of these texts by such people as feel that they need improvement in those lines. But the misfortune, alas! is that the temples are empty; for the people who would be most improved by the texts are occupied elsewhere, and those who do not need them stay at home to carry them into execution.

Wholly unlike this didactic and abstract system is the system by which Jesus Christ inculcated religion. He chose to teach by example. And his system has been carried out on the largest scale, a larger scale even than that of his own earthly ministry, in the method by which the world has, in fact, learned and maintained its religion. It is from those great dramas, in which nations rise and fall in thousands of years, that men learn the laws by which nations live. It is in the faith or the brutality of other men and other women that the people who come after them learn what it is to obey God and what it is to forget him. Men want to put all this into a code, to refer to the code by an index, and to teach the code by a catechism. But God chooses to teach his law by the Reported Cases. Those cases are the great dramas of history. The world never tires of them, never learns the lesson to the bottom, but never finds it can state it better. From the record of such cases, it brings together its Bible, and, in practice, learns and teaches its religion. What providence is, in the long run, the world learns, as it reads how Abraham left the beastliness of materialism and nature-worship behind him, and resolutely marched westward. How good comes out of evil, the world learns when it sees Jacob and his clans fed by the prudence and tenderness of Joseph. How tyranny dies,— and the great lesson of freedom instead of slavery, are the lessons of Egypt and the march through the desert. Law and the worth of law are taught, as that mob of slaves becomes, in a generation, a nation of freemen. And so you may go on through the Bible. Now, you cannot teach those lessons in the abstract. But, in the experience of thousands of years, you come to know what empire they hold over men's affections and their reason, when they are taught with all the picturesque scenery, with all the personal passion, with all the living intensity of the biographies of men and of women.

Of our Bible, one special element of value for our Western life incalculably is that it is written by men who are not afraid to speak of God as a Living Friend. They speak of God as HE, and not as IT. They speak of his presence in men's affairs. This is not natural to the Western races. In the *Iliad*, the men and women take their turns one day, and the gods and goddesses another. The Old Testament writers saw and knew that God could speak by Moses' lips, or rule in Joshua's leadership, or prompt Gideon's strategy ; and they did not fear to say so. The eternal God comes in as a present actor in human affairs. The Bible, therefore, is not merely a book of dramatic interest, teaching men by example ; but it is a book where the examples involve spiritual power. From end to end, it supposes and it states that the Idea creates the Fact, that Spirit rules Matter, that the Word makes and controls the Thing. This statement of what is the real substance,— namely, the soul or life,— with the corresponding statement that things, bodily and visible, are but transitory forms, gives dignity and character to what would else be petty in these histories. True, you can find the same lesson in all history. But you do not find it everywhere written in this Eastern naïveté or simplicity. This is indeed the distinction of Eastern thought, habit, and expression. It is the peculiar glory of Eastern literature. Those

Eastern nations were never startled by the idea of spiritual power, unseen, incalculable, but always present. So they never made the attempt which Western nations are always making, to simplify matters by supposing that such spiritual power acts by starts, comes in of a sudden, and is then for ages withdrawn, to wait and wait, and then to come in again.

Here is the key to the difference between the Eastern sacred books and our cold-blooded criticisms and commentaries upon them. Take the *Arabian Nights*, which are confessedly fictions. Those poets fill full their pages with superhuman action. Fairies and giants, genii and spirits, are woven wholly into the narrative. You cannot separate them. The worlds of the invisible and the visible, the worlds of spirit and of matter, are wrought in close together. And, though the whole is written as a fiction, it shows the habit and tone of thought of him who wrote it. But in any Greek or Roman poem, though written in as simple times and hardly less as a fiction, the author brings in now his gods and now his men, but with such careful distinction that they hardly appear on the same scene. The author is worried and ill at ease when they do. There is the habit of mind of Western nations, so far as spiritual conceptions go. The acts of God are read separately from the acts of men. The laws of God are one thing and the laws of men are another, to the careless eye. Religion is religion, and business is business. Sunday and Monday may be separated as quite different in spirit. The church and the street, the hymn and the song, sacred music and daily music, sacred history and profane history, sacred reading and profane reading, have been too long separated thus in general estimation. As if beneath all life, all action, all duty, there were not one spirit, one law, one God. All this is changed, when you read the Bible. God and man, man and God, God with man, man with God,— these are the actors — shall I say the heroes?— of the story, one and inseparable all the way through.

I wish some imaginative author, who should have humor enough to show the ridiculous side of what is absurd, would draw for us the picture of a colony, taken into a new region of the world, under the auspices of the Gradgrind school in morals and religion. One would like to have a fair statement of what the third or fourth generation would be in a world educated without fairy tales or the *Arabian Nights*, without Bibles or prophecies, on the hard-baked food of utilitarian ethics, demonstrated by the greatest good of the greatest number. This is, perhaps, not the place for such a narrative, as I am not the person to attempt it. But the lesson would be worth teaching and learning. Without working out that picture, you need only take the average Hymn-Book, and you have an illustration of what the world's Bible would be, if the trained teachers of the world had the arranging of it. The ghastly hymns, which they call "didactic hymns," which indeed sound like a school primer set to rhyme, are a prominent part of it. Why, in a collection of five hundred hymns, you shall not be indulged with fifty which have the rush of action, the ring of victory, nay, the picturesqueness of a common ballad, far less, anywhere, the energy and reality with which the Book of Exodus takes the Israelites across the sea, or the Book of Revelations overwhelms Rome in the ruin its sins deserve. The decorous and quiet men who compile the average Hymn-Book have no such knowledge of the world or what the world needs, to give you more than what their own stately and rather dreary language would call in the index:—

"Didactic Hymns on Fidelity to the Obligations of the Christian Life in general"; or,

"Devotion Sanctifying the Relations and Pleasures of the Christian Life in particular."*

It is, indeed, only the large borrowing from the more picturesque and dramatic Bible which saves the average Hymn-Book from decay and corruption.

It is no such fastidious and critical consideration in the abstract "of the obligations of the Christian life in general," which has saved the world, or taught it its religion, from generation to generation. Renan says with perfect respect to St. Paul, for whom he had a great admiration, that, since Paul died, his letters alone, which make half the canon of the New Testament, have not made a hundred converts to Christianity.† It is the story of the Master's life, it is his stories of the Good Samaritan, of the Prodigal Son, and the rest, which have taught men what life is, what divine life is, and have made them seek to be sons of God. Paul's letters have helped them, when they came to the detail of character. His epigrams have been texts for action and memory.* But it is

---

* These titles are copied literally from the "Index of Subjects" of what was lately a standard Hymn-Book.

† "Seules, les épîtres de Saint Paul n'eussent pas acquis cent adeptes à Jésus."— p. 100, *Evangiles*.

not a letter of Paul that sends John Augustus into the
prison : it is that he follows his Leader. It is no discussion
in the Epistle to the Romans which turns round yonder tear-
ful and repentant woman with the struggling hope of a new
life, to leave a house of shame : it is the story of Mary Magdalen.* Or when some Indian, coming in from the hunt,
stops in your frontier church to find what lesson the white
man's teacher teaches, he is not attracted by any discussion
about conversion or sanctification. He is touched, if that
day the preacher tells, though for the thousandth time, the
story of "I must walk to-day, to-morrow, and the day following." He believes in the love which was willing to die for
men unknown and far away.† I sat here on the platform
below, that evening in last November, when Miss Fletcher
was describing the Passion-Play as she saw it in the Ammer-
gau. As her narrative went forward, there was in it less and
less allusion to the peasants of the Tyrol, or to the adventures
of her own party. More and more, from the very nature of
her subject, was she thrown back to the unadorned language
of this simple narrative, as you would read it from any
Harmony of the Gospels. By a fortunate chance, as she approached the story of the crucifixion, the sun set without, the
church here grew darker and darker, and the only lights were
those which enabled her to read. She went on with the
simple narrative, just able to command her own voice as she
did so. And I, as I looked out from this light into the darkness over the crowd, saw every face eagerly and unconsciously
bent on her, every eye wet with tears. I felt the keen attention which would not lose one word of the story they knew
by heart. I heard strong men sobbing ; and I knew, in the
hush of the great assembly, broken only by that sound, how
it was possessed by the story. Then I understood once
more what is the God-ordered power of a book like the
Bible for maintaining the religion of the world.

I sometimes hear of some young gentleman, who has com-
pleted his studies of theology, proposing that we should
make arrangements for a new Bible. It is to bring in all the
sacred instructions of all the inspired men. Truly a large
collection! I never hear this suggestion from the older
men, who have advanced so far that they know that their

---

* This is not rhetoric. It is the literal statement of the result wrought by Mrs.
Greenough's poem "Mary Magdalen."

† This story is told very simply by Miss La Flesche.

studies in theology are hardly begun. For Bibles make themselves. They are not made by forethought or to order. This book made itself. Gospels there were, which are lost, alas! These four were so divine that men would not let them die. Hundreds of letters Paul wrote, and James, the secretary at head-quarters. These letters here, had in them that which men must have. The law of selection worked, and they kept these in being. Nay, you know yourselves how some parts of the Bible are strange to you, because they do you no good, while what you need is a household word and a blessed memory. It is by such compulsion, which no scholarship can overthrow or undermine, that a book like the Bible makes its own way into the affections of the world. And, whenever the world adds to its canon new treasures of wisdom or of imagination, it will repeat its old history. It will read, not the digest of a law-book, not the abstractions of a philosopher, but the intense visions of a poet, or the tale throbbing with pathos, which makes visible the struggles of a life.

I have chosen to say this to-day, because, in a few weeks now, the new version of the New Testament will be awaking a new external interest in the shape of the Gospels and Epistles, the Book of Acts and the Revelations. Happily, we shall not handle the book as an idol. Happily, we shall come to it for fruit, for medicine, as we need fruit or medicine; and, where we find neither, we shall not force the words for what they do not give. In the common-sense notion of the Bible to which the youngest child in this church is trained, it has a power far surpassing what it had in any of the days of superstition. That power is the power which narrative, dramatic or historical,— when it is the story of God with man, man with God, man's life hid in God,— commands of its very nature. Men must remember; and, if they remember, one day they will comply.

"Therefore speak I to them in parables, that hearing they may hear, even if they do not yet understand; and seeing they may see, even if they do not yet perceive."

"Happy are your eyes, for they do see; and your ears, for they do hear"

"What kings and prophets waited for,
And died without the sight."

INDIFFERENCE.

"Go ye into all the world, and preach the gospel to every creature."
— MARK xvi., 15.

In the early days of Christianity, the intensity or eagerness of the new converts roused the wonder and ridicule of lookers-on. There is many a jest in the classical writers at their habit of pushing things to extremes.

The truth was that, especially in the higher classes, eager or vehement action was then out of fashion. There was a fashion of indifference. In older times, a Roman gentleman had fought in person. He served in the army, led his own company to battle. But this was all over now. Any fighting was done by provincial regiments, and the average Roman gentleman stayed at home. Then, in old times, there had been the excitements of the annual political canvass. Porcius or Manlius was a candidate, and Junius and Livius were on his committee. Or, under the admirable civil service system of Rome, the young men were preparing themselves for higher duties by serving in the lower. If we lived under Roman law, no man could be governor of this State who had not been mayor of his city, nor mayor unless he had been superintendent of streets, chief of police, and superintendent of buildings. Thus they secured men of first-rate ability, even in subordinate offices. All such life had kept Rome alive in early days. But all this was over now. And now the fashion set the other way, in Rome and in the provinces. The fashion was to be indifferent, or to seem so. At Athens, Luke says, "they spent their time in nothing else but to hear and tell some new thing." In the capital at Rome, things might be described in much the same way. It was all what our modern world calls "loafing," and no other word expresses it so well. Such people dawdling through the day, wishing somebody would amuse them, and finding life very much of a bore, looked with amazement and amusement on such a man as Paul, pushing always from province to province,— nay, from continent to continent,— possessed by an idea. Scourged, imprisoned, stoned, shipwrecked, taken up for dead,— all the same this driving fellow is carrying forward his enterprise. The King's work must go on. And, in good report or evil report, he would drive it on. Freeman or prisoner, working in his shop or speaking from a platform, tossed on the sea or pleading for his life, first, last. and always, he would push forward the great idea, "Woe is me if I preach not the gospel."

The new stimulus with which the Christian idea broke up all such lassitude and indifference as then reigned is to this hour its first best gift to the world. It tells the sick world, or the world bored with ennui, to take up its bed and walk. To men and women in the highest grades of life, or in the lowest, it offers one great motive for life outside themselves. This picture of a possible, perfect world, of a world which shall obey God as perfectly as planets in the heavens obey him, a world in which men and women are to be willing servants, children, and princes of his, as loyal as the angels and archangels of poetry,— this picture, or real vision, is put before the eyes of the humblest and the greatest. Humblest and greatest are taught that they may do their share to bring it in. The languid young prince, who is tired of flattery, and the toil-worn day-laborer, who is tired of hard work and poor pay, see alike that here is an object great enough for the noblest. Once possessed with a passion for it, prince or beggar has something to live for. And, once enlisted in the service of him who leads the way to that perfect world, all lesser amusements pale, and all lesser ambitions are unsatisfying. The more they achieve, the more they seek to achieve; and passion grows with its own exercise and success. Nor is languor or indifferentism possible longer, to him who has seen the vision and enlisted in the cause, determined that God's kingdom shall come, and his will be done on earth as it is done in heaven.

The observation was early made that Christian men and women, embarked in this great cause, work from passion, work with the eagerness of their whole nature, and not simply under the cool control of mere logic. The determination of a Paul or a Francis or a Bernard, of John Knox or Fénelon or Wesley, is a passion sweeping away the whole man, and every power of his life. These are not statesmen who can argue for a constitution to-day, but to-morrow amuse themselves in society, turn over the best arrangements for their investments, or buy pictures for their galleries and discuss the last novelties in art. If they, by accident, do any one of these little things, it all falls into the sweep of the great determination that the Christian Commonwealth shall be established in the world. The critical world has been quite right in pronouncing that they are swept along by an all-controlling passion, and that they differ in every throb and in every act from mere theorists or men of prudence or doctrinaires.

It has happened occasionally that such a passion has swept nations away, perhaps they hardly knew how. When the cry reached Europe that the Pagans oppressed Christian pilgrims in the very region of the cross, that the land where the Son of God lived and died was desecrated by blasphemy, the Crusades, as they swept whole nations away, and made armies from peoples, showed in all their fervor, even with all their absurdity, that the Christian passion still ruled in the hearts of men. People, who could not be argued or convinced to change their daily lives by a hair's-breadth, could be summoned by the great invocations, "For the love of God" and "In the name of Christ," to leave every habit and surrender every comfort, to accept the worst hardships of campaigns well-nigh hopeless, under that passion's sway. It was infinitely stronger than any calculated appeals to personal expediency, or other merely worldly wisdom. Once and again, at its great epochs, the world learns the same lesson. Our people here knew it, when our Revolution began; people caught a glimpse of it in France, when their Revolution began, when one passionate appeal to the "Sons of Freedom" started a nation of peasants, just emancipated, on a career of conquest which defeated the armies of Europe recruited, and fought in decorous and calculated system. A finer instance than either was the great uprising of our own people, now twenty years ago, when every man forgot his own lesser duty to his family or to himself, in his passionate determination to serve his country. Those first three months of the war were worth everything to us who were happy enough to live in so great a time. To see the weakest vying with the strongest, the poorest with the richest, to show who best could serve in the hour of the country's need; to see the rare ingenuity of sacrifice by which man, woman, and child all found some way in which they could help in the great necessity,— this was to know of our own knowledge what is the abundant life which comes into play among sons of God, where there is common enthusiasm in one great cause. Even the courts of justice found that under this great emotion pickpockets and burglars forgot to steal and to rob. The meanest men were lifted above themselves; for a man was a man, and the worst man had a chance to show that he also could serve the country, the mother of us all, and God, who is our Father. "I have lost that which nothing can repay me," said a patriot American poet to me, on his return from France at that time, "because in my absence in Europe I lost the sight of this grand enthusiasm,— of this fanatic sacrifice of a nation of men."

The young American of to-day, ripening into manhood, is tempted to curse his star that he was not born into those fortunate days. His father charged with Kilpatrick or with Lowell, or sailed with Farragut or with Winslow, or struggled up the glacis with Shaw, or waved his hat and cheered when the rebel flag fluttered downward at Pulaski. And the son broods over all this, as he sits smoking in his club-room, or, lolling back with his feet on the window-sill, counts the passers-by from Parker's; and he asks why he was born to these degenerate days,— days of vulgar prosperity, where, he says, there is no chance for men. Even Literature takes on such ghastly purple hue of blood not oxygenated, and asks if life be worth living; sings her songs of gloom, and feeds us with novels about women uncomprehended and men without a purpose. For all which, our guardian angels must grieve and wonder. Is there no purpose worthy of adventurous manhood or womanhood but the storming of the walls of Jerusalem? Cannot a young man or a young women be roused to passionate life, unless a country be tottering to its ruin?

George Eliot was one day speaking to a lady about her hope for the future of mankind, and she said eagerly: "What I look to is a time when the impulse to help our fellows shall be as immediate and irresistible as that which I feel to grasp something when I fall." "The eloquent gesture with which she grasped the mantel-piece as she spoke remains in the memory, as the expression of a sort of transmuted prayer." Such are the words of her who was speaking with her.

The illustration is a perfect one of that eager readiness with which a man like Paul flung himself into service, or with which Saint Vincent de Paul took the place of the felon who had been chained to the oar. This is the "love your brother as yourself," which is the centre of the Christian ethics; and it suggests the great necessity that the effort and act must be, not cold obedience to an enacted law nor the deduction, as cold, from a logical investigation, but the passionate surrender of every power of the whole man to help the person who suffers. The quick eye and the sure foot and the strong hand and the ready wit and the sympathetic tear and the good-natured word and the wise counsel and the community of purpose which unites many in such help,— these are all to be twined together in the effort to relieve. It is not a fixed method, which men need to study or to resolve upon: it is abundant life which they are to consecrate to such a cause. Crusade, indeed! war for freedom, indeed! help of suffering, indeed! With all the passion of abounding life, the Christian theory supposes that each man enlists in the common service in the help everywhere and always of his brother-man.

And one need not go back to Paul for illustrations of the outcome of such effort. There are a plenty of little, halfway victories in this direction. The Washingtonian temperance movement was the sudden determination, eager and full of life, of a large number of persons, not themselves in danger of drunkenness, that they would come to the help of those that were. For the time, they would and did throw off other duty and other care. To find the man who wanted to reform, to be sure that he should not be alone, to surround the ray of his flickering candle with every screen and guard which should keep from it the wind, to strengthen by society and the quick stimulus of society — and that the best society — the trembling resolution just formed, and so easily abandoned,— these were the hopes of the Washingtonian reformers. They are hopes not planned out by wisdom or on theory, not possible to a commissioned functionary. A man flings himself into the gulf. A man! That is to say, a divine soul, using human wit and a human body. A man — that is, a child of God — says to this poor drunkard, Take my hand, and I will pull you through. And a woman — that is, another child of God — says, Take mine, and I, too, will pull. And another man offers his manhood, and another woman the divine force of her womanhood. They surround him, they refresh him, they inspire him, they encourage him, they feed him with new food, they excite him with new motive, they renew him with a new life. All this is because they do not work as functionaries, but because they are passionately determined. They give the omnipotence of life to the effort ; and life conquers death, as it always does.

To the young man or the young woman, then, who finds much learning to be weariness of the flesh,— who finds fashion a sham, society a bore, politics a fraud, who is weary of life and of self, and so sits by the wayside proclaiming his or her dolefulness,— the fair question is: "Have you, by chance, tried the experiment of the Christian Religion? Have you thrown yourself with hearty passion into a great cause,— the great cause of making this world a part of Heaven?" It is no affirmative answer to this appeal to say that one has fooled over social economy, has studied its statistics, or adjusted some of its machinery. It is no answer to say that one has sometimes offered advice which was rejected, or instructions which failed. It is no answer to say that you have offered a part of yourself, and kept the other part for certain purposes of your own. Nobody has asked for a part of you. God Almighty has asked for the whole. Jesus Christ, his ambassador, has asked for the whole. The demand is that you will squarely devote yourself, your life, that God's Kingdom may come, and his will be done on earth as it is in Heaven.

And do you tell me that you have no field, that the world does not need you? Surely there are ten thousand people right around you, nearer to you than any other ten thousand people in this world. Do you tell me that the kingdom of heaven has come to them and theirs? Where do they fall short? Where is the loose screw? Are there so many rushing to tighten it that there is no room for you? When you sprung to their place of need,— as George Eliot clutched that mantel that she need not fall,— were there so many that you could do nothing?

People talk of revivals of religion. It seems to me to be irreligion which is faint and wants stimulus, and there is nothing but religion which will revive it. Ennui, indifference, lassitude, will be quickened and revived, not by a new code here or a new method there, not by this system or that function, but by more abundant life,— that is to say, life from the fountain of life,— and this means more religion. The sickly revival of the churches is an appeal at the end of winter, when people's nerves and muscles are weakened by cold and by the absence of sunlight, so that bodies are faint and minds are morbid ; and it is an appeal to induce men or women to take up some new habits of prayer, of confession, and so far of Life. But how narrow the appeal, and how petty the object, compared with what it might be! If only some shot on some Sumter could revive, not ten men nor a hundred, but a whole community, to sweep out its iniquities, to put a stop to its debaucheries, to wipe out its temptations, to end its jobs, to give society to the lonely, to find homes for the homeless, to empty into the desert the crowds, to abate disease, to ward off pestilence,—in a word, for men to bear the burdens of their brothers, and live not for to-day, but for the years that are to come. And such a revival would not content itself with this little detail or that in the processes of observance, but would try to sweep in with a current of new life which should restore the whole.

I should think any life might be a bore, stupid and tedious, of which the centre was self-indulgence, self-approval, or any form of self-worship. To divide one's interest in the various rites or services of such worship must be monotonous. To share the sixteen waking hours between one's smoking, his dancing, his card-playing, his eating, drinking, and complaining, must be a stupid task ; and he who is immersed in it, certainly is entitled to the sympathy of men more fortunate.

But what Fate or what Devil condemns any man to this slavery? He has only to rebel, and to leave it. He has only to listen to his "marching orders," your marching orders, my marching orders. These good-tidings are what he needs, and the marching orders are that he shall make them clear to every creature. That God is, and is here ; that heaven is, and is here ; that these men and women round him are so many members of God's household, whose cares he is to soothe and whose pleasures he is to share,—this is what he is to teach, till men feel it and know it. He is to make his office-boy believe it. He is to make the waiter behind his chair believe it. He is to make the billiard-marker at the club believe it. He must make the girl he dances with believe it. With whomsoever he has to do, he is to carry life,—life more abundantly, the blessing God gave him,—and gave on condition that he should give it to his fellow-men. I should think life would be dull to the officer who has passed through West Point and acquired its accomplishment, has joined a marching column, and then, when the rest are pitching the tents, are seeking the water, are telling off the men, are dividing the rations, are writing the despatches, found himself by some devilish fatality always lounging round the camp, in the way of every worker and despised by every soldier. Striking no blow and rendering no service, varying the tediousness of his meals by his cigar and the tediousness of his smoking by his meals,— I should think this life would be dull. It was to save you and me from such tedium that the Saviour of mankind gave us life more abundantly. Machines move by processes. Men live with a Divine Spirit. That Spirit, for us, he quickened and made strong. To that life he assigned its duty: that we lift up this world; that we bring it to God; that I do not think of myself while we do it, nor you of yourself, so we only can bring in the Commonwealth of Love.

And we, if we accept this commission, find that this life is not bound in with the narrow range of this or that shop or office or club-room. Why, it unites me with him and with her who are on the other side of the world. It makes me partner with the nobility of all ages and all lands. My signal-flashes are read from the heights, which repeat them to all waiting eyes, just as I read theirs, that I may repeat them in my turn. My labor is not the humdrum toil of a separate machine: it is in the infinite life of a child of God, who lives with God, nay, who enjoys with God, in the abundant life of his united children. This is it to "go out to all the world, and preach the gospel to every creature."

THE POSSIBLE BOSTON.

"He looked for a city which hath foundations, whose builder and maker is God."— HEBREWS xi., 10.

THIS striking text has given the form to the ideal plans of Christian Reformers. Augustine, the great African leader, wrote a book called the *City of God*, which has held its place in literature as still a living book, with suggestions not all antiquated for civil society. Sir Thomas More's *Outopia*, which is his city of God, is not a mere play of fancy made for amusement of writer or reader. It is a profound study of social science, which, when presidents or governors or heads of bureaux choose to read to-day, it is well for those they serve.

Before such reformers there is a distinct vision of what civil order will be when God's will is done on earth as it is done in heaven. Where such a vision or plan exists, that man does not work wildly or from hand to mouth. It is true, on the other hand, that he is in danger of doing nothing, because he seeks for every thing. "The better," says Voltaire, "is the enemy of the good." It is a cynical statement, and dangerous. But it points out the risk which awaits Christian men and women, and all idealists. We are all to be careful, lest in our eagerness for the impossible best, we fail of that better, which is possible.

Among the people who have squarely addressed themselves to the building up a visible city of God upon this earth, the men who founded Massachusetts, and especially who founded Boston, are the most distinguished in modern times. They winnowed out from England about twenty thousand people of the class who were nicknamed "Puritans," because they meant to keep their bodies pure. They did not believe in drunkenness nor adultery, as the dominant party in England practically did. They did believe in a possible law of God on earth, and they meant to put it in practice in worldly legislation. For this purpose, they came to the end of the world. As long as they could, as long as they had power enough, they shut out from their jurisdiction all persons who did not prepare to join in their plans. And those plans, including all their legislation, went forward for two generations, in this hope of establishing here the pattern town or State.

When a year ago I was speaking here of Dr. Channing's early ministry, I said, in passing, that he and the men round him, fifty and sixty years ago, had this very hope for Boston, that they might make it a city without the faults, vices, crimes, and dangers which literature and history connect with city life. In the calmest and most resolute way, these men, in a little town of thirty or forty thousand people,* set about that business with the highest idea,— an idea nothing short of perfection. "Possible perfection of human nature" was the Channing motto. "Possible perfection of city nature,"— of the social methods of a large town,— that was the idea of this set of men. I ask you to-day to follow some of the more important of their theories and processes.

First, of course, was public education. They had, in the common school law of the State, the whole theory granted. But the practice was much below the theory. As early as 1813, Dr. Channing and the men around him went to work on the public schools of Boston. There followed the elevation of the Latin School, to be at that time the best school in America, the creation of the primary schools, the establishment of the English High School, which is spoken of in the pamphlets of the time as a new invention, the establishment of a similar school for girls, and the large improvement of all the grammar schools.† Of all this, we see the result to-day, when, from our whole population of the school age so called, from five to sixteen years namely, there are hardly fifteen hundred children in Boston not "present or accounted for" at the daily roll-call of the schools. This is a degree of success without parallel, I believe, in any country at any time since school education began.

That illustration of success shows what sort of perfectness these men expected in other lines of endeavor, as in

---

* In 1810, the population of Boston was 33,250; in 1820, it was 43,298; in 1830, it was 61,392.
† This school for girls, which began under the charge of Mr. Bailey, was afterward given up on the plea of economy, to be re-established in 1852.

prison-work, in houses of reformation, in the arrest of pauperism, in the suppression of intemperance. They thought they could make a clean sweep. Boston was a small city and a very rich city. It was a very prosperous city, when it was prosperous. And it happened that the rich and powerful men were in accord with this new theory of " honor all men." It is the only instance known to me, where the real aristocracy of a town held a religion which did not part them, either in practice or in theory, from the lowest of the low. The Channing theory of life is absolute democracy, and it happened to be held by the gentry of Boston. If anybody knew what was the right thing to do, such men as Jonathan Philips, Colonel Perkins, the Appletons, the Lawrences, and the rest, were behind that man with money, good-will, and power; and they meant to have that thing done.

Of course, the leaders of movement in such a town looked curiously and eagerly on the questions of poverty, the relations of the poor and the rich.

In view of our arrangements of to-day, it is interesting to see that they did not make the provisions we find necessary for the supervision and regulation of alms-giving.

They meant to prevent pauperism as a social disease.

As a military man would say, they did not mean to have the enemy advance beyond their outworks.

Dr. Channing, Dr. Ware, and the men around them, had studied with curious care the work of the social writers on the other side. They knew all about the plans of Fellenberg and Degerando and Robert Owen and, later down, of Fourier and Saint-Simon. They knew what is the truth,— that pauperism is a disease as much as scarlet fever is; one of those diseases, too, which you can prevent, but cannot cure.

They did not expect to prevent pauperism by feeding the hungry or clothing the naked.

They did mean to have a community in which men and women could feed themselves and clothe themselves.

There was not, therefore, any general arrangement before the year 1851 for what we regard necessary,— the general supervision of alms-giving.

The plans were all laid on the idea that alms-giving should be only accidental and occasional.

What shows the idealism of these men is that the two principal measures set on foot with this view relied on moral agencies. It was by making men more manly that they expected to rid their town of paupers.

These two measures took their form in a private club, from which much that is good in those days sprung. It was sometimes called the Wednesday Club, but it was not the club so called which celebrated its centennial a few years ago. It was a club of thoughtful men, all of them Unitarians, who met simply to discuss the desirable agencies for the moral and social improvement of this city. Among other things which sprung from its plans, this South Congregational Church of ours is one. The club voted that it was desirable that there should be another Unitarian church in this part of the town ; and from that vote this church grew. This club discussed the social, moral, criminal, and religious condition of the town and the best plans for its improvement, always having in view this possible perfect city, a city with foundations. Such men recognized the value of the established churches in this affair. They knew that people regularly trained in religious habits did not often become paupers or criminals. But, noticing the risk in cities of the existence of a class not so connected, the "Ministry-at-large" was established, to take in hand the people who had no church. It was not to feed them nor to clothe them : it was to minister to them morally. It was to give to them the self-reliance and backbone which belong to children of God who know they are his children. The original idea was that Dr. Tuckerman, who had volunteered, at his own charges, for this ministry as early as 1826, in a town where there were not five thousand people not on the visiting-list of some clergyman, should watch over the education and moral welfare of those "unchurched" people, with such aid as he could obtain from laymen and laywomen who were willing to work and visit with him. He was not disappointed. When Dr. Henry Ware first asked for such volunteers, Frederic T. Gray, George Merrill, and Benjamin H. Greene presented themselves, and while they lived did efficient service in the work proposed. Such men as Robert C. Waterston, Charles F. Barnard, and Charles Faulkner are among those who soon afterward joined cordially in this lay ministry. Three of these gentlemen were afterward ordained as clergymen. As you know, the organization which sustains this Ministry-at-large exists with increasing usefulness to this day. I am to speak of it further in a moment.

Side by side with this, to work on more secular affairs, the same group of men established in 1835 the "Society for the Prevention of Pauperism." This society was not to relieve hunger or cold or nakedness. It was to prevent them. I know of no other city in the world which has started with so clear-sighted an effort. The society was to see that intelligence offices were regulated, and that men who needed employment had a chance. It was to regulate pawn-broking, and see that the poor were not fleeced by usurers. It was to transfer labor where there was a glut to places where there was a need. It was to facilitate education for industry. In any way it could find, it was to prevent pauperism. This society also has now existed for near fifty years. I doubt if it has ever expended $5,000 a year. But it has kept down the ascending tide of pauperism. That is what it was for.

Both these plans were well in order when Boston was still a town of some fifty thousand people, of homogeneous English blood. There was one small Catholic church in the town. The men who established them were the same men who controlled, in those days, the politics of Boston and of Massachusetts. They had the confidence of the richest merchants and capitalists of New England. If any branch enterprise were needed to carry out such plans, it was at once established. If you needed a blind asylum, you had that. If you needed a deaf and dumb asylum, you had that. They had really good right to flatter themselves, in the insignificant population of their jails and their poor-houses, that they were working out the problem; and that here was to be a city which, for freedom from crime and freedom from pauperism, might challenge comparison with the most favored village or Arcadian valley in all the world.

But all such computations were doomed to disappointment, from an element wholly unexpected. In 1832, the wave of Irish emigration to America began. Within two or three years, Boston felt it. It was unexpected. It was disliked. Some of the least wise of our gentlemen here actually established an office on Long Wharf, and paid a secretary, with the purpose of dissuading Ireland from emigration. I knew this gentleman well. He sent out circulars, and wrote articles for Irish papers, to explain to Patrick that he had better stay at home. So Mrs. Partington swept back the tide with her broom! The wave increased. The famine of 1845 and 1846 made it a deluge. Of that deluge, Boston has received the largest proportional share. At this moment, in proportion to our numbers, our population of Irish blood is larger than that of any other city in America.

That is to say that, on your fine plans for curing pauperism before it existed, you now had with every year ten thousand people poured in, a fifth part of whom were paupers ready-made. On your fine plans of meeting such evils in advance by nobly educating the children, you now had poured in on you every year ten thousand men and women, who had been educated by penury, whose childhood was over, and whose characters were formed. And, again, on your fine plans for treating such evils by moral and religious influence, carried in personal tenderness to each separate home, you had ten thousand people in a year thrown in, who would not listen to the first word you said on religion, on the will of God, or the duty of man, without suspecting it,— nay, believing it,— as they were taught to believe it, to be damnable heresy. With this deluge of a population which Boston did not train, and for which old Boston was in no sort responsible, came to an end, a generation ago, the immediate hope that here should be a town in which alms-giving should be virtually unknown, and in which vice, godlessness, and crime should be at a minimum, steadily less and less, until the perfect end.

So far did the original aversion to any organized almsgiving give way, of necessity, that in 1851 it became necessary to organize the Provident Association. I am proud to say that, when the necessity existed at last, it was in this church and in the Warren Street Chapel, blood sister of this church, that this organization began, under the wise direction first of Mr. Charles F. Barnard, assisted then by our own minister, Mr. Huntington. The necessity was forced on them, and wisely and practically they met it. This was sixteen years after the Society for Preventing Pauperism was formed. So long and so successfully had that society and its sister, the Ministry-at-large, done what they were meant to do. In our own time, we find it necessary to make the fuller organization of the Associated Charities, which secures the intelligent co-operation of all these organizations, for the prevention of pauperism in the wisest relief of the poor.

All through this deluge, as I called it, the joint work of the Society for Preventing Pauperism and of the Ministry-at-large has gone bravely on, never flinching. To speak to-day of the last: it has now seven regular ministers, where it began with one; it has four regular chapels, and as many Sunday-schools, besides Warren Street Chapel, our own Unity

Chapel, and other kindred institutions. It has never proposed, in a single word, in a single report, any lower standard than the standard of the beginning. Nor has it used any lower agencies than the agencies of the beginning. By the word of God and by the help of God, men, women, and children shall be made freemen in Christ. Not by feeding them, not by clothing them, not by punishing them, no, nor by frightening them, but by renewing them, so that they shall come nearer the stature of a perfect man. Nor has this ministry failed in its hope of enlisting laymen and women to the direct ministry of Christ, by the side of those professionally ordained to that work. Such men and women are at work in connection with each of these centres, with a determination nothing less than that which I have cited,— the building a city of God on eternal foundations. Never was this work more effective and promising than it is to-day.

I have not, to-day, to say more than I have said on the secular sister of this ministry, the Society for Preventing Pauperism. I shall take another method to speak of its present position.

To-day is the anniversary of the Ministry-at-large. To-night, the churches which sustain it meet for its yearly organization. I have gone thus at length into its history, because I think that with this decade. which begins with 1881. we are to see the original work go forward on the original plan, as we have not seen it for twenty years. This wave of Irish emigration is well-nigh ended. From England, from Germany, come many more strangers than from Ireland. Boston is more and more an American city with every year. Our Catholic friends are less powerful and less bigoted, and their children are more truly naturalized. And, by the mere currents of emigration, of birth, and of death, it is certain that we have seen the end of an alien majority, either in our votes or in our counsels. The time has come again when, with courage, such as no year in the last forty could command, we may address ourselves to that larger ministry which levels up the people of the town. We can continue what we do. We could double it to advantage. We could meet the religious needs of persons dissatisfied with Rome, by a special ministry. We can take firmer hold than we have of persons released from imprisonment, and, at the very moment when they need moral help, supply it. We can take firmer hold on the details which lead to intemperance, and set forward in many ways the temperance reforms. We can be more ready than we are to welcome exiles on their arrival, and to place them in their new home. We can foster all the efforts by which the working-man becomes a land-holder, tied to the soil, and master of his home. We can quicken education and give it infinite life, so that those who learn how to count and how to read shall take in also honor, purity, truth, as eternal elements of life.

I hope we may enter on all such foundation-work for a city whose foundations are purity, honor, faith, and love. This is the subsoiling which is beneath all political advancement, all manufacturing or mercantile prosperity, all charitable organization. Never an autumn canvass for an election comes, with its free expense for partisan purposes, but one wishes that a tenth part of that money had been spent five years before in lifting up boys, in keeping girls pure, in opening noble avenues to life, in making manly men and womanly women. It is only in such work that your social advance has any hope, but with such work your social prospect is certain. You are working on the foundations, and your city stands.

If such a club as I described, for study and for action in subsoiling, should form itself again, you would not need five years to see in your statistics the sure fruit of its planting. I could name thirty young men — say from twenty years old to sixty-five or seventy, but still young — who would work together successfully in such a society: brave in theology; optimists by conviction; sure of success, because children of God; practical, because New Englanders; and strong with the strength of those who mean to lead and lift the people, and not to thwart them, to snub them, or to fool them. A club of thirty or forty such men, meeting, not like the Examiner Club to discuss philosophy, not like the Thursday Club to talk of science or manufacture, not like the Saturday Clubs to discuss politics, but to purify the moral tone, and to improve the social order of Boston has now its chance. The chance is as large as the work. The work is to make here the ideal city,— a city sweet as Arcadia, healthy, brave, and pure; a city which has the eternal foundations.

Of that city, the maker and builder is God.

INCREASE OF LIFE.

"Because I live, ye shall live also."— JOHN xiv., 19.

To Jesus Christ, the unseen world and the world which is seen are one world and the same. We talk of "the other world," "the future world," "the world above": he does not speak so. He speaks of heaven as if it were now and here, or might be; and, when they are confused with what he says, it is often because they see double where he sees singly. Nay: when he appears to be confused by what they say,— as sometimes happens,— the best account we can give is that they are talking of this visible world only, while he talks at once of the visible and invisible. There are a hundred texts which show his feeling,— "Lo! I am with you alway, even unto the end of the world." "It is my Father who doeth these works at which you wonder. You do not see him; but, all the same, he is here." "Father, I know that thou hearest me always. I would not have spoken aloud but for the help of these who are standing by." And, when he expresses his trouble because language and metaphor fail him as they do, it is in this very difficulty. Language, having been made by people who rely on their senses, to answer the purposes of the visible and tangible world, breaks down, and breaks down very badly, when it is applied to the range, vastly wider, of that unseen world, which permeates this world, and in which this world floats as a straw floats in the ocean.

Many of you remember our dear friend Starr King's celebrated discourse on "Substance and Shadow." He was at work there to remove exactly this difficulty which the Master tried to remove, nor is there work more essential for the Master's apostle. While we sat and listened to Mr. King, we felt and knew what Jesus teaches. The things which endure are faith and hope and love. Life is the substance, the hard-pan foundation, from which these forms and things around us are born. We cannot see life, nor handle it nor smell it nor hear it nor taste it. But life is; and without it nothing can even appear to be. In the beginning is the Word. Mr. King made us wonder that we had cared so much for this or that little thing, which is but a bubble tossed on the eternal ocean. For the moment, you said you would not be so fooled again. You would take fast hold on love, which you found to be a reality. You would live in hope, or in the infinite world, seeing that is the real world. You would trust wholly in God, seeing all being is from him; and these little things that perish in the using should fall into their own inferior place in your regard or thought or action. While that mood lasted, you caught the true Christian notion of life. There are not two lives,— a life of heaven there and a life of earth here. These two lives are one life. As the Lord's Prayer says, "God's will is done on earth as it is in heaven." This opens out the meaning of the more figurative phrase, "The kingdom of God is at hand."

The knowledge, that life is indeed larger than the little world we see, grows upon us in a thousand ways. The charm, always new, of watching a baby's life, rests in our interest in the steps of such growth. The little thing first learns its own hands, that they are its own. A little more, and it knows its mother's face, and that she also is its own. By and by, its world enlarges; and at last it knows the whole nursery, which seems a universe indeed, while it is a novelty, so much larger than the petty world the child was in before.

Such steps as these are really enlarging our life all the time afterward, though we do not perhaps note them with quite such eager curiosity. But it is just such a step, when the school-boy, who but yesterday was first in his class and could talk of nothing but the ambitions of the school-room, finds himself the smallest boy in a great mercantile house, where his existence is hardly suspected and nobody knows his name. He learns, by hard rubs perhaps, that the world is much larger than he thought. Yet his chief, the very "grand Cyrus" of them all, the master of masters, has to learn the same lesson. He takes his holiday on some favorable year, he crosses the ocean, he has or thinks he has some business with one of the merchant lords of London or of Paris; and, when the interview has been arranged, after some negotiation, he finds that he was never heard of before, that now his name is forgotten, that there are perhaps a hundred others waiting for their turn, and that he, the first tradesman in his own county, may be yet a very small person in the larger world. So in the world of politics, in the world of literature, in the ambitions of fashion and society, precisely because we are infinite beings,— beings whose nature cannot be limited,— we find all the time that there is far more outside of us in life than we have ever yet attained to. We cannot often enough say that life gives us more, nature gives us more, the more we take. Yes, and the more life gives or nature gives, the more they offer.

The robin in its nest looks into a world made up of a few leaves and boughs around. As the feathers of its wings grow, it flutters a little from the branch, and is astonished to find that the orchard is so large. The bird of passage, when the instinct bred by the season carries it far north or far south, learns that the covert of a few trees, orchard or grove, was nothing to this larger world. Man, of all animals, compasses the whole globe; and then man, in turn, studies the universe outside of it, and finds that this world is a speck, and only a speck, in that universe of whose laws he finds out more and more every day, for they are not beyond the ken of a child of God.

The village boy growing to manhood finds that he is a member of the State as well as of the village. He does not lose his interest in the base-ball club or the singing-class, because he has gained an interest in the politics of the State, or is at work for the State Fair, or has been chosen to the Legislature. Then a great crisis comes upon him, and his life enlarges again. Sumter is fired on, and he takes a commission from the President, and enters the service of the nation. Still, he belongs to the village, and to the State. His life as a citizen of the State does not cease because he is an officer of the nation. Such is the illustration of the common life,— life here and life in heaven,— which Jesus Christ is always trying to make us comprehend, even by symbols which he owns are inadequate. You do live in Chester Square or in Union Park; but you also live in Massachusetts, and have duties and pleasures which to that life belong. More than this, you are a citizen of the United States, and as such have other duties and relations. Nay: even if you do not cross oceans or continents, you are also a citizen of the world, and as such have a life yet larger. More than this, says the Saviour of men, you live in heaven, and have relations, pleasures, and duties, as a child of God, as a child of heaven. They are not apart from to-day's duties or pleasures. Rather they are all knit in with them. Nor are they the life of a to-morrow, unattainable until to-day is done with. They are the life of to-day, all mixed in with life which is visible and tangible. A woman's new life — when her first child is in her arms, wholly dependent on her — is, or may be, simply the life of a ministering angel. She does not care for herself, save as she cares for the child which depends on her. Her question is not, "Is the room too hot for me?" but "Is it too hot for him?" It is not, "What will entertain me?" but, "What will entertain him?" That measure of love is no more perfect in the ministry of an angel than is it in the ministry of any mother who surrenders herself to her child. So of the loyal, absorbed faith of a soldier going into battle. It is not, "Shall I best shelter myself here?" but, "How shall I best protect the men?" It is not, "Shall I get through easiest thus?" but, "How shall I best serve the cause?" No angel or archangel in any hierarchy of God can surpass that loyalty to a cause. And such faith as that, where it exists, manifests the law, the purpose, the system of God's own heaven. Such love as that mother's, such faith as that soldier's, are not to be spoken of as like the heavenly qualities: they are the heavenly qualities. What Jesus is trying to make us see is that heaven thus has its part and place in the world of time, and may wholly master it, if we will. To borrow a striking figure which I once heard Dr. Bush employ, the earth is as full of heaven as a sponge is full of water. Every pore is saturated and crowded with it. And the true child of God, who knows his own dignity, is not forever distinguishing between the sponge and what it holds, between things of time and things of eternity. How can he discriminate? Both are God's work. Both are in God's order. He can sweep a floor to God's glory as well as sing a psalm to his glory. As the true citizen does his duty, and does it of course and without question, never stopping to say, I do this as a Charlestown man, or I do this as a Massachusetts man, or I do this as an American, or this as a citizen of the world, but knows and feels that the one relation belongs to the other, reinforces it, and gains strength from it, just so the child of God lives his earthly life and his heavenly life at once and together. He does not define nor dissect nor analyze. There is no separation nor distinction. He speaks at once with the tongues of men and of angels. He does the deed at once of earth and of heaven. He does his own will,— yes, and he does his Father's will in the same act. For he has so wrought out the divinity of his own nature that his life is hid in God's life. Of which union the perfect statement was made, when Jesus said, "I and my Father are one." For which also he prayed for us, when we prayed that we might be one, as they two are one.

Careless people sometimes express surprise when they find the same man exhibiting what they call the most opposite characters, that he is at once so practical and so ideal. Mr. Emerson, for instance, idealist of the idealists, teaches the most obdurate common-sense in the homeliest Saxon dialect. So Professor Peirce, who could weigh one comet against another in his scales, who could count the oscillations of the rays of the Pleiades and untangle the cords of the attractions of Orion, was, through and through, an idealist, never so much at home as when he spoke of the foundations of ethics, and in most weighty phrase, rendered homage to the truth. It is only careless people who are so surprised. Earth being all full of heaven, the surprising thing would be if this were not so. The man really practical will be thoroughly ideal. The child of God truly heavenly will deal with things of time as simply and as certainly as God does. Here in your Gospels is Matthew, whom you call and call rightly a man of affairs, tax-gatherer, merchant,— gives you your parables of usury, and buying and selling and all practical affairs. Yes; and it is he who writes down your beatitudes, with that mystic, "Blessed are the pure in heart, for they shall see God." It is he who writes, "Fear not, little flock, it is your Father's good pleasure to give you the kingdom." It is he who sings, shall I say the eternal song of welcome: 'Come unto me, ye that labor and are heavy-laden; and I will give you rest. Take my yoke upon you, and learn of me; for I am meek and lowly of heart, and ye shall find rest to your souls." So easily and certainly does a child of God find the eternal truth, and speak it, in the midst of earth's affairs.

Film by film, shred by shred, this child of God lays off one and another of the environments which fetter him. The baby is not held longer in his mother's arms: he totters alone. At last, he is master of the house, and may roam where he will. Nay, the day comes when the doubtful mother must let him run outdoors under his own control.

He grows to youth or manhood, and makes his own home. Not even orders from father or mother rule him longer. Perhaps he passes from land to land, acquires the sway of new languages, and is not bound even to one country. Perhaps his word controls other men. What he writes is read by all thinkers, what he thinks is applied in all laws. Perhaps he startles a generation of sleepers, and they take up their beds and walk. All this steady enlargement of life and power is certain, because he is God's child. The soul in him controls muscle, nerve, sense, fibre, blood-vessels, and brain. The God in him controls the organic frame of an earthly tabernacle. One step more, and the sweet singer, who yesterday wrote some psalm of praise for a few companions, casts off this earthly house of a mortal tabernacle, and joins in the chorus of a nobler and larger worship.

The careful reasoner who, with the little tricks of two or three earthly algebras, untangled the problems of the universe, drops off the house of an earthly tabernacle, sees as he is seen and knows as he is known, and rejoices in the untangled heavenly verities. The faithful friend, who let no hour pass unless he had ministered to this orphan, had braced up yonder hesitant, had lifted him who was fallen, or comforted her who was starving, casts off this frail house of an earthly tabernacle; and lo! infinite resource with which to minister, no lack of time for endeavor, and no grinding burden of fatigue. She who, for months and years, lay gently on the sick-bed, who received from one and another a thousand tender ministrations to her pain, and repaid them all in her thankful patience,— she casts off this frail house of this earthly tabernacle; and lo! with the same love, with the same patience, with the same gratitude, she is ministering to them and to ten thousand more, in this glad freedom of disembodied life. As the baby passes into the boy, the boy into the youth, the youth into the man, so, in one more change, not unlike these others, the child of God stands free in the untrammelled life of heaven.

The revelation of life in Jesus Christ is not simply the fact of his personal reappearance after death. Before he died, he had quickened the life of the world, renewed it enlarged it. "I am the resurrection and the life: whoso liveth and believeth in me shall never die." Whoever lives with that control of sense and organ by the living soul which to the Christian man is possible, whoever rises superior to pain, hunger, want, whoever lives with the divine life of a son of God, that man knows he does not die. The answer falls fitly on the wretched plaint of Martha, dissatisfied, as well she might be, with the faith of her country and of her time. She sobs out her doleful creed: "I know that he shall rise again, at that distant resurrection, at that last day, which is, oh, so wretchedly far away!" How often has that mournful plaint of that Jewish woman been repeated by persons who have been taught the same Eastern doctrine of a suspended animation, even in Christian churches! Christ will have none of it. "Dead! Do you think I shall die? You believe in me! Do you think any child of God dies? If he once learns to live, if he live in the large life,— the life that believes, that loves, that hopes,— he knows he cannot die."

It is indeed a faith which it needs such as Jesus to instil. Those who knew him took it in and made it real. For us, we drink at the same fountain. The promise was not an empty promise; and when the moment comes, when the cloud opens and the heaven reveals itself, the Comforter, who is the Holy Spirit, speaks to us. Nor is it any new doctrine. It is the word which spoke from the beginning. The Comforter speaks to say that the world of God is larger than this world of man. The life of God is larger than this life, hemmed in by the powers of five senses only, and unable to know more or to do more. The Father of perfect love is always training us for that larger life and those fuller powers. Sometimes he shows us that this is possible. When he calls the careful thinker who has exhausted earthly processes, or the brave leader who has quickened a thousand thousand lives, nay, the loving boy who has shown me what the kingdom of heaven is and what it is like, or the unselfish mother whose life has been all made up of help and blessing to those around her,— when God lifts these into a life unembodied, and therefore unseen, he teaches me again the lesson which Jesus was teaching always. Such lives have larger sphere and duty; for God's purpose is larger than these cramped places and these passing hours. Who lives as they have lived, and with such faith as their faith, these never die.

THE KING'S WORK.

"I must walk to-day and to-morrow and the day following; for it cannot be that a prophet perish out of Jerusalem."—LUKE xiii., 33.

HOWEVER carelessly you choose to read the New Testament, you cannot but be impressed with the calm steadiness of the last march to Jerusalem. "I must go to-day, to-morrow, and the day following; for a prophet cannot perish out of Jerusalem." He must go, for he is about his Father's business.

Annas and Caiaphas do not expect him, do not want him. "He will not be here this time," they say, "to upset and confuse everything. He is no fool. We have given him a warning that his room is better than his company." For such men always put themselves in the place of him they judge. Caiaphas always thinks of Jesus as governed by Caiaphas' own motive. So, when people are guessing to-day about a public man, Will he do this, will he do that? you can see what the guesser is by his solution of the problem. But, in the great crisis of the world, Jesus moves on his own line, led by his own motive. To the surprise of all and the indignation of all, he appears again at the city, as surely as the feast comes round. "It cannot be otherwise. I must go." It is just as a gallant officer takes his column under fire, though he is to be the first man to fall, and knows he is.

Such is the central example of perfect devotion to the work God gives us to do,—work for that kingdom in which we are all citizens, and of which God is the King. It is one of the great compensations of our time for some of its supposed losses of faith, that it can see more easily than any other time has seen what this business of the King is, in which we are all enlisted. To our time there ought to be no danger that man or woman should fall back into an imbecile regret that God has no work for either of them to do. Every morning wakes us up to a life so large that the mystery is, rather, how the fifteen waking hours shall begin to answer its requisitions. Every man now sees the King's work every hour. The danger is only that he shall be attracted to too many parts of it, and shall not pull steadily at his own rope. For the inter-union of nations and tribes, and the ready communication between land and land, compel every man to see that he is his brother's keeper, and that his failure involves wide calamity. It brings the corresponding encouragement, that duty faithfully done is done in the King's work, and for a sphere no less than the whole world.

In conversation in a literary circle the other day, I heard the opinion expressed that the delicate work of those old essay-writers, who described with an exquisite finish the amusing niceties or pettinesses of village life, would never again command the interest of the great body of readers. Such detail as you find in Washington Irving's *Sketch Book*, in Miss Mitford's *Sketches of Our Village* and *Belford Regis*, or even the nicer studies of the detail of life by Charles Lamb and Leigh Hunt, or some of the descriptions most admired in the *Spectator*, are now considered by the younger generation as petty rather than fine. The opinion I heard expressed was this: that in Young America and Young England every youth and every maiden now feel what it is to be "citizens of the world." The English lad knows that the morning drum-beat of England is all the time resounding, as the sun rises on her different lands. The American lad knows that his kindred "vex every ocean" with their trade, push their gigantic game beyond the Arctic and Antarctic Circles; and that there is no dialect so barbarous but that men of his race have translated into it the oracles of his faith. This girl will be married, when her lover is well established in Japan. That minister mailed a pamphlet, which was asked for, to the Griqua diamond-fields. Your ladies' club in the vestry heard Miss Twitchell tell how the Papapigo girls made hard gingerbread at Hampton; and the young woman, who sang your Christmas hymns so prettily at the Unity, is to-day teaching Spanish children their catechism, under the shadow of the Andes. This thing is happening all the time. So there is not the old danger that people will be eaten up by the conceit of Nazareth, or will immure themselves in hermitages in Bethlehem.

In the analogies of war, the duty of working for the cause is perfectly understood. The great word "honor," in a soldier's interpretation of it, means that he subordinates himself entirely to the cause. Do you remember that little English poem which describes the martyrdom of a soldier of the Buffs in China? They had been taken prisoners by the Chinese, he and some Sepoy companions. All of them were bidden to perform Ko-tow — that is, to touch the forehead to the ground — before some idol. The Sepoys did it readily enough, and were let off. The English soldier would not do it.

> "Let swarthy heathen cringe and kneel,
> An English lad must die."

And he died. But I do not dare tell how many noble men that death of that unknown private fired to manhood. Regiments marching to war in our rebellion took up those words, took them to heart, and carried them to duty. The honor of the soldier was represented in the sacrifice. He must be about the business which is so much larger than his own life. And men learn in war to keep this idea before them always. Personal inconvenience takes its own proper and insignificant place. I remember an anecdote of twenty years ago, which has quite another tone, regarding one of the most finical and elegant young men I had ever known. I have not seen him since he was the most exquisitely dressed, the most elegantly nurtured, the most precisely ordered young man of my acquaintance about town. The clock struck for him. The gun fired. He was at his duty, and was placed on the staff of one of our most dashing leaders, perhaps because he knew all languages, and would entertain the French princes, if need were, without a slip in his accent. But the work of war is not talking with French princes. He had not been on duty a month, when at midnight he was summoned to direct a confidential party in a rapid movement to secure some contraband arms. The story of his soliloquy on his return has hung to me like a watchword, precisely because of the triviality of the detail. Soaked to the skin, covered with dirt from tip to toe, hungry, cold, cross, the elegant pet of society dragged himself upstairs to go to his bed at sunrise. His meditations were overheard through the thin plank of the barrack. "So, Alfred," he said to himself, "this is war. You've had nothing to eat. You've had nothing to drink. Nobody saw you. Nobody thanks you. Nobody will thank you. You've caught a cold that will keep you barking a month. You've spoiled a good suit of clothes. You've ruined a good pair of boots. You are frozen and hungry and mad. Yes, Alfred, — but you got the guns!"

No man who has served in the army will fail to appreciate his satisfaction and the point of the homely anecdote. The work in hand was done. Who cared for the cost or sacrifice? Of such experiences, of which the war was full, the moral value is in an inverse proportion to the importance of the end secured. It is not when the fall of Vicksburg is won by a night's watching that you learn the lesson. You do not need any lesson there. Then you see that the game is worth the candle. But it was in the lesser things that men learned how they also serve who only stand and wait.

But that sense of honor is not to be confined to soldiers. Eugène Sue, in his terrible novel, *The Wandering Jew*, made us all familiar, a generation ago, with the absolute fineness of organization in which the Jesuit community, one and all, are trained to obey the orders of their general. In the midst of the terror of the book, in the horror of that sense of an awful fate entangling and controlling every action of every person, as the snake in the Laocoön controls every limb of each child, the one redeeming and helpful element was the vision the book gave you of the consecration of noble men and women to a great cause,— a cause outside themselves, and vastly larger than themselves, for which they were willing to live, for which they were ready to die, if it were God's will. The excellence of the book, all that which was not sensational or morbid in it, was this success in transferring the notion of honor from half-feudal surroundings, from the association of armies or of courts, to what men call the mean details of common life. The postboy who harnessed a horse was on honor: the lackey was on honor, as he knocked at the door, and waited for an answer to his message. The method of the Jesuit Order, so ingenious and so sure to preserve itself, is well worth the study of any man of religion or any man of affairs who would learn how to co-ordinate men with each other, and how to assign to each his convenient place. And, when the faithful companion, no matter how low his grade in the hierarchy, feels that it is God's will he is doing, then nothing can be more grand than such devotion. But, when he has advanced so far as to see that it is the carnal ambition of men very low in their ambition, which orders him here or there as a chessman in their game, nothing can be more awful than his slavery. Of this awful picture, the redeeming side is in the possible devotion of man to a great cause. Because he is God's child, he is willing to do God's work. Because God's will is to be done by God's children, God's children volunteer. The King's work must go forward; and to the King's work are their lives devoted.

Where Ignatius Loyola stopped short, content with forming his little Society of Jesus, with its various centres, head-centres, and a general, Jesus Christ himself never stopped. "I go away," he said. The King would take command in person. Such devotion to the Father's work and will as he had shown, he expected that we could show, and it was all he wanted us to show. Such lifting this world upward as he had tried, not vainly, he believed that we should carry forward. Just such devotion to a cause as the soldier shows to his flag in battle, as the Jesuit shows to the poor paper order of his general, Jesus expects us all to show to that steady, heavenward progress of the world, which, as he shows, is God's purpose and command. "I must go about my Father's business," he says; "and you must go about it. As he has sent me into the world, even so have I, also, sent you into the world."

"The King's work must go forward. There is no stop possible. If it is in my hand, entrusted to me, I must carry it forward." Well for any man or woman who, early in life, works out this formula for the place or duty which is assigned to him in men's affairs. Duty is no separate business, no part of my self-culture, no service for which I am to be paid at the ticket office of heaven. Duty is my part of the infinite service, which an infinite number of God's children must render before God's kingdom comes. It is lifted from a little personal affair to its own place in close relationship with the movement of the universe. It seems to me not hard to make even children understand this, and enter into the enthusiasm of work thus rendered in the common cause for the Father of us all. Let the girl know that she does not do this merely to please her mother or to oblige her father, but that she counts as one in the great company who are pushing forward the King's work,— she also is an officer in the army, and to her also has he assigned work to be done. I shall never forget the enthusiasm of a young friend whom I had asked to carry forward some part of our work here for the families of soldiers absent in the war,— not a duty with any romance attached,— nothing which you would print in a newspaper or a biography,— the humblest of ministrations, in snuffy tenement houses of discomfort or need. But she said to me afterward, "I walked on air as I left you, for I was in the service also." She felt how great a thing it is to be fellow-workman with the King, to serve at his side in the place he has appointed.

Of this loyal service in the King's work, to-day teaches one of the central lessons. It needs consecration,— yes! determination,— yes! One must go to Jerusalem, though Jerusalem means Calvary and crucifixion. One must march to-day, to-morrow, and the day following. And then, when one looks down on the city, when one sees it in its glory and beauty, one may be, often will be, mocked by a false triumph. Here they are cheering him behind and before. Here are others coming out to meet him with the same enthusiasm. And it is not false enthusiasm: it is true. And it seems to mean so much! How easy to see that picture with the side-lights of our own time! I remember, to look back twenty years again, that it was my duty to preach in Providence on the 21st of July, 1861, when we knew that the first battle of the war was going on. I was speaking to the wives and daughters of fifty or a hundred men of the First Rhode Island Infantry, which regiment we knew was hotly engaged while we were in church. We woke Monday morning to pæans of victory. All had opened so well! A disgraced and defeated enemy was by that time in flight to Richmond. From hour to hour, as I came to Boston and afterward, these tidings of encouragement came in,— so many palm branches thrown before our feet,— till, at the office where I was working here in Boston, at one o'clock, there entered one of your merchant princes,— one of the men who has reliable private advices,— to tell us of the crash of Bull Run, that all our proud army was flung back in flight, and that Washington was swarming with stragglers and runaways.

I will not say it is always so; but it is so very, very often. The apparent triumph has to fade in failure before real victory comes. The French proverb says, it is true, that it is only the first step which costs. But nobody would ever say so, one who knows life in its reality and seriousness. Life has proved a thousand times that the triumph of Palm Sunday, the victory of the first step, is a false triumph and a false victory. It is only he who endures to the end who is saved. And he who is on the King's work expects and knows that he will meet the King's enemies. On Monday, the King's Son will meet in his father's temple money-changers and sellers of sacrifice, men who sell worship for money. They are the lineal descendants, the present representatives of that half of the patriarch Jacob which was cheat and truckster. They made his father's house a den of thieves. Tuesday, the Son of the King will meet captious priests, to ask who gave him his authority. He will meet crafty Sadducees who would catch him in his talk. He will silence these, only to meet others who would embroil him with the governor. They would be glad indeed to lay hands on him. It is Wednesday of the same week on which the King's Son tells these wondering brethren of his of the certain crash and fall of the glory that they see around them in this false Jerusalem. It is Thursday on which the lines draw tighter and tighter. Judas is dealing with Caiaphas and his crew; and the King's Son knows that he is thus wounded even in the house of his friends. Friday dawns, and sees him a prisoner, bound. The cock crows at sunrise; and he turns to look his reproaches on the faithless Peter who has denied him. The sun sets on Friday, on the tomb in which he is buried. Such is the week which follows your triumph of that beginning. And that test of our companions and partners, that test of ourselves, will come most likely to you and me. You must not say, "I will volunteer for the King's work, if the King will give me work which is distinguished and easy and agreeable." The stage-manager, who was asked to arrange a play by amateurs for some great charity, told me that all the ladies wanted to play Juliet, and all the gentlemen to play Romeo. The King's work admits none of that sort of volunteering. We must not say we will go and fight, if the King will assure us that there are no enemies or if we may fight in iron-clads. It is because there are enemies and are no iron-clads that the King needs his children. And these children — if the false triumph of Olivet do not turn their heads with vanity,— if they do not think the prize won because children cry "Hosanna" — may, with every new day, carry out the King's work more skilfully and win his purpose more completely. One could not but think of all this on Thursday. Mr. Brooks described to us the brilliant opening of his Union Reading Room, he described next its conflict with Pharisees and Sadducees and doctors learned in that dried-up law; and not till then did we see it come out strong, flat-footed, and manly on the working plane of real life. One could trace the same steps in Mr. Tilden's allusion to temperance reformation. That reform has a plenty of Olivet triumphs, mass-meetings, and wayside friends, cheering and promising. It meets its share, as well, of critics and cross-questioners,— doctors learned in the law and chiefs of administration, eager to send it back to the fastnesses of the rural valleys from which it came. It is not till, in the gray of a cold morning, after a night of tears and horror, there meet together in some garden of a new life some child of God, all broken with despair, and the other child of God, who is eager in the Father's work,— it is not till then that the true new life asserts itself, and, for the repentant, new hope comes in.

Our Easter rejoicings of next week are but painted upholstery, unless we be thus enlisted in the King's work for weal and for woe. Who seeks a lesson in Palm Sunday and in Passion Week must learn that lesson of manly, of womanly endurance,— that victory is not in the shouting or in the multitude. The real victory is sure when a loyal child, for darkness or for light, for death or for resurrection, goes steadily about his Father's business.

THE VICTORY OF THE FEW.

"And the number of names together were about a hundred and twenty."—ACTS i., 15.

IF this little company had simply preserved its own existence, at this modest standard of the beginning,— with its simple worship, its loyal faith, and its hearty mutual love,— if it existed now after eighteen hundred and fifty years, one hundred and twenty men and women, honoring while they loved the Leader of their lives, wherever it held its meetings, whatever its language or its home, it would be to-day by far the most interesting society in the world, as it would be the most extraordinary. No other organization of men and women exists, which existed that day, excepting the Jewish Church. And the Jewish Church, without priest or temple or altar or sacrifice, without Pharisee or Sadducee, and without the expectation of a Messiah, is so changed in its old age that its best friends could hardly recognize it in these surroundings. If the hundred and twenty of the beginning had never added one to their number, had they simply testified through eighteen centuries and a half that God is our Father, heaven our home, man man's brother, and Jesus the leader of his life, here would have been a spectacle for men and ages. Our wise men would wisely study, our poets and artists would rejoice that here was one relic of a pure age and one memorial of a matchless life, and our men of religion would see that here was the mystery of mysteries. "This handful of people," we should say, "has proved, so far as eighteen centuries of time can prove, that somehow they are allied to eternity."

Precisely this thing has happened in these centuries, with some noteworthy additions. This company still exists, proclaiming the central truths of life,— that we are children of the Power that rules the universe, that among ourselves we bear a common life, as brothers with brothers, and that this life is unending or infinite. This company, thus united, proclaims now as it did then that God is our Father, that we must bear each other's burdens, and that we live forever. It announces now as it did then that from Jesus Christ, whom men crucified on Calvary, it gained that enlargement of life to which these infinite conceptions belong. And to-day as then, when men tell you he is dead, this company who take his name says that life is infinite, and that man, who is an infinite child of an infinite God, can never die. It maintains for him the love and the gratitude it maintained then. It calls itself by his name. It tenderly remembers the crisis days of his life and fate. But it is with this addition to what was then in the upper chamber in Jerusalem. It is not to-day one hundred and twenty poor people, frightened by a catastrophe, hiding from the police, doubtful about to-morrow, who thus honor him and remember him. There is no petty tribe of savages, nor empire stretching round the world, which does not know his name either in fear or in joy. It is not a company like that of strangers to each other,—a few Jerusalem citizens, with a few fishermen from a lake-side far away, an outcast Samaritan here, and an outcast Tyrian there, a centurion speaking Latin, and a traveller speaking Greek, who have met with an Edomite Arab or with the grateful, gentle-woman of Cesarea. It is not such a mixed company, attracted from so many different lives by the magnetism of his life. Whole nations acknowledge that life and its power, quickening every drop of the life of national being. Codes and constitutions are construed by jurists, with careful reference to his instructions, which have become the foundations of law. New enterprises of reform recommend themselves by showing that they obey his suggestions or are by his spirit inspired. So that, if our cold Western tongues could quicken themselves to use the strains of Eastern fervor, we should sing alike, with the understanding as with the spirit, the words which call him King of kings and Lord of lords, and say more certainly than ever that he shall reign whose right it is to reign.

We do not mean that this wave of steady triumph shall stop with the end of the nineteenth century. There is no danger that it shall. We may fairly use our festival to-day, by considering the infinite means which have created this advance of the power of Jesus Christ, and by considering as well the way in which these same means shall advance his kingdom in the future. People say that the belief in a historical record grows fainter as time passes by. So let it be. But, on the other hand, the certainty of the majesty of life increases with each new exhibition of its sway. The thing that has been shall be ; and the course which the world has taken in nineteen hundred years of its history may well be taken as an indication of its course in centuries which are to come.

I need no better statement of the means which have enlarged the Church of Christ and extended his power than the statement now fairly celebrated, made a century ago by the historian Gibbon. Men of my profession were scandalized by it then, and well they might be ; for never was a more witty or a more true exhibition of the narrowness, bigotry, and cruelty which have, alas ! too often connected themselves with the priestly functions. But, for all that, the essential truth of the statement remains,— a statement which, like Renan's statements, has ten thousand times the value of any plea of any advocate, however loyal or sincere. Gibbon says that the growth of the Church at the beginning was favored by the five following causes : —

By the inflexible zeal of the Christians.

By the miraculous powers ascribed to the primitive Church.

By the pure and austere morals of the Christians.

By the union and discipline of the Christian republic, which gradually formed an independent State in the heart of the Roman Empire.

By the doctrine of a future life, improved by every circumstance which could give weight to that important truth.

In this enumeration, I use Gibbon's own words.

1. Now, to see how far these traits are effective, and to speak of them one by one ; — we may well be grateful to-day for that "inflexible zeal" which carried the new life everywhere. It is easy for a lazy and an indifferent age to criticise it. But, for one, I am glad that I am not a savage, half-dressed in a wolf-skin, tracking a wild boar somewhere in Kent, or taking my chance for life, as I might or not find a few oysters left by an ebbing tide. And that is certainly what I should have been but for the enthusiasm of the men who, by their Christian enthusiasm, made Britain the garden of its time. Indeed, in whatever cause, I am fond of saying that I have never known any enterprise succeed, which had not a fanatic hitched to it somewhere. And the world knows perfectly well, in a thousand experiences, what becomes of reasonable systems, well-balanced and propor-

tioned, which have trusted to their own decorous propriety and even roundness to force them upon the attention of mankind. Such lessons speak to us, in our time, as to our duty upon the age before us. Not without zeal, inflexible indeed, and intolerant so far as vice and dirt and disease are concerned, are we to lift this age up to be a nobler and better age than any which has gone before. If Paul had waited at Antioch till Nero sent a delegation to him with a "letter missive" to say that the first Congregational Church in Rome had organized itself in the palace, and wished to ordain Paul to its ministry, Rome would never have been a Christian city, and we should never have been here. And, if we propose to wait here till blackguard boys and criminals just out of prison come to us to say that they have found by experience that the way of transgressors is hard, and that they hope we will kindly baptize and reform them, Boston will never be a Christian city. This is certain. It is not such a city to-day. And not Athens in its lazy quest for something new, not Corinth in the scandalous lust of its by-ways, not Rome beneath the heel of a Cæsar, ever offered more prizes than Boston offers for inflexible, nay, for intolerant zeal.

2. "The pure and austere morals" of the early Church make another of the causes assigned by Gibbon for its success. This, again, was in the Master's line and purpose. No zeal will achieve a permanent victory, if the man behind be not through and through reliable. As Jesus himself said, no amount of talk in God's service compares with work in his service. Your prophet may be a matchless preacher; but the first John Baptist who prepares the way of the Lord is greater than he. The world has been teaching that lesson ever since in these centuries. This and that prophesier has risen and proclaimed; and, if he had the weight of character behind, if, to the word which proclaimed, he added the energy of the life which did, he has succeeded. But the world has rightly held every John Baptist, every Saint Francis or Saint Bernard, every Fénelon or Vincent de Paul, to that terrible test of the Master,—"Why do ye call me Lord, Lord, and do not the things that I say?" The same test applies to-day, and comes into the horoscope by which Christian successes are to be prophesied. Man or woman, preacher or poet, church or society, must expect to be judged by it. Character first and creed tested by character; not creed first and character tested by creed. That is the Jewish system,

and that system failed. The Christian system and the Christian future depend to-day, as they depended then, on the pure and austere morals of all who have it in hand.

So far does the present age recognize this truth, that the one new demand made in our own immediate generation is the interesting appeal for the formation of schools of ethical culture,— congregations even, of people who, while they want to do right, do not mean to be annoyed by worship or logic or creed or ritual of religion. Both in Europe and America there are men and women who are so heartily wearied by the endless quarrels of churches, by the unwarranted assumptions of priests, and by the unmeaning formalities of old worship, that they squarely say they will have none of them. "Give us pure and austere morals, and we will ask no more." That request could be granted, but for the presence with us of God almighty. The Holy Spirit is here as well as these men and women and children whom we see. And this Spirit will speak; and man will answer to the end of time. All the same is it sure that this Spirit will exact now, as he exacted from the hundred and twenty in the beginning, pure and austere morals. "Thou shalt do this." "Thou shalt not do that." And the true children will obey.

3. Again, Gibbon recognizes the effect of the miraculous powers assigned to the primitive Church. And well he may. True, he believes that these powers were falsely so assigned; but he knows that the men of that time admitted the claim. We need not go into any definition of miracle. And we need not weigh, for the thousandth time, the testimony which can be piled into the scales of history. What the world was glad to believe then, it is glad to believe now. It believed that the spirit ruled the thing: it believed that life swayed and moved matter. To that latent scepticism about the power of spirit, which surrounded Abraham in the nature-worshippers of Uz, which was at the bottom of the beastly rites of Syria, which spoke out in the materialism of Epicurus and Lucretius, the Church opposed its steadfast testimony. "Man's soul is greater than his body. The God of the world is greater than the world is. Any son of God who uses the divine life and trusts to the Infinite Spirit sways body, flesh, world, and devil." This was, at bottom, the reason why the world was perfectly willing to accept what apostles, who were martyrs, told it of the wonders which came from Jesus' love. The same world, to-day, chooses to believe that spirit is stronger than flesh; that God's spirit

is greater than the frame which it inspires. Not but there are men now who take the brutish notion, and stand against the heavenly truth. There are men who believe in the machinery of their mills, and mean to make it control and overmaster the men and women who are the workmen. "Let these men and women die," they say: "there are more to be found." "Steam and iron," they say, "are more than men and women." These are the heathen of to-day. There are other men who believe in the men and women who guide the machinery: they care for their health and homes, care for their children's education, care for the immortal soul. "The soul," they say, "is more than wood and iron." These men hold the Christian theory, and these men succeed. One nation believes in improved muskets and cannon, in the machinery of war and tactics. Another nation believes in schools for boys and girls, in the careful training of men and women. When this Christian nation meets that heathen nation, the heathen nation goes under, and the Christian nation stands. A heathen politician to-day believes that money is greater than men, that bribery at elections and the skilful distribution of patronage will win success. A Christian statesman believes that men are worth more than money, that he can do more by convincing minds and alluring souls than he can by place or intrigue. This man believes that spirit sways matter, and this man succeeds. And so, in the future, man, or society, who will pledge themselves to the eternal principle of all that is called miracle — namely, that the spirit shall sway the thing — will succeed, as the primitive Church succeeded in the beginning.

4. Of that primitive Church, as Gibbon says, another secret was "the union and discipline of the Christian republic." They believed in the "together." This was of course. They were not atoms, knocked here and there by tempests, as Lucretius said they were. They were children of God, and shared his nature. Because children of one blood, they were brothers in one family. Into a political system so unsocial that a fire-club was the only association permitted by the law, and that of mere necessity, there came this loving family of men and women who bore each other's burdens, and loved to do so. And they succeeded. Like success is for us, in proportion as we use the same talisman. And, as it was then, is it true to-day that the youngest "Lend a Hand" Club, which unites its common forces in a common purpose, advances the King's work more than the

largest or richest church, where men and women meet without meeting, unite without uniting, and do not share in one campaign for the service of the Father. In those simple days, if a man did not accept the "together," he did not pretend to be a Christian. In those days, the believer who went into solitude to "commune with nature" came back more ready to work for man. It was left to weaker days, of faith unsettled, and for our days,— when instead of faith a poor sentimentality comes in,— before men or women supposed that they could bear the pressure of life, or could do its duties alone.

5. And easily chief among all the victories of the primitive Church in this catalogue is its certainty that man is immortal. Every preacher in every land began and ended with this glad cry of Easter day:—

"Now Christ is risen from the dead. He is the first-fruits of them that sleep." It was the message the world waited for, longed for, perished for the need of. And, when the message came, it taught "the doctrine of a future life, impressed with every circumstance which could give weight to that important truth." These are, again, the words of the sceptic historian. One can well see what dignity spoke in the words even of the meanest preacher, when he found that to eager listeners he had this certainty of life to proclaim, "as with authority, and not as the scribes." "Here was my Master, oh, more kind and thoughtful than your dearest friend,— they cannot be compared; more wise and ready than your wisest,— oh, they cannot be compared; he could do such things as no other man did than he,— they cannot be compared. We are all God's children; but he,— why, I tell you,— he knew what it was to be Son of God! We have all asked God's blessing; but he, why, he lived in God, moved in God, and in God had his being! And do you think he died, or could die? This is what he said, 'Because I live, ye shall live also.' This is what he said, 'God is before all, and because God lives we live.' Well, they tried it: they nailed him to the cross, they laid his body in the grave. And he loved us so — loved you so, loved me so — that he came back to that body. He spoke to me, spoke to her: he walked with us, and he talked to us. We know now that in reality God's children never die. Does a grain of wheat die when it is cast into the ground?"

In the finest passage in Bulwer's poem of "King Arthur,"

the spirit of a brave man passes from this earth in struggle and victory, rises through ineffable splendors nearer and nearer to the Centre of Being and Light of Life, and there is just ready to witness and enjoy the glory of perfected being, to receive an answer to every question which human nature asks, when a message is brought of some act of human ministration, for which his service is required on the earth. The ready friend, just girt with the glories of his spiritual body, does not hesitate, and to the earth returns.

> "What rests? The Spirit from its realm of bliss
> Shot down to earth, the guide to happiness.
> Pale to the waiting King, the Spirit came.
> Its glory left it as the earth it neared.
> In living likeness, as its corpse it came;
> Wan with its wounds, the awful Shade appeared."

The story is taken, of course, from this vision of Easter morning. To give to a world this blessing of life assured, life unbroken, the Saviour Spirit returns to his friends, to say once more, "I am the resurrection and the life." The men who told that story won the world. The world of their time accepted the truth and the testimony to it. And, in all time afterward, the words of this morning are the words which speak in every chamber of bereavement. "He is not here: he is risen. This is only the place where he lay." Or "I ascend to my Father and your Father, to my God and your God."

The world was hungry, thirsty, and faint: the whole heart was sick, and the whole head was sick. It heard this voice of these teachers, and it took up its bed and walked. Jesus Christ gave it life. Doctrine? yes; social order? yes; morals? yes; new strength? yes. He gave these because he gave life, life stronger than death; life because we are living children of a living God; life which cannot be fettered in forms, swayed by palaces, or buried in tombs. Life gave his cause the victory, and makes him Ruler of Mankind.

I MUST SEE ROME.

"Paul purposed to go to Jerusalem, saying, After I have been there, I must see Rome."—ACTS xix., 21.

EVEN now, when Rome is a ruin, the yearning to see Rome often becomes a passion. Around the fallen piles where were her palaces, there huddles only a handful of people, if they are compared with the millions who lived there in Paul's day. In the wreck of those palaces, they have found a statue here, a vase there, now a mosaic, now a gem ; and, from such raking in the ashes, they have collected museums which attract the world. "See Rome and die," is a proverb which speaks for this yearning. Most of you who are of my age will remember a pathetic story, in the First Class Book, of a poor student, who sold all his books for money to travel to Rome, looked once from a neighboring height upon the dome of St. Peter's and on the contour of the seven hills, and then went home not dissatisfied. Such is the passion now. Is it not a pleasure to think that Paul felt it then,— Paul, who has made our modern life? This text is not the first glimpse that we have of the eagerness in choice of objects for travel of this prince of gentlemen. There is a glimpse of it as he seeks Athens, with the eagerness with which a man of letters seeks Athens now. There is a glimpse of it as he goes down to the field of Troy to read his Homer, where Alexander read his, where Hecuba wept and Hector died. In his after life, in this little glimpse of hopes and projects, it is quite of course that he who has seen Corinth and Athens should long to see in their places the masters of Corinth and Athens. With him, it is not what it is with us, merely the wish to see masterpieces of art which have been carried to the capital to adorn her galleries. Paul has dealt with Gallio, and he would be glad to deal with Seneca. He has seen pro-consuls, he will be glad to see the emperor. And then what Rome is to-day gives only the outline of what Rome was then.

Cæsar's palace stood glorious, where we now trace its ruins with difficulty. Temples, gigantic piles for baths, aqueducts which carried rivers of water to supply them, where we see only lines of broken arches; the forum crowded with loungers to be counted by thousands, where to-day the traveller presses a fern or picks up a bit of marble; ranges of statues, from which we admire a single torso,—all these glories were in their exact perfection. It is in the eagerness to see all this with his own eyes that Paul so confidently speaks. There is an earlier intimation of the same yearning in the epistle to the little handful of Christians in Rome. He tells them that he shall stop and see them, when he makes his journey into Spain. There is the eager pressure on him to carry over the world this gospel which is to renew the world. And, of course, to a man who had the just pride of a leader, there was the eager desire to stand in the city which commanded, and to deal with leaders. "I must see Rome."

Two or three years pass by, and Paul does see Rome. And he comes not as he had expected. To Athens he had come, a solitary traveller, in advance of his companions; and he waited for them there. When he landed at Neapolis, with the eager curiosity with which an Asiatic must always look on Europe for the first time, it was with these same companions,—two or three of them,—glad to leave the discomfort of a Greek fishing-boat. In both these cases, he had come because he chose to come; and, though it were in simple array, still he had travelled as a freeman travels. But, when he sees Rome at last, where the Appian Way passes Albano, it is under the escort of a company of soldiers, in a travelling party of prisoners, of whom he is one, in the weather-worn array of those who left the East some six months before, and who have been shipwrecked since. He comes, because he must come,—a file of soldiers before and a file behind. To carry his humble packs, there trudge at the right and left a glad company of Christian disciples, who have come out from the city to greet him and to meet him. It is the cordial welcome which the poorest give the poorest; and this welcome has already given Paul courage. They rise on the gentle slope of the roadway; and one of the most experienced runs forward and points to the north, where the towers rise white against the blue. "Ecce, Roma!" he cries; and Paul sees Rome.

So different is the fulfilment of our most careful plans from the hope and prayer with which we make them. Paul means to go to Rome as a leader and teacher. He comes here as a prisoner, waiting his trial. Such certain result, steady and unflinching, achieved in ways most unexpected, is the delight of poetry and imaginative fiction. The astrologer prophecies that the prince shall be killed on his birthday. The fond father shuts him up in his palace, that there may be no possible murderer. And on the morning of the birthday, as the young man lifts down a melon from the shelf, the fatal knife slips, falls, strikes his heart, and his father finds him cold in his own life-blood. All such tales spring from such experiences as Paul's. The end comes by ways the most improbable. Man proposes his course, and that course fails. But all the same, in the steady march of days and years, the end is sure. He sees Rome. Men and women of intense purpose come to hate slavery. They combine against it, they preach and prophesy against it. Their method is the dissolution of the Union and the downfall of the Constitution. And they live to see their purpose accomplished, in a war for the preservation of the Union and the maintenance of the Constitution. Every method they proposed is thrown on one side, but the great purpose for which they prayed is granted. The Pope is eager to do something for the glory of God worthy the see of Rome. He builds St. Peter's, with its matchless architecture. To meet the cost, he sends out the agents, who shall sell indulgences North, South, East, and West. This profligate offer of tickets, sold for money with which to enter heaven, touches the torpid conscience of the world. Half Europe rises in protest against him and his, turns them out of doors forever. And so the real glory of God is advanced, and his true worship secured, as it could not be by a thousand shrines more glorious than St. Peter's. All the history of the world is thus the history of progress which no man has dared foresee. And history owes its charm to such surprises. Who reads wisely is always coming upon the story of men who have "builded better than they knew."

In grateful recognition of the share of a good God in such unexpected victories, men refer them naturally to what we call "Providence," for want of a better word. What we mean is the underflow and constant presence of the eternal law of right, the same yesterday, to-day, and forever. Of course, we puzzle ourselves, if we imagine an outside God contriving, centuries in advance, a certain mechanical success, like checkmate on the chess-board of history, and for hundreds of years pushing up pawns and pieces till he has secured it. That is only a puzzle. But there is no such puzzle when we see God as the present conscious power which works for righteousness, when we see that right because it is right must produce right and succeed, while wrong because it is wrong can produce nothing, and must fail. If we see this, we find real meaning in the Scripture statements that we are working together with God. Those statements are not figurative. Paul, for instance, is at work in this way. Paul knows what he wants: he wants to strike at centres. As Jesus bade him, he wants to work in the cities, and not stand chattering with wayfarers. He has seen the little cities: he must see the great city. He has seen pro-consuls: he must see the men who sent them. His own plan is to weave enough tent-cloth and to make enough tents, to hire a wretched steerage passage to Ostia, and then to throw himself on the kindness of the Roman Church. But he is no stickler for method. What is important is the object, and he keeps his end in sight. At last, a prisoner before Felix and Agrippa, he sees his chance. "I appeal to Cæsar," he cries. And from that moment he is Cæsar's ward. Rome must care for him, Rome must protect him, Rome must feed him and clothe him. In that happy word, Paul compels Nero to bring to Rome the man whose word and work are in the end to overthrow Nero's throne. This is it for a man like Paul to be fellow-workman with a present God.

It will help you and me in our frequent discouragements, if we can remember these great instances, whether in Scripture, in history, or in our own seeming failures, where the perfect end comes, steady and glorious as the march of Orion across the sky, though every device of ours to secure it seems to have broken down. I have no doubt that Paul was a good tent-maker. I suppose he knew how to choose his stuffs, where to buy the best needles and the best thread, how to cut the patterns with least waste, and how to meet the rightful demands of purchasers. But it was not by tent-making that Paul was to save the world. It was by this steady persistence of which this text gives one little sample. You see it in this trial before Felix, where he sacrifices the chance of immediate acquittal for what he values so much more,— the chance to plead before Seneca and Nero. He never forgets the underlying purpose to proclaim God, and

God at hand. And, because he never forgets it, this God who is at hand, this eternal Power who works for righteousness, always works for him. Here is the infinite alliance: if you do "accept the universe," your own method fails, but your infinite purpose is accomplished.

A father watches his only son as he might watch an orchid in a green-house,— never a frosty night, never a blast of cold, never sunshine too hot, never a draught of unaccustomed air. Ask him his purpose, he will say simply that he hopes himself to help in answering the Saviour's prayer, and makes these arrangements all in the wish that the boy may be shielded from all temptation. Loyal and thoughtful father! What he can he does, as best he sees and knows. But, as it happens, God knows better. One night the father dies. The wind blows the next morning, and the whole card-castle of his fortune falls. That petted boy is turned out upon the street with nothing, as we say. By which we mean he has nothing but the memory of an earthly father's integrity and the certainty of a heavenly Father's present love. If he has these, he has the whole,— he has enough and more. It is enough to put him on the very path his father sought for him. It is enough to train him in that integrity which made his father's only prayer. It is enough to teach him how to stand upon his own feet, fight his own battle, and with his own arm win God's victory. The father's method has failed; but his wish is answered, because he did not work alone, but was a fellow-workman with God.

Or you find it hard to lift your daily life above things, things that "perish in the using." Bread and butter, clothes and fashion, house-rent and insurance and fuel, the summer's journey and the winter's repair, are too much for you. You hear preaching and hymns about another life, but it does not seem to be for you. You know people who talk of heaven as if it were as near them as the next room, but it does not seem so to you. Still, you wish it were; and you try for it. You go to the minister's Bible class, and that does not help you. You read Thomas à Kempis, and that does not help you. You try the bold experiment of a revival, and that does not help you. Dear child, the good God is as eager for you as you are for yourself. He has his ways, as you have yours. What if it happen, that, in face of your best provisions, nay, without granting your most eager prayer, he lift your darling baby from your arms, and fold the child gently in his own? What if he take your treasure from your home here to your other home there? What he means is that where your treasure is your heart shall be also. Life is where those are whom we love. And from that moment the heaven is nearer to you which seemed so far away. You had your way to seek it: he has his for you to find it. And you will find it, if you trust these constant currents of his love.

From every place to every other place there are a thousand possible ways,—nay, a million. It is not the little choice of the township in the wilderness, where the puzzled traveller is told that he may either take the hill road or the meadow road or the road between. In those courses of life which we are studying, our problem is more like that of the navigator, when he has come into the offing and taken his "departure." His home is blue behind him, his port is on the other side of the world, and the ways thither are infinite in number, not two or three alone. The great circle is the shortest. But the great circle may cross a continent,—most likely will,—and he must go by sea. He must take a part of another great circle, and then a part of another, and then a part of a third, and even more. And he must consider the great sea-currents, the gulf stream, and the rest. He must remember the trade winds, and he must avoid centres of calm. Nay, when he has started on the best plan which an angel could propose to him, there may come a tempest which shall drive him from his track. It may leave his vessel so shattered that she can only run before the wind. So that his choice is to be made between so many courses, not to-day only, but every day. Each day will have its right course and its wrong. And the tack which was the right tack with the wind of yesterday may be the wrong tack with the wind of to-day. But here the parallel with the voyage of life ends. For the voyage of the seas, before we trust ship and cargo to such varied contingencies, we insist that the commander shall have had experience of every sea, and of calm and storm. But, for the voyage of life, we need make no such demand. In that voyage, all that is asked of any of us is a loyal desire to succeed. The man who intentionally turns backward, and tries to go backward, succeeds in going backward. The man who tries for nothing, but lies as on the painted surface of a painted sea, goes nowhere. But the man who loyally tries to make the voyage God proposes, finds in the vessel beneath him and the skies above him an infinite purpose and power which commands success. He may not gain it by the route he first proposed. He may be disappointed in his second. But he cannot go wrong. He works with God, and in God's time he finds his goal. He starts to see the city which hath foundations; and in the end, though he be storm-tost on the way, shipwrecked perhaps, stung by serpents or deserted by friends, in the end he rises, like Christian in the story, or like Paul when his long task is over, the last height is surmounted, and the city is there.

Only let a man have a purpose, and that purpose a godly purpose. "I must see Rome!" Must, because there was the best place to work, and the most work to do. As a greater than Paul, on a journey more critical, said, "I must work to-day, to-morrow, and the day following; for a prophet cannot perish out of Jerusalem." The prospect is death. The certainty is what men call failure, "cruel mockings, and scourgings"; but the result as certain is the salvation of the world.

It is not the way you or I would have devised. No Tacitus or Seneca of those times would have planned it. The world is to be lifted to a nobler life. Men are to rule themselves, not to be ruled by princes. Women are to be free, not prisoners or slaves. There is to be no slavery. Sickness is to become less and less. Pain is to be forgotten. Men and women are to live for each other, and bear each other's burdens. For this, a carpenter from the hills of Galilee is to proclaim the present God. For this, he is to come to Jerusalem to proclaim him. For this, he is to be nailed to the cross, and die. Yes; and because he comes, because he dies, man is free and woman is free. Sickness, pain, and even death, are less frequent and less. Men live as brothers more and more; and in a common life they bear each other's burdens. So orders his Father and our Father, his God and our God. So rules the infinite Power which makes for righteousness.

HONOR AND IDOLATRY.

"This people honoreth me with their lips, but their heart is far from me. But in vain do they worship me, teaching for doctrines the commandments of men."—MATT. xv., 8, 9.
And in another version, Isaiah xxix., 13.

JESUS describes what is passing around him. Enthusiastic crowds of Galileans listen with delight to what he says, and then go back to their homes to do much as they did before. And here, in the moment when he speaks, he is in sharp conflict with a troop of smooth-spoken spies from the city, glad to catch him in his talk, if they can. They are over-civil, even, in their manner, perhaps a little as one is apt to overdo respect, when he talks to a crazy man. They honor God with their lips; but, as to his real empire over the world, they are at best indifferent. To describe them, Jesus uses the words with which Isaiah described their fathers seven hundred years before.

As it happens, and perhaps, as he foresaw, he describes precisely the way in which the world was going to treat him. More and more did the passion grow for honoring him — with the lips. Honor passed through all the stages of human veneration, and then passed beyond them. Worship passed from the worship of a teacher, even from the worship of an emperor, to the worship of a God. The Nazarene carpenter — whom his own townsmen turned out of the meeting-house, whom his countrymen wanted to stone, and did at last crucify — was lifted, by after-ages of lip-service, to sit on the throne of God as God's equal, and at last to be worshipped as God himself. Yes, and of the men who did this he would say so sadly, "Why call me *Lord, Lord,* and do not the things which I say?" The humblest vine-dresser who gave him a cup of cold water, in thankfulness for his tenderness to a child, was more apt to do the things that he said than those purpled and crimsoned bishops, who, in their liturgies, bent their heads in reverence of his name.

Such experience is not without parallel in other affairs of

men. The history of human sovereignty repeats it in one or another form not widely differing from each other. Charles the Great of France conquers Europe, and his court is the grandest in the world. In the course of a century or two, his descendants receive all the honors he received, and more. But honors are not power. And, while the sovereign sits almost fettered on the throne, some master of the palace orders the troops here and there; and the poor sovereign cannot so much as send a message across his own kingdom. The Japanese for the last two centuries, up to our own time, had reduced this thing to a perfect system. The emperor, supreme in rank, if rank were all, was venerated as not even gods were venerated. At one time, he sat motionless for hours every morning on the imperial throne, thus to typify and to preserve the peace of his kingdom. If he turned to look right or left, by misfortune, calamity was threatened by his imprudence. His food was brought to him in new vessels every day. And, once in seven years, the acting sovereign of Japan made him a state visit, with every expression of homage. From time to time, in the intervals, the same acting sovereign sent him embassies with presents. But, all this time, this supreme emperor, so called, this High Gate, or Mikado, who represented the dynasty which for more than two thousand years had held the rule in Japan, had not a shred of power. He could not appoint a servant in his own household. Far less could he send a soldier here or enforce an edict there. Such luxuries as power and command belonged to the tycoon and to other "inferior" princes.

To precisely such barren homage did men reduce Jesus Christ in the course of ages. Throne? Yes! King of kings and Lord of lords, if calling him King and Lord would answer; "Very God," if a sounding name will answer. But, when any son of man would know what he said, proposed, wished, or prayed for, that son of man must go, not to him, but to his viceroy. For a thousand years, the Pope of Rome held this viceroyship for Western Europe, and the patriarchs of the Greek Church for Eastern Europe; and whoever needed help or direction went to them. And, when this awful tycoonship broke down, still, for two or three hundred years, a host of inferior princes have struggled for the same viceroyship, and, under the forms of one or another infallible Church, have kept men parted alike from Saviour and from God.

All this time, these people — prince, bishop, priest, and all — reverenced him with their lips, called him "Lord, Lord," rendered to him every form of homage. To this hour, men shall bow their heads in the creed when his name is named, who, before the same service is over, shall acknowledge that some viceroy of human imperfection is to interpret his instructions, and administer religion in his name. But suppose I go to such viceroys or vicars. How much do I learn,— whether of his spoken instructions,— or how much even of the spirit of his life do I imbibe? Suppose you had an eager pupil, not harassed by scepticism, certain in his regard and love, who wanted only to reproduce Christ's work in this end of this nineteenth century. The last thing you would do with him, if you knew what you were about, would be to set him upon studying the proclamations of Popes. Nay, the worst thing you could set him to would be the study of Calvin's Institutes, or of the canons of any Church now existing. If you do know what you are about, and what he wants, your wisest course is to show him the men and women who have shown the most moral force in history,— who, as we wisely say, are most Christ-like. Show him the steadiness and perseverance of John Eliot. Show him the faith of Saint Francis. Show him the quaint good sense of Oberlin. Show him the tenderness and resolution of Mary Ware. Show him the daring of Selwyn. Show him the breadth of purpose of Xavier. Let him find out that to be a follower of Christ is to carry manhood to the highest power, to work out the highest heroism of the hero, the finest chivalry of the gentleman,— that all these things follow to the son of God. And if, by such lesser examples, you bring him to the central example, if he find there the most tenderness, the most manly manliness, the most chivalrous chivalry, and the noblest triumph, why he will learn the "noble lesson" which the first and best of the world have learned, exactly as they learned it. Sad enough that he is not led to it by any men, because they are honoring Christ with their lips! That service is worthless, unless they are honoring him in their lives.

The true way to honor Christ is to follow him. Do as he did. Then you show that you love him, and hold him in reverence. See him as he was, and do not bury him behind your purple robes,— no, nor crown him with your thorny crowns,— no, nor give him a reed for his sceptre. That was what Pilate did; and how many men have done it since who pretended to revere him! He needs no monarch's robe to give him command. He needs no crown and no sceptre. He leads because he is leader. And when you see him as he is, and know him as he is, you will follow.

The living generation of men has undertaken, in good faith, to produce Jesus Christ again to the world he served. From the beginning, in nineteen centuries, there has been no such loyal effort to show him as he was as we have seen in the last fifty years. This work has wrought much destruction of what had been called sacred. There was some necessary dust and much noise, as the scaffolds and upholstery of centuries were pulled down. Criticism has been sometimes irreverent, and often foolish. But the result is that men know Jesus Christ the better, and the result will be that they will know him more. They honor him more, even if they worship him less. I spoke here three months ago of this determined Christian realism of our time, the resolution "to see with the eyes of those that looked on." I read that day from Mrs. Greenough's poem of Mary Magdalene, one of the recent efforts to tell the story in this realistic way. Well, the next morning I sent the copy of that poem which I had here to a distant city. God so ordered that the pretty volume fell into the hands of a woman wholly broken down in the vice which men say is most incurable. My friend, who had the book, had been pleading with this poor creature; and, with the hardness of despair, the girl had bidden her go her way, and had said, "I have chosen mine." But, as God ordered, at the same moment the girl took this book from her, and read it. When she had read it, that very night she said to the Christian friend who lent it: "Where you lead, I will follow. What you ask, I will do." That softening of a rebellious heart, that readiness to follow Jesus Christ, was what came to her when for the first time, probably, in her life she was able to get some glimpse of what he was. I dare say she had bowed her head in the creed. I think very likely that she had been taught to repeat, that

"The Son, which is the Word of the Father, begotten from Everlasting of the Father, the very and eternal God, of one substance with the Father, took man's nature."

But neither the act of homage nor the statement of doctrine had saved her from temptation or had loosened the power of sin. When she saw what his way of saving people was, she chose that way of salvation. She did not love her sin. Poor wretch, nobody knew better than she the depths to which it sunk her. And when she saw him, and when she knew something of that life, she yielded herself to it as those did in his day, of whom the whole record is they "turned and followed."

It is almost a thing of certainty that, as the world chooses thus to take its Saviour by the hand and to look in his face, we shall hear the complaint that we treat him with irreverence. "Master, rebuke the multitude." This is what the people, fond of outside pageantry, said then; and what they say now. Of this remarkable book of Dr. Clarke's, *The Legend of Thomas Didymus*, we shall be told that he takes undue liberties with the person and character of Jesus Christ. "He has placed words in the Saviour's lips which we do not find in St. John." Yes; and did not St. John tell you that he had only written a fragment of the history? So a chambermaid of Queen Elizabeth might complain that the royal robes of State were hung in the closets and that the throne-room looks dreary, when the Queen dresses herself for service and rides out to command her army. So the priests of Apollo did complain that no man came to do sacrifice before the Image of the Sun, when the rejoicing world had gone after the Son of Righteousness. The habit of the first school of painters was to invest Christ's figure with different raiment and coloring from that which became a man. Later down, a sacred "glory" had to be painted around his head. And to this hour there is scarcely a picture of him which is not either too soft to be strong or too rugged to be tender. Whoever does try to lead us to a more real sense of his manhood, which is to show us better how divine he is must not dread such criticism. He must do his beste that we may see the most tender tenderness, the most rugged manhood, the most firm resolution, the most living life. Then only do we know why and how he moved the young man who had great possessions, the poor woman of Tyre, the tax-gatherer at his office, or the centurion at the cross. Into the market-place of Capernaum, or under the shade of the orchard in the country here, came one whom men called the carpenter of Nazareth. The children were not afraid of him, for his welcome was such as they had never known before. Young men and women talked with him, found him cordial, sympathetic, so wise, and so hearty. Puzzled people, who had handled back and forth all the problems, talked with him. He was not puzzled, and to him there were no problems. Timid people talked to him, and found him all courage. Sick people talked to him, and found such vitality as was a fountain of health. Some of these people were so fascinated that they could not leave him. What he did, they tried to do. What he said, they tried to obey. He wanted them for a purpose he had in hand, and to that purpose they devoted themselves.

The purpose was to make all men and women like him,— more manly, more womanly,— till they were perfect as is the living God. Of all that company, the one who knew him best was sure to be the one most like him; who knew him best, was sure to be the one who followed most heartily; who knew him best, was sure to be the one who succeeded most completely. Yes; and he who knew him best would certainly honor him most as he would wish to be honored. It might not be by calling him "Very God of the substance of God"; it might not be by clothing him with a robe of purple; it would not be by banishing him to sit in majesty on some secluded throne. Honor would come where obedience was rendered; and when Oberlin made light shine in darkness, when John Eliot buried the tomahawk, when Mary Ware watched by the dying peasants at Osmotherley, then was it and thus was it that they rendered to him the fit and only homage.

It has been my good fortune once and again to know the pupils of a great artist, who loved him, honored him, and would have died for him. I have known the aides of a great general, who believed in him, honored him, and would gladly die for him. I have had the good fortune to know men who loved great women with all the passion and energy of life; and I have known women who, with all the passion and energy of life, loved great men. But never, in any such cases of life enlivened by life, does he who so drinks at the fountain expect to honor fitly with the lips him or her who has so quickened life and inflamed passion. Always, where passion is perfect and life is true, always this is the wish and prayer: O God, that I may be worthy of that which he has been to me! O God, that I may do something to show him that I apprehend and comprehend! O God, help me to carry out his purpose! Help me, indeed, to make real the life which from him I have derived. Well! Is that the law of life in these separate instructions and inspirations? All the more is it the law of life when Mary or Martha sit at Jesus' feet, when Mary Magdalene finds the devils are cast out, when Simon and Matthew find what life is and what it is for. Those men and women do not go about shouting "Hosanna!" They are not constructing creeds,— nay, they are not so much as writing hymns. Hymns write themselves, and creeds compose themselves. They are not taking thought how they shall best build him a monument. Rather, with all their might would they live in his life, and carry out his unfinished plan.

This is as true to-day as it was then. Nor does the detail seem difficult. No man need say the days of miracle are gone who sees how one act of love repeats itself to-day, or how any loving life lifts up what is fallen down, just as his did. You and I cannot work his miracles, you say. Then we must work ours. There are no lepers for us to cleanse, but there is dirt enough all around us for our cleaning,— homes grimy with dirt, which you and I might make cheerful; nay, hearts impure, which you and I might sweeten and freshen. He opened the eyes of the blind. Yes; and there is not one of us but may provide one page more for the reading of the long midnight of these brothers and sisters of ours whom we vainly teach to read if, when their fingers can trace the letter on the page, there are no letters for their tracing. He cast out devils in his exceeding love. And you and I,— are we sure we have exhausted all our power in that direction? He made another place of that Samaritan village; he made another woman of that Samaritan outcast. And you and I? How many outcasts from other lands cross our lives every day! And have we tenderly and manfully done all we can do for them? He gave to sinners new courage, because he had hand and word and promise for them all. There are enough left for us to try the same experiment.

And all this may be without a man's once bowing head in his honor; nay, without a man's naming his name. What does he care for that? "Blaspheme me, if you choose," he says proudly to the world: "that is easily forgiven." Only carry forward the work. Build up the perfect kingdom. Come yourself to his Father, as he came, and do the thing he did. No fear but there will be sufficient honor. Yes, the honor most grateful, when all tears shall be wiped from all eyes, when every man shall sit under his own vine and fig-tree, when God's will shall be done on earth as it is in heaven.

THE UNITARIAN PRINCIPLES.

"Endeavoring to keep the unity of the Spirit in the bond of peace."
— EPHESIANS iv., 3.

WE are God's children, not merely his creatures. That is, we inherit something of God's nature; in the Bible phrase, we are partakers of the divine nature. When we feel and own this, we know that we are of the same nature with other men and women. We are drawn to them and they to us in unity of the spirit.

In every-day life, we see some people who feel this, and like to feel it, and some who do not want to feel it. Some people like to draw together, to act with others and to agree with others. Other people hate to agree. They take you up on the first word where discussion is possible. They do not listen to the end of the sentence. Such men never form partnerships; or, if they do, they quarrel with their partners and dissolve. They do not join in societies. They do not subscribe to contributions. Such a man never crosses the street to speak to a friend. Indeed, he does not know what the word "friend" means. He might be a partaker of the divine nature, but he does not choose to be. He chooses to live apart from his fellow-men.

A similar type of men, not living in absolute loneliness, separate in groups from others. They are partisans, sectarians. The type of these men are the separatists in Scripture whom our Bible calls Pharisees. "We are holier than thou," — this was their motto. "This people, which knoweth not the law, is cursed," — that is their theory. "Rule or ruin," — that is their plan.

Paul had tried this plan very thoroughly. He was well sick of it. He had worked through, and come out upon the great Christian theory, which is that God is Father of us all, that we have all something of the divine spirit. There is, therefore, a unity of the spirit, which we can all preserve, and in which we may live and move and have our being as one. It is with this hope that Paul writes so largely in this text, and begs them to all keep the unity of the spirit in the bond of peace.

This idea of unity of the spirit is at the bottom of all our modern systems of toleration in religion. Jew and Gentile, Quaker, Episcopalian, Methodist, Romanist, and Greek,— all, in our time, share equally before the law. They may quarrel in their weekly newspapers, but the State does not care. The State acts as Gallio did. The State says: "You must keep the peace so far, that every man may worship as he pleases. You must keep the unity of the spirit in the bond of peace." So far has Christianity triumphed in law. For this is the Christian principle.

It was first asserted in political combinations, in the Kingdom of Hungary, as late as the year 1563. After hateful discord between different religious parties, in which Roman Catholics, Lutherans, Calvinists, and Socinians were all engaged, the three Protestant bodies agreed on a basis of union. This secured to all denominations, or to all persons, freedom of religion, whatever their belief. For a while, the Protestants held by each other in standing for this toleration. Because they were thus united, and were also agreed in maintaining unity, or the unity of religion, they were called "Uniti" or "Unitarii." It is in this union for toleration to all, that the word "Unitarian" first came into existence.

In that particular case, the Lutherans and Calvinists, so soon as they came into power, gave up the decree of toleration. The Socinians only, the party which, in controversies about Jesus Christ, held that he was the Son of God, but not God himself, were the only body which held to the "Unitarian" position. The name "Unitarian" thus attached itself especially to them; and, by gradual dispersion from Hungary through Europe, it now designates the religious body to which we belong. It is in this first struggle for toleration that the word has its honorable origin.

The word is itself so good a word, it refers to a truth so great, and is in its origin so honorable, that our title to it has been seriously challenged. Thus, I find in the English "Church Dictionary" of Archdeacon Hook, a most estimable clergyman of the English Church of our time, representing in that Church the old-fashioned Anglican view, or what is familiarly called in England "the high and dry division," that he gives this definition of "UNITARIANS": "A title which certain heretics, who do not worship the true God, assume most unfairly, to convey the impression that those who worship the one and only God do not hold the doctrine of the Divine Unity. Christians worship the Trinity in Unity, and the Unity in Trinity." Thus, Dr. Hook would be glad to have the Church of England known to be a Unitarian Church. But Dr. Hook is certainly mistaken in saying that the Unitarians have "assumed" this name. The earliest account of the historical origin of the word seems to be that which I have given. The doctrine known as the doctrine of Unitarians is, indeed, as old as the time of the apostles; but the name came, as almost all names come, without anybody's previous device. Just as the names "Methodist" or "Quaker" or "Episcopalian" have attached themselves to different branches of the Church, the name "Unitarian" has attached itself to our branch of the Church. We could not help it, if we would. Fortunately, we would not help it, if we could. Simply, it is ours to remember that the name which the world likes to give to us stands for as great a reality as the oneness of God, and the consequent oneness of man, who is the child of God. It follows from our very position that we ought to be the last people in the world to cavil about names. Our central statement being that all men are children of God,—the statement of the divinity of human nature,—we are, of all believers, those who should be most shy of partisanship or of sect, which is to say, of Phariseeism.

All the same, however, Unitarians exist, and have a religious life parted as far as the poles from the religious life of people who believe in sect and rely on dogma. I have sometimes found myself in correspondence or in conversation with persons relying on creeds, and as sure of their doctrine as the high-priest Caiaphas was of his, who did not seem to me to have the faintest idea what I meant by the word "Religion." Thus, if you train a man to consider that forms are the essence of religious life, you cannot make him understand what you mean by "spirit" or "spiritual communion." The religious life of Unitarians, and what is properly called their faith, cannot, from the nature of the case, be defined in a creed. For a creed is limited and means to be limited, and the religious life and faith of Unitarians are unlimited and mean to be unlimited. Still, truth is truth, life is life. The divine life, shown in human order, will show itself in ways resembling each other. And so it is that, even without a written creed and without any authoritative statement of form or dogma, the position of the Unitarian Church is probably more intelligible than that of any other communion in Christendom. True, in bringing together the writings of any religious communion, it would be found necessary to throw out on the right or on the left what the florists would call "sports," — the fanciful or exaggerated statements made by strongly marked individual men, fond of showing their independence, and afraid to work in harness. The same liberty would be necessary in comparing Unitarian writers. But I believe that, with all our freedom, we should have fewer occasions to ask this indulgence — if it be one — than any other religious communion. And, as I have said, the religious system which has gained the name "Unitarian" seems more intelligible, because more harmonious within itself, than is any other religious system now known under a Christian name.

What is this religious system?

First and chiefly, the Unitarian Church regards man as the child of God. This is a fact, and not a metaphor. God is our Father in truth, and not as a matter of affectionate expression. We are his children in truth, and we are all his children. From this central truth, all statements of total depravity or original sin fall away, as water drops from hot iron. We have no part nor lot with them. We take the new-born child as the child of God, train him as the child of God, treat him as a child of God, bid him pray to God as a child prays to a father, and trust him as a child trusts a father. He is never to be afraid of God: he is to consult God about everything, and work with him about everything. Man and God are together, and nobody and nothing are to part them. Least of all shall any form of religion put them asunder.

It is the fashion to say, with a sneer, that the Unitarian system is a system of negations. But what can be more positive than this, its central statement,— that man is son of God and God father of man? You must contradict lies. If the devil comes before you, you must rebuke him. And if ten or twelve dark centuries, which come to be known as the "dark ages," culminate in that awful negation that man is incapable of good, that he is unlike God, that he is lost and is exposed to damnation, then, if you know you are God's child, you must deny such a negation as that. And, as always, your two negatives become an affirmative. Your Church stands on the infinite affirmation of the "humanity of God and the divinity of man." *

2. This, as I have said, is the centre; and it is the most important statement of the Unitarian position. It is probably held in the private convictions of almost all Christians; but it is contradicted in words in all the written creeds, excepting those of the liberal churches. It states the relations of man with God. This follows, of course, that man with man, each of us, must honor his fellow-man. He must bear his brother's burdens. Thus, all men must be equal before the law. So far as the Declaration of Independence and the Bill of Rights proclaimed this equality, they were Unitarian documents. So long as slavery was the law of the Southern States, the Unitarian Church was virtually impossible in the Southern States. No religious system which divides priesthood from people, as the Roman Catholic Church seems to do, can fairly mount to the lofty height of this principle. The Unitarian Church of necessity recognizes the brotherhood of man.

3. It follows, almost of necessity, that it devotes itself to building up the kingdom of God in the world. For this, it certainly has good authority. It does not wince at any of the great texts which ask us to be perfect as our Father in heaven is perfect, which ask that God's kingdom may come on earth as in heaven, which say that Christ's disciples will do greater things than he does, which say that the King meant that all should come to his supper. It accepts them fully, without any attempt to tone them down. Really believing that God is at hand, the Unitarian Church really believes that God's kingdom is to come here, and says that its business is to make it come. If it had no such business, it would have no right to be.

4. From the belief that man is of the nature of God, it follows that man is immortal. "God is not the God of the dead, but of the living." To the Unitarian Church, death is an accident, important, but not critical. Like the change when an infant's body becomes the body of a man, is the

---

* I had occasion to use this happy expression some months since, and was sorry to find it cited in the papers as if the choice of the words were my own. The idea, of course, is perfectly simple, and as old, at least, as the New Testament. But I quoted this exact statement from a very instructive and suggestive essay by my friend, Rev. Edwin C. L. Browne, of Charleston, S.C.

change when a man throws off the earthly house of this tabernacle and puts on the heavenly house. But the man remains, child of God and of his nature. His character or stamp remains. If improving, well. If failing, ill. But the man lives, of his Father's nature, in his Father's care, and under his Father's law.

5. Again, from the certainty that man is child of God and of the same nature, there follows a certain evident comparative indifference even to well-approved human methods of worship or of education. To the Unitarian Church, any form must be judged by its power to express the present truth: it must be tried by its fruits, and only so. Or, in other words, if we are all God's children, if we are "all kings and priests," we shall certainly come to God, each and all, with our own questions to receive from him his own answers. And it is certain that he wants us to. It is here that there comes in a certain eclecticism in the choice of worship, which may look like arrogance, and is sometimes so called. Thus, in the Unitarian chapel at Cambridge, they venture to sing the Latin hymns of the Roman Church, which a High-Church Episcopal college hardly dares to sing, for fear the hymn should be misconstrued by somebody. And thus, on the other hand, it is very certain that the Unitarian Church accepts its preachers and other ministers only for the good they do, and cannot claim for them any functional merit or authority.

6. But instruction, help, progress, will come in from all history, precisely because the Church holds man to be God's child. Such help will come from the noble lessons God has taught to his noblest children in history. Nobody is to be set aside as "common or unclean." Something will be learned from every one who has really sought God; for to this Church it is certain that that man has really found him. What God has said to Wesley or Whitefield, to Fénelon or to Francis, to Bernard or to Ambrose or Augustine, thus becomes God's word, and not the mere fancy of a man. All history thus becomes sacred, and is studied with a tenderness and care with which no Pharisee can study Gentile history. Here is it that there comes in that respect with which the Unitarian Church regards men not Christians, such teachers of the world as Spinoza, as Philo and Plato, Buddha and Confucius,—a respect for which it is often calumniated. "Honor all men" is a direction which cuts low down. And the instruction given to Peter on the house-top ranged much fur-

ther than the mere etiquette of the intercourse between Jew and Roman. "Honor all men" makes it easier to-day for the Unitarian missionary to deal with a Ute Indian or with a Fiji Islander or with a Brahmin in Hindoostan. They meet, not as enemies on two sides of an entrenchment, but as the common children of one God.

It is thus that the Unitarian Church, naturally recognizing Jesus Christ as Leader and Lord of the whole Church, makes him the most Real Being in history, while the Church of the dark ages has succeeded in making him the most Unreal. As God visits every soul and gives help to every child, how certain is it that this Son of God, who receives the spirit of God without measure, who shows in his energy, his purity, his tenderness, and his unselfishness the fulness of every attribute of life,— how certain it is that he will be able to exhibit to us God's will and law completely! There is nothing unnatural in such an exhibition of perfect manhood. It is, on the other hand, perfectly natural. The world was not deceived in expecting it. It was precisely what the love of God would have intended. The world was not wrong in believing it had come. It was precisely what the world had a right to wait for. True, the world was wrong in worshipping him, who bade it worship his Father and his God. But it is easy to understand the origin of such homage. When the world sees its mistake, all the more it sees that the Son of God, who has stood nearest to God, who has understood him completely, and relied upon him implicitly, is its sure guide in the interpretation of God's wishes and his kingdom. It is thus that, as it happens, the latitudinarians, the men who were not sectarians, have been in all ages those who have led back the Church to that tender allegiance to Jesus which the pretences of Schoolmen had made well-nigh impossible. Such men as the Waldenses, in their mountain valleys, broke from the Roman Church because the Pope came between them and their Saviour. And you find, when you look up their confessions, that these men would not let their Saviour take the place of their God. So Thomas à Kempis, and the brethren of the life in common, were dreaded by their own time as heretics. It is doubted whether they are not outside the fold. All the same, it is Thomas à Kempis who shows every believer how he may commune with God as Jesus Christ did; and has done, who shall say how much, to help forward such communion. It is John Milton, who will hardly enter a house of worship, who can find no church broad enough for his heresies, who writes for you your Hymn of the Nativity, and in Paradise Regained brings you face to face with your Saviour. And in these later days, in our own generation, all saturated with what you called the Unitarian Heresy, when you can hardly find a scholar who, in good faith, is willing to repeat the language of the Athanasian Creed as to Christ's person, you find such Christian realism as no age has known before. You find that the heretic of a century ago is he who is making your Saviour to be more near to you and more dear than he has been for ages.

7. From all these convictions, it follows as matter of necessity that the Unitarian Church demands purity of character from those who belong to it. Strictly speaking, this is all that it demands. It asks for other things; but character is essential. It is glad to have good sense in its members. It is glad to have intelligible theology. It is glad to have the results of the study of the past. But it must have purity of life. Idle to preach the possible perfection of mankind, if the man who preach or the congregation who hear are satisfied with imperfection. Idle to bring to Jesus Christ the reverence due to the Leader of the world, if we do not follow in his footsteps. "Why do you say, Lord, Lord, and do not the things which I say?" In a Unitarian church there might be forty theories as to predestination, but there must be one determined resolve for purity of life.

I see that people are as eager as ever to condense the foundations of religious life, in brief and hallowed sentences. Fortunately for us, the Unitarian Church has no reason to dread the severe simplicity of Scripture. The common phrase, "The Four Gospels are a good enough creed for me," has for us a substantial meaning and foundation. To those who ask a briefer statement, I am apt to say that those are convenient texts which Jesus taught at the well-side: —

"God is a spirit, and they that worship him must worship him in spirit and in truth."

"I must do the will of him that sent me, and finish his work."

"Lift up your eyes and look upon the fields: they are white already to harvest."

It would not be difficult thus to state all the special principles of the Unitarian Church in such expressions, at once venerable and familiar. That Church, in brief, exists, —

"To do the will of God, our Father, who is in heaven";

"To follow Jesus Christ, his well-beloved Son, who is the Saviour of the world."

It looks on all men as made of one blood in all nations of the world, and it teaches all men "to bear their brother's burdens." To those who try, it promises that the "spirit of God, the holy spirit, shall lead them into all truth."

It is, of course, at once the hardest religious system, and the easiest,— hardest, because it offers no short cuts to favor, no leap into heaven, no sudden completion of all duty. Man's duty is as eternal as God's life: man must walk with God. But this is easiest, because it is the spirit of God which works in the life of man. Man's life is hid with Christ in God, when he loyally devotes himself to his Father's purpose. And from the Infinite Fountain man receives infinite supply.

The Œdipus Tyrannus and Christianity.

"There hath no temptation taken you but such as man can bear."—
I. Cor. x., 13.

The University has devoted loyal pains, study, care, and time, to the reproduction of a great Greek tragedy, which in the last few weeks it has exhibited to those most interested. The occasion has its lessons for us all here, as well as for scholars.

The tragic dramas of the Greeks were founded almost without exception on one idea, which now, when spoken of among scholars, is named by their name. These tragedies describe the struggle of a brave man against the Absolute Fate which involves his certain ruin. Such a struggle, wherever it appears to exist in life, is now spoken of as tragic, or sometimes as Greek, because from such struggles the great Greek tragic poets—Æschylus, Sophocles, and Euripides—made their plots. Such struggles have been treated by modern authors, but not exclusively. But they are the frequent and almost only subject of the Greek tragedy.

In the case of the tragedy of King Œdipus, which was chosen for exhibition by the University, an oracle, announcing the will of the gods, had pronounced at his birth that he should kill his father. To avoid that destiny, his father exposed him to the beasts to die at his birth. As always in such stories, this exposure insured his life. In young manhood, he, having been also warned by an oracle that he should kill his father, leaves the court of the king who had brought him up, and in a brawl kills his own father, not knowing who he was. He then marries his own mother, equally unconsciously. He and she are wholly innocent in purpose; but, as the two or three hours of the play prove to them the horrid truth, she kills herself and he blinds himself, that he may never see his own children. Such is the penalty, or sacrifice, by which they avert the wrath of the gods, or buy back their favor for Thebes. You see that from the beginning Œdipus is innocent of intentional wrong. In the fatal brawl in which, unconsciously, he kills his father, he acts on the defensive, one against three. All the same, parricide is to these gods a crime, incest is a crime. All this time, he must not plead that the gods ordered his guilt in advance. He must do penance, though, according to the story, he is a pure-minded ruler and innocent of intentional wrong. The tragic interest of the story turns on his real innocence and that of his poor wife, Jocasta.

Such in the great Greek tragedy was the fate of one innocent man and one innocent woman.

Such notions of the gods above them sank deep in the mythology of those countries and times. Our special interest now with such tragedy comes from the fact that, near a thousand years afterwards, the superstition of the Dark Ages transferred to all men and all women the same horrible fate which in the play fell on Œdipus and Jocasta. The greatest victory of Christian faith had been the dethroning of the Greek gods, Jupiter, Apollo, and the rest, and the acknowledging of one God only, of whom a Jewish writer said, "In sum, he is All." From their petty realms, God's empire was so enlarged as to include all heaven and all worlds. And then, as if to match this magnificent enlargement, the ages, darkest both in reason and in faith, extended such little curses as oracles could pronounce on Œdipus or on Orestes, and, with the fell sweep of universal cruelty, damned all mankind in one condemnation. According to this later fable, when one man, Adam, committed one sin, all his descendants were condemned to a common penalty. In that lesser case of Œdipus, he had committed unconsciously an act which, if he had meant it, would have been a crime. But, in this most comprehensive and most horrible fable, all men and all women, without doing anything, had sinned. Nay, before they did anything, they sinned. They sinned when Adam sinned; and, in his sin, they were damned. The purest, the most unselfish, the most spiritual, men braver than Œdipus, women more loving than Jocasta, might struggle against this fate imposed by the Ruler of the Universe, but they struggled in vain. The terror and the grief which held captive a Greek audience, as they witnessed the conflict of one man wound in the gripe of this awful doom, are multiplied in the theology of the Dark Ages a thousand-fold. All mankind are damned. All mankind struggles. And all mankind fails.

To add to such accumulated horror, the theology of the Dark Ages contrives one terror more, to make more complete the blind cruelty of its God. The Œdipus of the play, to take the convenient illustration now before us, is innocent in intention; but still he has done the deed of which he is charged. Nay, the hot passions of youth led him to that deed. It may be excused, but it has been committed. In the larger and more horrible fable, by which the Dark Ages reconstruct the history of the world, it is a Son of God, absolutely and wholly innocent, confessedly innocent, innocent in fact, innocent in appearance, innocent in intention, who is seized upon for punishment. And the punishment heaped upon him is not any poor blinding of the eyes. It is not the mortal struggle of his crucifixion. It is, by an ingenuity of which no Greek dramatist was ever capable,— the accumulated and infinite punishment which all men ever deserved for all sin ever accomplished,— it is this which, to accomplish the needs of a cruel Divinity, misnamed justice, is heaped all at once on one absolutely sinless and pure.

By an exaggeration so awful do the Darkest Ages of the world parody horrors, little in this comparison, of the Greek tragedians.

We owe this awful parody, in the first instance, to the genius and passion of the African Augustine, who credited the race of men with such depravity as he supposed he himself was born to. That would be a curious study which should show how far the idea of Fate or Destiny, as a god above God, stronger than the God of men, was borrowed by the Christian Fathers from this Greek Destiny, stronger than Jupiter and Apollo, and holding them in its iron rule. But I have not the scholarship for that study; nor is this the fit place for it, if I had. For our present purpose, it is enough to say that, if Jesus Christ is an authority in Christianity, that idea of Fate is no part of the Christian system. There is no reference to it in the Four Gospels. There is even no refutation or reply to it, more than any affirmation of it. You would say that the danger of such a doctrine had never been called to Christ's attention. It is certain that the fear of destiny is not a Jewish term. The Jews believed that their God was all powerful, and could do what seemed good to him. As a metaphysical subtlety, the discussion between free will and foreknowledge is played through in the book of the Wisdom of Sirach. But it did not trouble the Jewish conscience. So that all Christ's illustrations point exactly the other way. With him, God is Father, and is Father of infinite tenderness. He forgives where he chooses. The prodigal has only to return sorry, and to say he is sorry, and he is clasped in his father's arms.

The child, however weak, however fallible, is still sent into his Father's harvest field, and told to work with his God. He may doubt as to his own skill; but, by every word of parable and every personal direction, he is encouraged. He is assured of the infinite alliance. That God has any prejudice against him is never implied. That anybody has sinned for him in advance is never implied in the Gospels. All that is extorted by preposterous misreadings from Paul's letters. But Paul, too, like his Master, steadfastly tells the child that God is eager to reverse every injury which human failure has brought upon the world, and to bring in the empire of perfect love.

If this tragic fable of one oracle of fate, damning with depravity all mankind before they were born, had ever really commanded the faith of the Christian world, there would have been the end of the Christian religion. "Any thing rather than that," men would have said, and said justly. Happily, the Master was stronger than his interpreters. Happily, the life of Jesus Christ himself was known of all men. The words he spoke, the stories he told, were on all men's lips. And the simplest clown, who could make nothing of the long-drawn inferences of the theologians, could make out, were it only in a poor picture, the story of the Marriage Feast, and could take to heart the tender forgiveness of the Prodigal Son. The Christian world was better than its creed, as, thank God, it is to-day. A loving God, indeed, was not willing to leave it to any accident which might bring or refuse the message of the Christian gospel. As Paul said to those savage Lycaonians, God never left himself without witness in that he did good. "In that he did good." Say what you please of sorrow, pestilence, famine, still, on the whole, men know and acknowledge that whoever rules this world rules it well. He does good. Put it in another phrase, men love to live. They are eager to live. The love of life is their strongest passion. To save it, they implore tyrants, they sacrifice wealth, they exhaust ingenuity. Our age is the first, indeed, which has reduced to a scientific statement the other theory,— that this world is the worst possible world and this life the worst possible life. We owe this argument to the philosopher Schopenhauer, who did his best to make other people believe it. But that he did not believe it himself was clear enough from the simple fact that he continued to live out his threescore years and ten. On his theory of morals and of life, if it had been more than a philosophical ingenuity, he would have put a pistol to his head, and there should have been an end to life. But he, too, loved to live, as all men love to live. It is clear that the fly loves to play in the air, the fish loves to swim in the sea, the bird loves to soar, the kitten loves to play, the dog loves to bask in the sun, the horse in the pasture loves to run, the cattle on a thousand hills love to crop the herbage. I believe that grass loves to grow and flowers to open. Certain is it that man loves to live. Never a sun rises but it rises on a landscape of beauty and a world of happiness. And the "mists and exhalations," the diamond in the dewdrop and the daisy in the grass, the sparrow on the twig or the bee in the blossom, consciously or unconsciously sing the praise of the power who gives them food and life, and makes up a world in which they are glad to live.

From this simple faith, men lapse,— and this is a terrible misfortune,— when they separate their God from the world he made. The carelessness of selfishness, or the narrowness of priests, or the subtlety of philosophers puts God outside his world, sitting on some Olympus or in some seventh heaven; and, inside of it, another set of powers, which they call "Nature," works its will, God supposed to be ignorant or indifferent, or, as in the case of Œdipus, impotent. For Jupiter himself, in that fable, could not have saved Œdipus from murdering his father. Such danger does not belong to those times alone. It was the danger of the Pharisees' precision. Jesus points out to them that they have one religion by which they pull a sheep out of the pit, and another religion in which they conform to the traditions of their law. If Œdipus and Creon and priest and people could have understood, alike, that they were all at that moment crossing the purpose of their God; if, in whatever solemn inquest, they had found from what filthy mill-pool or man-made Gehenna came the malaria which was poisoning their city; if, in whatever solemnity, they had restored its conditions to the sweet salubrity of the forest or of the wilderness, working with their God for the good of his children,— they would have learned and have taught the eternal lesson that it is in him, and only in him, that we live and move and have our being. All the idea that our sacrifices are to pacify him or our prayers to move him, when he is far away or does not wish to be pacified, belong to our separation of him from the laws of the world that he has made.

Of course, the circumstances to which a man is born dictate, to a certain extent, his early temptations; and the moral condition of the world as he finds it dictates his temptations afterward. But temptations are not sins. You have heard, in the Scripture lesson, how sternly Ezekiel challenges and refutes the idea that the iniquity of the fathers is to be visited in punishment or as guilt upon their children. Whatever the second commandment implied on that point, Ezekiel insists that each man stands for himself, and by his own sins stands or falls. Of course, for instance, that man has horrible temptations, who has been born from drunken parents to inherit, from their lust and intemperance, appetites which he has to resist his life long. But he is a child of God also, and with the divine spirit he inherits from his heavenly Father he can resist these earthly enticements. He has power to loosen sin and to retain sin, if he will. "There is no temptation appointed him but such as he can bear." He lives in God, if he will. He shares God's nature. He is God's child.

Slowly but surely, the world learns that great lesson. It lives in him. It has no other life. He lives in the world. He has no purpose but its good. As the world feels that perfect Love more perfectly, there are not so many tragedies nor subjects for tragedy,— that is true,— but there is life more successful because more simple, more glad because more divine. Nor let us, because we are impatient of the slowness of the world's advance on this line,— let us not persuade ourselves that it fails. If any oracle to-day sent word to any city that its ruler's son or any beggar's brat in its gutter was damned by a fate which would compel him to commit murder, the men and women who uttered that lying oracle would be haled before its courts and punished to the utmost. If it were the Archbishop of Canterbury, if it were the President of the University, if it were the most learned philosopher in the land, if all three of them united in such slander against the love of God, they would be tried for defamation of the character of the baby about whom they prophesied, tried for conspiracy to defame if they united in their oracle, and they would all be justly punished for forecasting woe. Thus to press to the ridiculous the most solemn of these superstitions of the past is wise and fair, if we learn, as we ought, that at bottom in the hearts of men is more of the surety of God and of his perfect love. On that surety, laws have made themselves, customs formed themselves, and States been founded. As the world goes forward in that surety, the little children learn that this is God's hand from which they take the dandelion and the buttercup, that these are God's leaves which are dancing on the trees and his blossoms which perfume the air, that this miracle, in which a month since the bare twigs of the winter budded, bourgeoned, and blossomed in the fresh glory of the spring, was the present God, giving, as he always gives, new gifts unto men. As the children grow in this knowledge, as young men and maidens are happy in it, as hard-working men and women consecrate their daily labor in this certainty, the more certainly will there die away even the memories of the old curses, whether pronounced by priests or argued out by logicians. Sorrow will come,— yes! It is the gate of wisdom, and man must pass through it as he ascends to higher life. But no man knows so well as he who passes through it that in the goodness fresh every morning and new every evening, the goodness which makes the heavens blaze with light, and makes every inch of the earth a miracle of wonder, there is the constant assurance of unchanging love. It is the repetition of constant blessing which we never asked for nor imagined, which surrounds even our remembered sorrows with the light and glory of God's tenderness. It teaches us that they were no curses of any avenger, but that they also have their place, though it be not for us to tell where, in the courses of his unvarying tenderness. It is not any arguing away of pain that enables us to bear our sorrows. It is the constant renewal of the gifts — call them great, call them small, infinite, and unceasing — of a Father's love.

Just in proportion as any man knows that God is spirit, just so far as he separates him from the limitations of Time and Space, so far do the worries vanish about his going hither or resting there, about his looking backward or his foreknowing. He IS without time. I do not say that any man understands how God IS. But I do say that a man used to the contemplation of the infinite, were it only in mathematical study, knows why he cannot understand it. It is no more strange that I cannot see how God exists in all time than that I cannot imagine his existence in all space.

The world will have fewer subjects for tragedies, as it feels more and more that God is ; as it feels his presence in all Nature, and knows that it is he whom it praises as it extols her wonders,— fewer subjects for tragedies, but it must be one of the last objects for loving wisdom to provide its children with subjects for lamentation. Literature changes, manners change, science changes, governments change. All things become new, as the world comes to feel that in him we live and move and have our being, that in sum he is All, and that this All loves every child with equal tenderness, and leads every child with perfect wisdom.

INDEX.

Abolition of Pauperism,	70
Abraham Lincoln, quoted,	2
All Things New,	61
America, Religion of,	127
Apostles' Creed,	89
Arthur Clough, quoted,	105
Benevolent Fraternity,	159
Boston, the Possible,	154
Brown, Howard N., quoted,	10
Brown, E. C. L., quoted,	203
Charles I., Sunday Proclamation,	4
Children in the Wood,	44
Christian Realism,	76
Christian States,	72
Christ, Leader and Lord,	205
Christ's Plan,	67
Christ, the Friend,	52
Christ, the Giver,	44
Commonwealth,	76
Commonwealth of Love,	153
Davidis, Francis,	1
Easter,	177
Eastern Mystery,	127
East Tennessee, Gospel in,	27
Elias, Revelation of,	87
Eliot, George, quoted,	149
Ellis, Rufus, quoted,	18
England, Decrease of Crime,	14
Established Church in Boston,	16
Eugene Sue, quoted,	172
Faith, Hope, and Love,	38
Follow me,	194
Four Mottoes, The,	39
Fuller, Margaret, quoted,	125
Furness, W. H., quoted,	135
Gadarenes,	29
Gibbon's Account of Success of the Gospel,	179
Gibbon on Preaching,	94
Gifts unto Men,	46
God is a Spirit,	113
Holmes, O. W., quoted,	22
Honor and Idolatry,	192
Hook, Archdeacon, quoted,	200
Hungary, Edict of Toleration,	202
I must see Rome,	185
Increase of Life,	162
Indifference,	146
In the Name of Christ,	148
King's Work, The,	168
Law and Gospel,	20
Lives of Saints,	2
Living God,	141
Look up Legion,	39
Louisiana, Territory of,	62
Mary Magdalene, a Poem,	97
Men of Gadara,	29
Ministry at Large,	159
Missionary Hospital at Canton,	49
New England's Genius,	65
Newspapers, Sunday,	6
New Year's, Sunday,	61
North American Review, cited,	25
Not Less, but More,	86
Œdipus Tyrannus,	208
Parable and Bible,	137
Peter Parker, Dr.,	48
Pork Market in Gadara,	31
Possible Boston,	154
Predestination,	211
Renan, Ernest, quoted,	143
Religion of America,	127
Revivals of Religion,	151
Ritualistic Clergymen,	91
Sartor Resartus,	106
Send me,	122
Sermon on the Mount,	75
Son of Man,	57
South Congregational Liturgy,	79
Sterling, John, quoted,	87
Substance and Shadow,	162
Subsoiling,	13
Sunday Laws,	3
Sunday Travel,	7
The King's Work,	169
These Three abide,	36
Things Above,	78
Thomas Carlyle,	104
Together,	111
Unitarian Name,	200
Unitarian Principles,	199
Victory of the Few,	177
Vineland in New Jersey,	74